Every Investor's Guide to Wall Street's Hottest Phenomenon!

Understanding Electronic Day Trading

Carol Troy

McGraw-Hill

New York   San Francisco   Washington, D.C.   Auckland   Bogotá
Caracas   Lisbon   London   Madrid   Mexico City   Milan
Montreal   New Delhi   San Juan   Singapore
Sydney   Tokyo   Toronto

McGraw-Hill

A Division of The **McGraw·Hill** Companies

1 2 3 4 5 6 7 8 9 0   AGM/AGM   9 0 9 8 7 6 5 4 3 2 1 0 9

0-07-135152-3

It was set in Garamond by North Market Street Graphics.

Printed and bound by Quebecor Martinsburg

 This book is printed on recycled, acid-free paper containing a minimum of 50% recycled, de-inked fiber.

McGraw-Hill books are available at special quantity discounts to use as premiums and sales promotions, or for use in corporate training programs. For more information, please write to the Director of Special Sales, McGraw-Hill, 11 West 19th Street, New York, NY 10011. Or contact your local bookstore.

This book is dedicated to those two devastating brothers from Cornell, Francis Troy, '29, and Hugh Troy, '27, and their father, Professor Hugh Troy, Class of 1898.

For the memory of my Uncle Hugh, "an artist of the practical joke, with a refined touch and a sense of the profoundly satirical . . . all in addition to the main business of his life: painting murals, writing and illustrating books, serving his country in mysterious ways . . ." in the words of his friend Tom Wolfe.

And for my beloved father, Francis Troy, who was not a CIA agent, for his artistry at taking life one day at a time, with a refined sense of forensic accounting and a sublime touch of the profoundly silly.

Drawing by Tom Wolfe, 1983

CONTENTS

THIS BOOK'S FOR YOU

If you think online trading in stock is:

> Too confusing
> Too risky
> Too expensive
> Too revolutionary . . .

this book is for you.

Understanding Electronic Day Trading walks you through the exciting new ways you can profit through online trading—right now—starting with a modest online brokerage account from your home computer, up through a five- or six-figure account online or even with an electronic trading brokerage.

ONLINE TRADING: WHAT, WHEN, WHY, HOW

This book will answer your questions about online trading and help you get your feet wet with as little as $1000 in an online trading account, just one click away from trading with real-time market feeds and instant access to buying and selling stock at the lowest cost to you.

The only requirement? If you don't already have a home computer linked to the Internet, you're going to have to summon the guts to take the leap into cyberspace. Once you've done that, this book will guide you through the entry-level steps of choosing an online brokerage account with features similar to true electronic direct-access trading. You can now experiment in the privacy of your own home with small, manageable trades in stocks.

You already have an online discount brokerage account? Then you may want to review the capacities of the various companies with an eye to online trading. Ask exactly how quickly they can get you in and out of a stock and where, how, and how fast your orders are executed.

To supplement your online account for trading stock on the New York Stock Exchange and Nasdaq, this book will lead you to the cutting-edge sources for real-time market information, news, and analysis, giving you the online traders' top picks of real-time information providers—including the free ticker you can program to keep you up to date, second by second, on the stocks you're watching. Charting and technical analysis will add another dimension to your understanding of the stock market and the online trading universe. You'll find out what you really need to read and what you should scan to stay current with global macroeconomic trends.

Understanding Electronic Day Trading discusses some of the most popular software tools now available—tools that will help you refine the list of stocks you watch, concentrate your energies, and alert you to sudden, potentially profitable movements in the market.

We'll wake up one morning with a cautious online trader who has picked off over $1500 a week over the past five months—at a desk in her bedroom—before driving off for work at her job downtown in San Francisco. That trader is me, the author.

Your author removes profits from her $25,000 trading account along the way. She doesn't like to gamble anything more, now, than the total of those profits—about $31,000. (For an inside peek at the details, see the Transaction History for TROY8527 in Figure P.1.)

Had this trader kept all the profits in her account, that $56,000 would have been barely enough to buy a space at the big boys' tables: Landmark, Heartland Securities, Momentum, On-Line Investments, and Broadway Trading, the biggest day trading brokerages nationwide. (I'll share a cautionary tale about the time I spent working at a computer at such a trading firm.)

To open an account at a professional electronic trading brokerage, you may need $50,000, $100,000, or $150,000, depending on the firm. These professional freelance EDAT (electronic direct-access trading) traders—making money for their own accounts, not for Wall Street—tend to work with blocks of 1000 shares or more, trading every few minutes. They mirror their counterparts on Wall Street—coming into work at the crack of dawn, grabbing fast food at their desks in the trading room, keeping their eyes glued to the computer screen nearly every second the market is open, tearing themselves away every few hours to rush off to the bathroom.

The job requires enormous amounts of education, market savvy, and fast reflexes. But they say they're making glamorous amounts of money.

FIGURE P.1 *The account summary keeps your records back to the date you opened the account; your tax accountant will appreciate you.* (Datek Online.)

Date/Time	Action	Qty	Symbol	Price	Amount	Balance	Flag	Reference
10/29/1998 14:13:03	Credit		Cash		$25,000.00	$28,552.62		W-000-0466-2697
10/30/1998 13:16:50	Bought	200	SPY	110 5/16	$-22,072.49	$6,480.13		G-200-AADO-8351
10/30/1998 15:48:27	Bought	100	SEEK	29 9/16	$-2,966.24	$3,513.89		B-300-AABA-0515
10/31/1998 23:59:59	credit				$3.88	$3,517.77		W-000-0525-8518

Account Summary

Date/Time	Action	Qty	Symbol	Price	Amount	Balance	Flag	Reference
11/01/1998 00:00:00	Balance		Cash		$3,517.77	$3,517.77		W-000-0601-2820
11/01/1998 00:00:01	Long	25	CNWK			$3,517.77		W-000-0601-2816
11/01/1998 00:00:01	Long	100	SEEK			$3,517.77		W-000-0601-2817
11/01/1998 00:00:01	Long	200	SPY			$3,517.77		W-000-0601-2818
11/01/1998 00:00:01	Short	20	YHOO			$3,517.77		W-000-0601-2819

Account History

Date/Time	Action	Qty	Symbol	Price	Amount	Balance	Flag	Reference
11/02/1998 09:54:05	Bought	20	YHOO	132 9/16	$-2,661.24	$856.53		B-100-AABR-7821
11/02/1998 09:54:05	Bought	10	YHOO	132 9/16	$-1,335.62	$-479.09		B-100-AABR-7821
11/02/1998 10:44:24	Bought	100	DLJ	35 7/8	$-3,597.49	$-4,076.58		F-200-AAED-4348
11/02/1998 11:33:10	Bought	100	MER	60 1/16	$-6,016.24	$-10,092.82		F-200-AAED-5936
11/02/1998 12:27:02	Bought	100	EGRP	19 5/16	$-1,931.25	$-12,024.07	2	G-200-AADK-9161
11/02/1998 12:27:19	Bought	100	EGRP	19 5/16	$-1,931.25	$-13,955.32	2	G-200-AADK-9161
11/02/1998 12:27:36	Bought	100	EGRP	19 5/16	$-1,931.25	$-15,886.57	2	G-200-AADK-9161
11/02/1998 12:35:36	Bought	200	EGRP	19 5/16	$-3,872.49	$-19,759.06		G-200-AADK-9161
11/02/1998 12:45:12	Bought	50	AOL	132 3/4	$-6,647.49	$-26,406.55		G-200-AADH-9728
11/02/1998 13:12:27	Bought	10	CSCO	64 1/4	$-652.49	$-27,059.04		G-200-AADI-0577
11/03/1998 11:14:38	Sold	400	EGRP	18 13/16	$7,524.74	$-19,534.30	2,3	B-300-AABC-0391
11/05/1998 09:33:22	Bought	30	AOL	137 3/4	$-4,142.49	$-23,676.79		B-400-AAAY-1025
11/05/1998 09:36:45	Bought	25	YHOO	147 1/4	$-3,691.24	$-27,368.03		B-400-AAAY-0965
11/06/1998 10:19:30	Bought	25	GERN	23	$-584.99	$-27,953.02		0-000-AAAF-5664
11/06/1998 14:15:36	Sold	100	EGRP	23 1/4	$2,314.93	$-25,638.09	3	B-300-AABJ-6369
11/06/1998 14:28:28	Sold	200	SPY	114 1/8	$22,814.24	$-2,823.85	3	B-300-AABJ-6893
11/06/1998 14:30:43	Sold	100	MER	63 9/16	$6,346.04	$3,522.19	3	B-300-AABJ-7224
11/06/1998 15:37:18	Sold	100	SEEK	34	$3,389.89	$6,912.08	3	B-300-AABJ-6970
11/09/1998 12:13:25	Sold	100	DLJ	36 13/16	$3,671.13	$10,583.21	3	B-300-AABH-5155
11/09/1998 12:23:10	Sold	25	GERN	13 7/8	$336.87	$10,920.08	3	B-300-AABH-5642
11/09/1998 12:50:37	Bought	20	AOL	142 1/4	$-2,854.99	$8,065.09		B-300-AABH-7179
11/09/1998 12:57:41	Bought	50	YHOO	159 5/16	$-7,975.62	$89.47		B-300-AABH-7562
11/09/1998 13:04:47	Bought	50	XCIT	44 11/16	$-2,244.37	$-2,154.90		B-300-AABH-7939
11/10/1998 14:34:27	Sold	85	YHOO	176 7/16	$14,986.70	$12,831.80	3	B-400-AABI-2503
11/10/1998 14:38:57	Sold	50	XCIT	53 9/16	$2,668.05	$15,499.85	3	B-400-AABI-2701
11/10/1998 14:39:44	Sold	100	AOL	147 3/8	$14,727.01	$30,226.86	3	B-400-AABI-2574
11/10/1998 14:39:58	Sold	25	CNWK	50 11/16	$1,257.15	$31,484.01	3	B-400-AABI-2756
11/10/1998 14:43:52	Sold	10	CSCO	67 11/16	$666.86	$32,150.87	3	B-400-AABI-2966
11/10/1998 19:02:55	FundRqst		Check		$-7,132.00	$25,018.87		W-000-0525-2588
11/11/1998 14:36:19	debit		Cash		$-10.00	$25,008.87		W-000-0525-5833
11/13/1998 09:39:38	Bought	200	SEEK	32 7/8	$-6,584.99	$18,423.88		B-400-AABO-7304
11/13/1998 09:43:08	Bought	100	AOL	140 3/4	$-14,084.99	$4,338.89		B-400-AABO-7254
11/13/1998 10:37:48	Bought	35	GNET	50	$-1,759.99	$2,578.90		B-400-AABF-7170
11/13/1998 10:37:48	Bought	15	GNET	50	$-750.00	$1,828.90	2	B-400-AABF-7170
11/13/1998 11:27:31	Bought	50	YHOO	171	$-8,559.99	$-6,731.09		B-400-AABO-7308
11/13/1998 12:04:23	Bought	100	AOL	138 1/4	$-13,834.99	$-20,566.08		B-400-AABO-7262
11/17/1998 13:00:41	Sold	200	SEEK	36	$7,189.77	$-13,376.31	3	B-400-AABQ-4337
11/17/1998 14:19:12	Sold	50	YHOO	174 15/16	$8,736.59	$-4,639.72	3	B-400-AABC-7892
11/18/1998 00:00:02	Fwd. Split	200	AOL			$-4,639.72		W-000-0541-8919
11/19/1998 11:33:34	Bought	100	CNWK	63 3/4	$-6,384.99	$-11,024.71		B-300-AACK-8714
11/19/1998 11:35:52	Bought	100	MCOM	7 7/16	$-753.74	$-11,778.45		B-300-AACK-8911
11/19/1998 11:48:11	Bought	100	SOF	15 15/16	$-1,603.74	$-13,382.19		B-300-AACK-9756
11/20/1998 10:56:05	Sold	10	CNWK	57 1/4	$562.49	$-12,819.70	3	B-400-AAC8-3258
11/20/1998 10:56:05	Sold	90	CNWK	57 5/16	$5,157.95	$-7,661.75	2,3	B-400-AAC8-3258
11/20/1998 12:39:35	Sold	100	SOF	16 15/16	$1,683.70	$-5,978.05	3	B-400-AAC8-2397
11/20/1998 13:47:44	Sold	400	AOL	82 5/8	$33,038.90	$27,060.85	3	B-300-AACO-8258
11/20/1998 14:21:36	Sold	50	GNET	35 1/16	$1,743.08	$28,803.93	3	B-300-AACO-9813
11/20/1998 14:22:47	Sold	100	MCOM	6 3/4	$664.98	$29,468.91	3	B-300-AACO-9855
11/20/1998 14:28:17	FundRqst		Check		$-4,469.00	$24,999.91		W-000-0544-8655
11/23/1998 13:59:18	debit		Cash		$-10.00	$24,989.91		W-000-0545-9407
11/27/1998 11:16:06	credit		Cash		$10.00	$24,999.91		W-000-0549-9108
11/27/1998 15:56:05	Dividend		MER		$24.00	$25,023.91		W-000-0550-6457
11/30/1998 23:59:59	margin				$-29.33	$24,994.58		W-000-0617-4246
12/01/1998 14:25:26	Bought	100	ASPT	18 3/8	$-1,847.49	$23,147.09		B-400-AADD-0731
12/01/1998 14:29:25	Bought	100	DBCC	10 5/8	$-1,072.49	$22,074.60		B-400-AADD-0953
12/24/1998 10:45:53	Bought	15	SEEK	52 3/8	$-795.62	$21,278.98		B-300-AAFH-9485
12/24/1998 10:45:53	Bought	85	SEEK	52 5/16	$-4,446.56	$16,832.42	2	B-300-AAFH-9485
12/24/1998 12:46:48	Bought	500	DBCC	12 13/16	$-6,406.25	$10,426.17	2	B-400-AAFH-8672
12/24/1998 12:46:53	Bought	500	DBCC	12 13/16	$-6,416.24	$4,009.93		B-400-AAFJ-8672
12/24/1998 12:57:51	Bought	1000	DBCC	12 15/16	$-12,947.49	$-8,937.56		B-300-AAFJ-0631
12/29/1998 13:50:39	Sold	900	DBCC	15 13/16	$14,230.77	$5,293.21	2,3	B-400-AAEZ-2195
12/29/1998 14:11:01	Sold	1200	DBCC	15 13/16	$18,974.36	$24,267.57	1,3	B-400-AAEZ-2195
12/30/1998 10:40:03	Sold	100	ASPT	15 7/8	$1,577.45	$25,845.02	3	B-400-AAFA-7854
12/30/1998 10:43:41	Sold	100	SEEK	52 3/8	$5,227.33	$31,072.35	3	B-400-AAFA-8375
12/31/1998 23:59:59	credit				$66.11	$31,138.46		W-000-0717-6288

Account Summary

Date/Time	Action	Qty	Symbol	Price	Amount	Balance	Flag	Reference
01/01/1999 00:00:00	Balance		Cash		$31,138.46	$31,138.46		W-000-0874-4713

Account History

Date/Time	Action	Qty	Symbol	Price	Amount	Balance	Flag	Reference
01/05/1999 14:42:14	Bought	1000	DBCC	18 1/4	$-18,275.00	$12,863.46		0-000-AAAH-4917
01/13/1999 10:39:09	Sold	180	DBCC	35	$6,299.79	$19,163.25	2,3	B-400-AAGD-6525
01/13/1999 10:39:20	Sold	820	DBCC	35	$28,689.05	$47,852.30	3	B-400-AAGD-6525
01/20/1999 09:26:47	Bought	100	YHOO	324	$-32,409.99	$15,442.31		B-400-AAGT-1695
01/20/1999 09:46:08	Bought	200	SEEK	77 1/4	$-15,459.99	$-17.68		B-400-AAGT-1834
01/20/1999 12:40:02	Sold	200	SEEK	75 7/16	$15,077.00	$15,059.32	3	C-300-AACB-9920
01/20/1999 13:20:16	Sold	100	YHOO	318 3/4	$31,863.94	$46,923.26	3	C-300-AACC-1803
01/31/1999 23:59:59	credit				$74.91	$46,998.17		W-000-0889-1308
01/31/1999 23:59:59	margin				$-4.92	$46,993.25		W-000-0889-1309

Account Summary

Date/Time	Action	Qty	Symbol	Price	Amount	Balance	Flag	Reference
02/01/1999 00:00:00	Balance		Cash		$46,993.25	$46,993.25		W-000-1032-5357

Account History

Date/Time	Action	Qty	Symbol	Price	Amount	Balance	Flag	Reference
02/25/1999 13:58:48	Bought	100	SEEK	72	$-7,209.99	$39,783.26		C-300-AAEC-7971
02/26/1999 11:59:49	Sold	100	SEEK	72	$7,189.77	$46,973.03	3	C-300-AAEE-4948
02/26/1999 23:59:59	credit				$126.17	$47,099.20		W-000-1041-5413

And in the evenings they can relax, because they've gone flat before leaving for the day: they've sold off everything in their accounts to avoid any ugly surprises from Mr. Market the next morning.

Later in these pages, you'll find yourself at the elbow of a hot Houston day trader during one market opening. You'll be right in the middle of the action on the floor of a day trading firm. And you'll see an honest accounting of just how much this gunslinger made, or lost, by day's end.

"I'm looking at a trader now who's done 450 trades so far this morning," said James Lee over the telephone from Houston, Texas, back in the fall of 1998. Lee heads Momentum Securities and represents the ETA, the Electronic Traders Association. Traders at Momentum often start with an account of $250,000, and trade on margin.

"My trader's up $13,000," said Lee. "But it's a good morning. The markets are bouncing around. Yesterday our average trader did about $18,000. But that's an extraordinary time!"

A decade of corporate downsizing is driving the individual investor from an attitude of trust and reliance on his or her stockbroker to one of self-education and self-reliance. The security of retirement benefits has been replaced with the responsibility of growing individual investing profits. The pressure is on, but the rewards can be enticing.

Thanks to the silent cyberrevolution transforming traditional markets into online cybermarkets, anyone with a home computer can now start to trade stock alongside the professional traders on Wall Street. In fact, this new electronic access to the market floor has put the individual investor one-up on Wall Street. Online investors buy wholesale. They nip away at the traditional markups between bid and ask that market makers once pocketed on the prices of Nasdaq-listed stocks like Cisco, Amgen, Intel, and Microsoft.

The lure of becoming an insider has always been irresistible, especially when it promises the riches of Wall Street. The Wall Street insiders used to wear Saville Row suits paid for with your brokerage commissions, drive Porsches financed by investment bank profits made on your stock trades, grab the best table at Elaine's, and generally lord it over the rest of us. There was Michael Douglas as Gordon Gekko in Oliver Stone's *Wall Street,* complete with beach house in the Hamptons. Tom Hanks brought one of these insiders to life in the movie *Bonfire of the Vanities,* playing the greedy and terrified self-proclaimed Master of the Universe who lived above his means in a splendid Fifth Avenue apartment, on the glittering profits shaved from the billions flowing through Wall Street each day.

The insider was the man with the stock tips, the man who told you when to get into a stock and when to get out. Of course, you could never reach him on the phone after his two-martini lunch. And you were expected, back then, to hand over something like a $300 commission every time he bought you 100 shares of stock.

Your full-service broker/salesperson is not the insider any more. Today, that 100-share trade could cost you less than $10 to $30, depending on whether you're online with a 1990s discount broker or using a professional day trader's dedicated line and Level II information. Real-time quotes, analysts' ratings, and company earnings and reports are free for all on the Internet. Today, the online trader is the insider. It's power to the people time.

COVER STORIES AND CHAT ROOMS

Every week, cover stories in *Forbes* and *Business Week,* and articles in *The New York Times, Time,* and *Fortune* are buzzing about how the person-in-the-street can become the insider, thanks to new open market rules from the SEC (Securities and Exchange Commission) and innovative online brokerage accounts.

In chat rooms across cyberspace, day trading is the hot topic. If you can go online with a home computer, the moneymaking powers of the stock market suddenly start to reveal themselves. Wall Street traders used to pay thousands of dollars a month for access to this "insider" information, breaking news, and real-time quotes that are now available free, online.

How did all this happen? First, SEC prompting caused brokers' fees to drop in the mid-1970s and 1980s. This era saw the advent of discount brokers like Charles Schwab in San Francisco (see Figure P.2).

Then the explosive growth of the World Wide Web in the mid-1990s made online brokers the fastest-growing segment of the business. And electronic communications networks (ECNs)—the little electronic stock markets whose best bid and ask prices are entered on the Nasdaq Level II quote montage along with those of all the top market makers—blossomed in 1999 so dramatically that the New York Stock Exchange itself declared an interest in creating its own.

Silicon Valley companies like E*Trade opened for business online, using up-to-the-minute marketing to enroll new customers.

WHAT'S THE CATCH?

The only drawback for the dedicated online trader today is the lack of control over your price and entry time into a trade. Most of these online dis-

FIGURE P.2 *Schwab's new home page brings visitors into a first-rate financial portal.* (Charles Schwab & Co., Inc.)

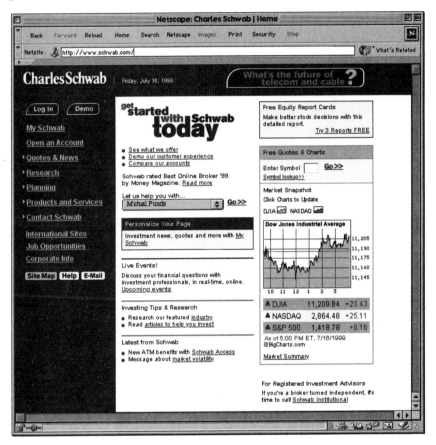

count brokers continue to send their customer orders to a middleman, in exchange for a fee for order flow—or a "kickback," as a top Internet stock analyst calls it. The hidden costs of that extra percentage—that little slice taken by the middlemen, Nasdaq market makers, or the New York Stock Exchange specialists—can end up costing you an extra couple of percentage points on some trades—a cost of thousands over several years of compounding. But now this drawback is dissolving.

The EDAT day traders—those who use electronic direct access for their orders to the Nasdaq screen-based cybermarket—average 1000+ share buy orders, send their orders through the Nasdaq Level II market, and see them pop onto the Nasdaq screen immediately. There they can choose between the various ECNs and the market makers on the Nasdaq Level II screen—whichever has the better price. They're at the center of the action, in the whirling vortex of the game. In 1999, the advantages once held only by this EDAT day trader are available to the little guy. The small investor now has online access to the ECN called Island, at www.island.com, with more soon to come.

At home or at the office, you can have an online broker feeding you a real-time, second-by-second ticker, with a trading window in the middle, to follow the stocks you're interested in. At the time of this writing, there's only one such Streamer, from Datek Online, that's capable of passing through almost all corporate firewalls so you can sneak a trade in your office before work or at lunch. Combine that with a peek at the Island ECN *limit order book,* the list of all the bid and ask prices in their order-matching service, and now the small guy can watch that order flow—for free.

That new middle ground between the new discount online brokers and the EDAT day traders—paying a $300 monthly bill to support their software and dedicated access lines—first emerged in 1998 when one online broker didn't sell the order flow to a middleman for a kickback. This new-style online broker executed trades within about 10 seconds, at the click of a mouse, with routing direct to the Island ECN.

America Online popularized the Fool.com (see Figure P.3), while the Fool's best-selling *Motley Fool Investment Guide* (Fireside, 1997) gave readers a clearheaded view of how Wall Street had often played the wolf in sheep's clothing. Online brokers and AOL started providing free charting, technical analysis, company backgrounders, and even analyst recommendations. Merrill Lynch, long a laggard in the online investing arena, made proprietary company reports written by its high-paid stock analysts available on the Web—free. And portal companies like Yahoo! opened free full-service investment sites like Yahoo!Finance, while Microsoft rolled out MSN Personal Finance Investor.

DILBERT GETS RICH QUICK

During high-tech and biotech investment conferences, money managers and investment bankers now dash to banks of computers to punch up Yahoo!Finance during their 10-minute coffee breaks. Meanwhile, hundreds of thousands of Dilbert fans are punching up the same information in their office cubicles. The market's playing field is leveled by this free flow of information.

During 1999, thousands of men and women—teachers and marketing directors, CEOs and car parts distributors—decided to become market insiders themselves. These students of the markets were empowered by two key innovations, using the new powers of (1) instant access to market prices with streaming real-time quotes or the Nasdaq Level II screen, and (2) near-instant executions available through an online broker's ECN.

These insiders don't work from wood-paneled Wall Street offices or deluxe brokerage firms. You'll find them in a bedroom in Los Angeles, sipping coffee as the sun rises, watching CNBC, and making a trade or two on their home PC. You'll see them in an office cubicle in St. Louis, tearing into an Egg McMuffin, using the company's superfast T1 line, and hoping the boss doesn't come in early. And like the Wall Streeters who preceded them, these highly focused new stock market insiders are amassing wealth using the electronic access previously available only to the very rich and the very Establishment.

Why are the markets becoming so wide open? Because this new electronic world magically allows the new insiders to see into the markets. Market transparency, the ability to know what everyone around the world is doing in a certain stock, has become an electronic reality. The new online trader can see into the best bid and offer prices at Nasdaq, where most of the technology shares are listed and where higher volatility often gives a better chance of quick profits than the New York Stock Exchange.

The online trader who takes a profit of $300 during morning coffee knows when to get into and out of a stock, because today's instant elec-

FIGURE P.3   (The Motley Fool, Inc. www.fool.com.)

tronic market access gives him or her a direct line into the market—a virtual ringside seat in the cybermarket.

TAKING THE LEAP

Many online traders working out of their homes or sneaking in a few minutes in the office prefer to keep things simple. They choose to trade one, five, or ten times a week. They don't toss and turn through sleepless nights.

Others find the momentum of success hard to resist. They trade 10, then 20, then 30 times a week. Then one day, these traders buy some proprietary software and online feeds, guarantee their online connections by avoiding the "World Wide Wait," and go straight to a dedicated connection through a day trading firm direct to the market. Now, splashed across their ever active screens like the killers in a video game, color-coded visual cues indicate exactly who is selling how much stock at what price; and likewise, who is buying. Here come MLCO, Merrill Lynch, and MASH, Mayer Schweitzer, Charles Schwab's wholesaler.

At this level of play, the traders enter the game as serious players, EDAT professionals. They begin to know their opponents, anticipate their moves, note their mistakes, and profit. Some choose to trade online before going to work; others insist that learning the markets well enough to trade successfully is a full-time job.

TRYING IT OUT WHILE PLAYING IT SAFE

The magic of this new world is that anyone with a home PC, an Internet hookup, and the ability to concentrate can start profiting with online trading. By riding a stock up one or even two points, the small investor can start to play the game from home, without spending hundreds and thousands on day trading programs, questionable seminars, and complex data links.

The beefed-up computer, training, and data feeds may get you further, faster—if you're willing to put in thousands of dollars and thousands of hours. Instead, you can read this book and meet people who trade from day one, putting the least amount of money at risk and getting the most reward.

Maybe you'll become one of them.

Let's take a look.

ACKNOWLEDGMENTS

To the many people who have added spice to this editorial stew over my years in journalism. In New York, Lucian K. Truscott IV, Caterine Milinaire and *Cheap Chic,* John Haskins at *New York Times CyberTimes,* Betty Prashker, Tim Seldes, Ki Hackney, Susan Peterson, Brooks Riley, Alan and Sally Lubell, Bruce Harris, Roger Black, Sandy Socolow, and the fabled Belinda Breese.

Other New Yorkers include Susan Heath, Richard Merkin, Harold Evans, Lloyd Ziff, Lala Coleman, Michael Kamen, Betsey Johnson, Tina Bossidy, Harry Benson, Diane Smith, Ruth Reischl, Charles Churchward, Tom Werts, Blair Sabol, Anthony Haden-Guest, Gully Wells, Michael Schnayerson, Bud Lee, Joan Juliet Buck, John Lombardi, Gay Bryant, Tom Wolfe, Jacque Leo, Pat Carbine, Jaime Raab, Dick Lemon, Gail Zweigenthal, Francois de Menil, Rhoda Grauer, and my former partner in *Rags* magazine, Mary Peacock.

In Houston, B. K. Dillingham and Fred T. M. Hofheinz, Esq.

The Long Island contingent, including Clive Irving, Andy Port, Robert Sam Anson, and the gracious Pucci Meyer (and Lola).

In London, Clive Irving, Andrea Adam, Russell Harris; Jean Orr in Edinburg.

In Los Angeles, my splendid lawyer, Eric Feig, Esq., Deanne Stillman, Anne Beatts, Andy Meisler, Bill W., Nancy Allen, Dianne Partie, Lydia Cornell, Lynda Obst, Hunter Drohojowska and David Philp, Ron Meyer, Gillian Anderson, Darien Lum, Jennifer Grey, Alec Benblock, Anne Bardach, and Wallis Annenberg. Thanks also to Marie Werner, Rod Friend, Esq., Emil Soorani, and Vivian Geiger.

In Moscow, Artiom and Svetlana Troitsky.

San Francisco spawned Gregor Bleimann, Jon Carroll, Susan Subtle, Maura Thurman, Pat Steger, John Burke, Rosalee Wright, Hans Severeins of the Band of Angels, B. K. Moran, Steven Scheer and Eric Beresford-Wood at Landmark, Velveteen Rose, and Frank Robertson, plus friends at Robertson Stephens, Softbank, Hambrecht & Quist, E*Trade, Discover, and Charles Schwab.

For wending through the early drafts, Joyce Sasse-Wood, Esq., Juanita Madara, and Jeffrey Dunne.

The McGraw-Hill editorial team of Stephen Isaacs, acquisitions editor, and Jeffrey Krames, publisher, investing and finance; for that final spin, Ginny Carroll, project manager at North Market Street Graphics; and the New York production team of McGraw-Hill, Ede Dreikurs, art director, Eileen Kramer, and the editorial panache of the peerless Meredith Moran.

And for launching this book into the world, great thanks to Lydia Rinaldi, with McGraw-Hill New York public relations, for all your enthusiasm, plus the strategic thinking of San Francisco's Kerry McGagin of KMA Communications and Michael Whitehouse of Connections Corp., Menlo Park.

I could not have pulled this together without the fantastic screen shot research and art direction under the supervision of Craig Anderson, USC Film School.

Finally, endless kudos to Candace Lewis of the Annenberg School for Communication and now VP, Editorial, troy.com, who pulls it all together.

And thanks to all who shared their wisdom and knowledge about the online world. May your investing be blessed with both a peaceful glow and a Zen attitude of delight.

For a glossary, suggested reading list, and further information and goodies, go to the Web site at www.caroltroy.com.

CHAPTER 1

WHERE'S THE MONEY?

TRADING BEFORE BREAKFAST

The alarm rattles me awake at 6 a.m., California time. A pearly gray light is barely seeping into the sky, and already those optimistic birds are out there chirping. I roll over, click on the television next to my bed, yank myself out from under the warm comforter, and dash to the kitchen to make coffee. I can't afford to miss a word of Maria Bartiromo's wisdom, offered daily on the CNBC "pregame" show that precedes the opening of the New York Stock Exchange at 9:30 a.m., New York time, 6:30 a.m. where I am.

I punch on my PowerBook, its modem cord plugged into the phone jack near the bed; prop myself up on some pillows; swallow a slug of steaming French roast; and get to work. Thanks to my laptop, the discount online stock trading revolution, and a fierce curiosity to see if I can actually make money this way, the stock market is not a spectator sport for me any more. The computer revolution has given me a front-row-center seat. I'm there.

The New York market opens in 20 minutes. I click onto America Online. I've got mail: TheStreet.com—a new online-only market newsletter featuring the economic outlook and preopening rants by Wall Street's estimable professional trader/writer, James Cramer. Here's a small sampling of Cramer. Speaking of brokerages, he says:

> . . . in the world of financial information and brokerage, I have to tell you that when the Net is finished with these businesses, you

won't recognize them. . . . You may have heard the phrase "wake up and smell the coffee." Well, with these guys, it is wake up and smell the formaldehyde . . .

I check for e-mail from the *Wall Street Journal* Interactive Edition. They'll zip off a note if anything earth-shattering has rocked the markets overnight. I read the Motley Fool's e-mail, then click over to Ziff-Davis for technology news, and Silicon Investor, ditto.

I dash across the World Wide Web "front pages" of *The New York Times* Business and Technology sections; then the *Wall Street Journal* Interactive.

It's time. I take a deep breath and fire up the home page of my online brokerage, Datek Online, push the green-and-white log-in button, type in my account number (issued to me a few days after I mailed in my application and check, minimum $2000). Then I type in my secret code (the VeriSign logo tells me the information is secure) and take a look at my portfolio.

I swallow another gulp of coffee. My heart is pounding. Maria's bobbing center-screen on CNBC now, buffeted by hordes of traders and specialists rushing across the floor of the NYSE. The camera cuts to a reporter a few blocks away, standing in front of the Nasdaq board, the market that lists most of the high-tech companies. The starting bell's about to ring. Why did I think I needed coffee?

The entire Internet sector has taken a beating these past few days. The analysis I've been reading in The Street, *The Times, WSJ,* and elsewhere has me convinced it's a good time to buy back in. I consult my little black book where I pencil in my notes every day: what's down, what looks good to go up.

I click on the "quotes and trades" page in my online brokerage account and type in the symbols of the stocks I'm interested in this morning. Then, just like magic, the current market quotes—the best bid and ask—on those stocks pop up on my screen in a neat little column. To the left of each line are icons linking to "news" and "charts" and "fundamentals." I click on "charts," get a feel for my stocks' performance over the past year, then ask the free online charting to show me how the performance of each stock compares to the others, and to the Nasdaq index, over the past 10 days only. The graphing line for each company scribbles across my screen in green, turquoise, pumpkin, scarlet, and black, an M&M bag of possibilities. I back away from the stock that has already "popped"—jumped up in price—and do my short-term investing in those companies I consider to be undervalued today. I may keep them for a day, a week, a month.

I click back to the same quotes page, type in the symbols of the beaten-down stocks, enter each with a *limit order* price only, go right back to set an emergency *stop-loss market order* in case the bear mauls the bull today, make a note of a polite and ungreedy sum that would please me as a trader, *pencil in my sell price,* and then go about my day. I call these steps Troy's Three Trading Tips, or T3 (more about these steps in an upcoming chapter).

If I don't like what I see on the chart, or read in the paper, or hear Maria talking about on CNBC, I'm out of there. There's always next week. The market will always go up, and the market will always go down. My very cautious style of trading keeps me in tune with market rhythms and increases my odds of making better choices than the mutual fund managers make. I might even beat the Standard & Poor's (S&P) 500, or the Nasdaq index. I'm not sure, of course. But I'm willing to try.

WHAT'S A NICE GIRL LIKE YOU DOING IN A CYBERSPACE LIKE THIS?

Looking back at my rather striped past, I find no clues that would have led me, or anyone who knew me, to believe that someday I'd be rolling over in bed in the morning, reaching for my laptop, and working up a sweat trading stocks before I've even put the water on for coffee.

For starters, I grew up female in the 1960s. If there were any female stockbrokers, female market analysts, or female venture capitalists they certainly weren't visible to me and money matters weren't considered proper dinner table conversation in our middle-class home. Uncharacteristically for a woman of her time, my mother took a great interest in the stock market; she tried to pass it on with the only bit of career advice she ever gave me. "Get a job in a brokerage," she said, "and you'll meet a rich man."

I ignored my mother's advice. Instead I became a writer; I also married one. Both moves proved unexpectedly lucrative. Following the success of my book, *Cheap Chic,* and my husband's best-selling novel, *Dress Gray,* we were an investment disaster waiting to happen. Sure enough, a good friend of ours, who worked on Wall Street, advised us to buy stock in a company I'll call "Fly-by-Nite." The next day we opened an account with Muriel Siebert, the first woman to buy a seat on the New York Stock Exchange. The day after that we went back to writing books and forgot about our investment.

The next time we remembered it, we discovered that every penny invested in "Fly-by-Nite" was gone. You'd think that experience would have been enough to keep me away from the stock market for the rest of my life. It might have, if two other unexpected things hadn't happened.

First, in the mid-1980s, I went from being an affluent, free-spending married woman to a single woman with no divorce settlement and a sudden appreciation for penny-pinching.

Second, in 1997 when my mother died, I made a horrifying discovery. As my parents had aged, they'd turned their money over to a full-service stockbroker. During one of the longest bull market runs in history, the "expert" my parents had trusted to manage their money had kept them barely treading water. And their retirement plan, funds invested into a Wall Street trust, was performing even worse than Social Security.

My determination not to let what had happened to my parents' hard-earned money happen to mine coincided with my burgeoning interest in the amazing new world, cyberspace, that was exploding to life all around me. As a journalist, I was fascinated by the Internet and the technology that made it possible. In 1996, when I hired a high school kid to set up my new $1400 Mac Performa with a 28.8-bps modem and a Netscape browser, *The New York Times*'s new online publication, *The New York Times CyberTimes*, popped on my screen every time I went online. I started reading columns on digital commerce by Denise Gilbert and breaking news stories about Silicon Alley by Lisa Napoli and about Silicon Valley by John Markoff. Before long I was watching the one-hour technology program broadcast nightly throughout 1996 with Soledad O'Brien from San Francisco on MSNBC, the cable news network launched by Microsoft and NBC. Nerds whose names I was starting to recognize from the mastheads of computer magazines debated the size of "pipes" that would speed the "World Wide Wait." MSNBC and *CyberTimes* were making the cyberspace culture visible. Viewers and readers were picking up the lingo, speaking a new language—and so, increasingly, was I.

I undertook a campaign to convince the wonderful, harried editor of *CyberTimes*, Rob Fixmer, to let me write stories for him. Finally Rob gave me my first assignment: follow Mac evangelist Guy Kawasaki to a Santa Barbara Web design conference with Kai Krause, and I drove off to simultaneously learn and write about the new technology. Over the next two years I did a stint in self-education that was a little like freelance graduate school, with the Internet standing in for the professors. Writing a *CyberTimes* story often took me several months as I struggled to get myself up to speed on the topic.

Eventually, writing stories about the Internet led to writing stories about the financial element of the Internet, a realm that was cracking wide open as the forces of Silicon Valley invaded the staid bastions of Wall Street. In late 1997 and 1998 I wrote a series of three pieces on the intersection of the Internet and investing: one about a futurist predicting the death of the stockbroker at the hands of technology; one about the chairman of Nasdaq setting up "markets in a box" worldwide, based not on the specialist auction system of the New York Stock Exchange but on the kind of electronic order matching possible with the Nasdaq computerized stock exchange; and the final piece, on the speculators in a Los Angeles EDAT day trading shop. One of their star traders was a former pro basketball player for the Los Angeles Lakers who called this style of electronic direct-access day trading "a twitch game." In this professional-level electronic order-entry screen world, I realized, the successful cowboy day trader needed the reflexes of a professional athlete and the mental prowess of a scholar.

This last article caught the attention of Stephen Isaacs, an editor at McGraw-Hill, who called me to ask if I'd write a book about online trading. I agreed, and told him that I didn't want to write a book about something I wouldn't do myself. And so I began. My goal was to try it—both online trading and EDAT—and while trying, to keep my investment nest egg intact.

EARNING BY LEARNING ONLINE TRADING

When I sat down at my laptop in November 1998 with a gleam in my eye and my $25,000 investment at stake, the warnings of the naysayers were ringing in my ears. *Fortune* pronounced that for the little guy (or gal, presumably) who's trying to make money day trading, Wall Street is a "rigged game." The paternalistic brokers on The Street swore, "You can't outsmart Mr. Market." My father's broker said I'd be "taken advantage of" if I tried to teach myself to trade online. Friends told me that online trading is the fastest way to part a fool and her money. And when I started to mention the success I was having, the skeptics said, sounds great—but where's the money?

The answer is, I got it out. $31,500 total. I wasn't making the money as an EDAT but from trading online with an online, Web-based broker, just like millions of Americans. Before Christmas I got a check for over $4000. And then another one for almost $7500. Between Christmas and April I got two checks for $5000 each and one for $10,000.

That's pure profit.

So, to *Fortune* magazine I say, I believe you're sadly mistaken. The technological revolution is unrigging the game, opening the markets wide to small fry like me. To my father's broker I say, it wasn't online trading that took advantage of me—especially compared to my savings account, my credit card interest, and my cash card fees. In fact, by online trading I'm taking advantage of an entry point that was never before available. And to the naysayers who swear that the market should be left to the big boys, I say: Merrill Lynch, watch out. Salomon Smith Barney, mind your flanks. Because I'm no big boy, and in four months of trading I made 130 percent on top of the money I started out with.

Annualized, as they say in the financial industry, that's about a 400 percent return on my investment—a whole lot more than I would have made if I'd put my $25,000 in money market funds, mutual funds, or other traditional safe investments, and about 100 times better interest than I would have earned at my local Citibank or Bank of America.

DO TRY THIS AT HOME

I'm not technologically gifted. I'm not a professor of physics or a computer geek. And I'm living proof that you don't have to be any of those things to use the Internet to make money in the market. It's time for us scared souls to take the money out of the shoe box under the bed and give investing and trading a shot. As a wise friend once said, "Nothing beats a miss like a try."

Just as you can gradually educate yourself about the milieu of finance and the Internet, you can learn about online trading. The successful student is self-taught, using some key books, online resources, discipline, and guts. In the chapters that follow, I'll outline this self-empowerment, self-education process and give you the tools you need to put it to work for you.

You'll be in good company when you do. The market is full of baby boomers—accustomed to instant gratification, to figuring things out as they go, with an independent, sassy attitude. Rushing to make up for lost time, astounded at the continuing strength of this bull market, people my age are finally facing a reality the '60s generation never planned for: college for the kids and retirement.

And then there's Generation X, the children of the boomer generation, who take to technology like surfers to waves and snicker at their elders' inability to set the timer on the VCRs, install a new version of Microsoft Word, or sail boldly into the seas of Internet online trading. Now Generation Y. These generations, and their elders, are meeting up at online trading sites. Retirees, single mothers (like the one depicted in the Ameritrade ad, who sits at her daughter's computer at nursery school, making several thousand dollars while the nursery school teacher looks on in awe), and child-supporting dads are turning their small investments—the sum they can afford to lose totally, in the worst-case scenario—into significant profits.

Before we go on, a few words about my hidden agenda. I don't have one. I haven't written some fancy stock-picking software I'm hoping to sell you. I don't own a day trading parlor, as do many authors of books about day trading. I'm sharing what I've learned with you, the reader, because it works for me, and I believe it can work for you.

A FEW IMPORTANT TIPS: THE T3

Today, the new trader doesn't have to be a "cowboy" working in a day trading parlor or with an EDAT connection. The new online trader can start practicing one or two trades a day, privately, at home, very slowly and with little risk, using a discount broker like Schwab, Datek, or E*Trade. A portfolio of $250,000 will demand a different trading style than $2000, $1000, or even $400. But both can profit online.

Watch your costs: all new traders can use these T3 rules for managing risk. Keep your stock—one minute, one day, overnight, or over the weekend. But also keep these three simple risk-reduction elements—the T3, otherwise known as Troy's Three Trading Tips—in place:

1. *Limit order:* Know how to place a limit order when buying stock. No surprises. You buy only at the exact price you specify, usually somewhere between the bid and ask price on your screen.
2. *Stop-loss market order:* After you buy, immediately turn around and place a stop-loss market sell order with your online broker (or hold it mentally with EDAT trading). This 30-second act of typing in symbol, price, shares, and the time period during which you want this order in place will automatically sell your stock later, at the price you have predetermined, if the market suddenly plummets.
3. *Sell order:* Decide on the price at which you'd like to sell—don't get greedy—and keep it written on a piece of paper next to your computer. If the stock zooms up further, you can always buy back in for $8 or $10 or $30 commission—better than getting greedy and

losing your entire investment. Then circle back through steps 1, 2, and 3.

Troy's Three Trading Tips will be your beginner's safety net while you taste the highs and lows of trading. Determine for yourself if online trading might become your early-morning passion, an after-hours obsession, a treat with your morning decaf on a break . . . or something better suited to your husband, your wife, or the teenager next door.

In the next chapter we head to an EDAT trading parlor for a visit with the cowboy day trader, the gamer who watches his computer screen obsessively from 9:30 a.m. market open to 4:00 p.m. market close, trying to pick off a teenie (¹⁄₁₆ of a dollar) here; an eighth (12½ cents) there. This high-wire act, gambling blocks of 1000 shares or more, paid for with leveraged, borrowed money, is riddled with pitfalls for the nonprofessional—and is fascinating to the curious. . . .

•   •   •

INTERVIEW WITH EDWARD J. NICHOLL, CEO OF DATEK ONLINE HOLDINGS CORPORATION

An experienced Wall Street executive, cofounder and longtime president of Waterhouse, Ed Nicholl never went to college, but managed to graduate from Yale law school anyway, a first in modern history. He was recruited to Datek to bring some wisdom and experience to that company of twenty-somethings.

How'd you get to Datek after Waterhouse?
I started with Larry Waterhouse in 1978 as a discount broker after an earth-shattering event: May Day 1975. Prior to that date there was a legal monopoly fixing brokers' commissions. The SEC's goal was to unbundle commissions, to separate the cost of advice from the cost of executing. There was an inherent conflict of interest, of course, with brokerage commissions, because they never get paid to tell customers to do nothing.

At Waterhouse we used to try to figure out ways to put more information into the hands of our customers. We wanted to mail out charts to compare three companies' performance against the Dow. The cost to distribute that through the mail was astronomical, and by the time the customer got it, it was too old to use. Even five years ago, for me to get a chart of three companies and compare that against the Dow, I'd have to go to a sophisticated econometric boutique that provides the kind of information that was only available to professionals and institutional investors.

I've been in this business since the beginning of the evolution of discount brokerages into online brokerages. It's a remarkable time of change, analogous to the industrial revolution. We're really evolving into an information economy. People are more empowered, have more information, more access, than they've ever had. The key to the change has been the Internet itself. It's a distribution revolution, not an information revolution. The cost of distribution is so cheap now, thanks to the Internet.

What is an ECN?

An ECN is an "electronic communications network," an efficient vehicle that allows customers to meet among themselves. It also creates transparency and price competition—highest bid, lowest offer. All offers are published on the Web site (island.com). Island has its full book on the Web. All investors have equal access, competing with the same information set, so the spread is narrowing, and price discovery is extra efficient.

How do the trading desks for Nasdaq market makers and wholesalers operate?

Traditionally Nasdaq is a dealer market. The dealer buys the stock from customer A, sells it back to customer B, and profits from the difference. The spread is so profitable that they actually pay from 2 to ½ a penny a share for that order flow, so the dealers have to make more than what they paid the brokers to send them the order flow. By definition, the executions have to be worse than they are with an agency auction model like Island. It's why online brokers using an agency auction model ECN are winning the market share game. Customers go where the broker best represents his client, or they'll go to a brokerage firm that uses Island or Instinet.

How do you see the difference between EDAT day trading and using an online broker?

Day trading shops have direct access to the market. The difference between online and day trading is that the Internet puts another barrier of communication between the investor and the market. You still get that intrinsic delay that has to do with being on the Web, your ISP, the load levels. One second saved is very valuable for someone doing massive amounts of trading. People don't understand that a day trader routinely does 300 to 1000 trades a day. I cannot believe that anyone would want to do that! They turn into animals! It's just a horrible life.

What is it that EDAT day trading firms do?

They provide their clients with more complicated market momentum tools than the typical online firms do. And they allow their customers to choose (or "hit") the market venue exactly where they want it executed. An online firm has "best-execution" responsibility from the SEC. You give me an order and, as your broker, I've got to choose where I can best execute. The day trader says, "Here are the markets; you pick the best one."

Can an online trader choose where his or her execution goes today?

There's a movement afoot to empower the online investor to choose the market where they want to execute their order. AB Watley is trying to bridge that gap. E*Trade will allow customers to choose which ECN to go to. And we [Datek] are working on similar products, though we haven't yet had any public announcement to that effect.

The online trader must tread carefully. It's extremely complicated for the retail customer to decide which market venue is best. The majority of customers still expect their broker to make that choice. Part of what you get for the 10 bucks you pay Datek is a quality execution—we direct your order to where it will get best execution. Remember, the places for best execution change all the time: Island at one time, market maker at another.

Datek scans the market on a real-time basis. When your order comes in, Datek looks at all the market alternatives and directs it instantaneously to where it will receive best execution: one of the 500 registered market makers; a couple of exchanges, for example; Chicago trades over the counter. The order goes to where it will sell to the highest bidder or go to the lowest offer.

Yes, sometimes you will benefit from choosing where to have an execution. That's for really sophisticated traders. We're moving in that direction but we don't want to unnecessarily burden our customers with too many choices.

What's the difference between sending your order on to an ECN like Island and sending it to a market middleman who pays your broker for order flow?

The difference is huge! ECNs are auction markets. They allow customers to meet without having an intermediary who takes out a slice for his participation. Island "disintermediates." The customers meet; Island charges a small fee. Island's net fee is .00075 a share, less than one-tenth of one penny a share. On Instinet the institutions pay from 1 cent up to 6 cents a share. Buying 300 shares costs 22 cents on Island. On Instinet, where a typical institution pays 2 cents, it's $6. Look at the difference: 22 cents or $6.

Why do you say that Island is like eBay?
In both cases, people are empowered with information. They don't need to go through middlemen. There's no longer any need to give one set of capital market players the kind of advantage market makers and specialists have, by giving them superior information. Now the market makers (on the Nasdaq) and specialists (on the NYSE) actually impede efficient price discovery, in our opinion. Think of the automobile market. Do we need the dealers to tell us about the features of a particular car when they're all out there on the Web? Why not sell amongst ourselves via a mechanism that allows buyer and seller to meet efficiently? The most efficient price would be found when all the buyers go to this one centralized venue. It's called disintermediation.

How do you react to recent warnings from Levitt, chair of the SEC, about day trading?
There's nothing about disclosure that I don't like. I think it's the right way to go. People need to understand that there's a lot of risk, and be aware. At Waterhouse over the last 20 years the belief was that most people are best served by measuring their own risk/reward curve—by trying to understand, then acting on their own. I've always believed in disclosing as much information to investors as possible. If investors want to set aside $30K of their $300K portfolio to go crazy with day trading, there's nothing terribly wrong with that.

THE WILD RIDE OF
THE EDAT BANDITS

ON THE SCENE AT MOMENTUM

The mood is laid-back here in Houston, as the traders wait for the markets to open on a Friday morning in May. Dressed in their usual assortment of jeans and T-shirts, shorts and polo shirts, they sit at their computer stations sipping coffee from Styrofoam cups, crackling the pages of newspapers (the *Houston Chronicle* Sports section is a must-read before beginning a busy trading day), studying their screens. A conversation breaks out in a corner of the room, as a cluster of traders share information on some IPOs—initial public offerings of new companies making their debuts in the markets—that are scheduled for today.

Bennett Rowe, one of Momentum's best traders and the instructor of the firm's day trading training course, arrives and settles in at his station. In the final minutes before the bell, he scans various indicator charts—S&P Futures and Nasdaq—on his three computer screens to see where things stand and get a feel for where the market will open.

With Instinet active after standard trading hours, a lot can change between yesterday's close and today's opening.

"Some people take advantage of that after-hours Instinet trading and hold positions overnight," Rowe says. He doesn't, but he does run through his portfolio of stocks to see if there have been any changes since he left here last night.

Less than five minutes to go. The activity level in the room picks up. News is being called out by traders and by Momentum's full-time news announcer.

"One minute till the market opens," intones the calm voice of the announcer.

"E*Trade up 5. Ameritrade up 3 or 4," he adds.

And then, "Market's open."

For the first few minutes nothing much seems to be happening—in the market or in the Momentum trading room.

"I usually sit on my hands a little at first to get a feel for how the market is going. It's easy to get fake signals at the beginning," Rowe explains.

"THDO up $^{14}/_{16}$ on earnings," calls the announcer.

"Maxxam going up?"

The room is still fairly quiet except for the voice of the CNBC reporter on the New York Stock Exchange floor. But then the traders begin an intermittent commentary—some of it obviously meant to be shared, much of it muttered to themselves—about what's happening to various stocks and to their own trades. One trader wearing a baseball cap bursts forth with a stream of profanity.

"You have to get used to that," says Rowe, who is intently focused on his screens. "The air can turn pretty blue when traders are on the wrong side of trades."

As the first hour of trading progresses Rowe will not fare well, but his demeanor and discipline will remain unchanged: even-tempered, sanguine, focused.

An electronic bong sounds repeatedly at each trader's computer, signaling that their trades have not been executed. A computerized female voice seduces with "You got it!" when a trade is successful. These signals are part of the proprietary trading system used by Texas-based Momentum Securities.

"I messed this one up," Rowe remarks. By 9 a.m. the Nasdaq is up 25 and the Dow up 20, but traders can be heard muttering comments like "wishy-washy," "doesn't know where it's going," and less savory phrases.

"The market has no real direction this morning," says Rowe. "It's one step forward and two steps backward." Today is an especially quiet day. This kind of day can be tricky, tempting traders into ill-advised moves followed by activity insufficient to correct their losses.

"I've lost money this morning. I'll be spending the rest of the day trying to make it back," Rowe says a bit glumly.

On active market days, information updates pour out in a constant stream from the news announcer and from the traders. Unlike the hubbub of the open-outcry stock exchange floors, where shouted bids are still the rule, online trading is primarily a game of intense concentration and minimal movement or sound, as large amounts of money are gained or lost with a keystroke. It's deceptive. It's beguiling. And it's definitely not for the faint of heart—or assets.

Momentum Securities in Houston, Texas, is one of the oldest day trading firms in the country. Founded in early 1994, Momentum is still run by Jim Lee, who also represents the day trading constituency in Washington, D.C., as head of the ETA.

COWBOY TERRITORY

Online traders and EDAT day traders use very different tools and very different strategies, and occupy different camps. EDAT, again, is the defining element of the real day trader. The real day trader never uses the Internet to place orders, but rather uses electronic direct-access trading, a dedicated phone line to the market, wired through the broker. Many of the online traders described in Chapter 1 pay retail, have no idea how their trades are executed, use market orders, and often face unpleasant surprises. Here we visit the land of the cowboy day trader, also called the EDAT (electronic direct access) trader or the wholesale trader (so named for the prices he gets on his stock).

EDAT day traders are customers of an NASD-member brokerage house—a specialized small brokerage house called a *day trading firm*. The cowboys rent the computers and trading software they need to day trade, either in the firm's trading room or at home, using a dedicated phone line into the private telephone system that their broker/dealer uses to access the Nasdaq market directly.

These customers of day trading firms are not trading online through the Internet. They trade using a dedicated communications line that guarantees them instantaneous access to the "floor" of the cybermarkets, where they can execute a trade with the click of a mouse. And though they are customers of a brokerage house—just as you might be a customer of Charles Schwab's online brokerage—this is a special brokerage house that allows the cowboys, with their direct access to the market, to pay wholesale prices lower than the retail prices paid by the retail customers at Schwab and most of the other online brokers.

Despite the massive publicity heaped upon these EDAT day traders, the fact is that there aren't very many of them—analysts estimate there are

4000 full-time EDAT day traders in the United States today. And no wonder they're a rare breed: the cowboy trader's life is no quick ride into the sunset.

His work is performed quickly and directly, like a player in a game of Doom. (I say "he" because few women have the stomach to hang in there and pay the high commissions, although I've seen several be quite successful in trading rooms.) The EDAT trader's trading screen interfaces directly with the Nasdaq Level II quote montage, including the ECNs. He doesn't go through any middlemen. No market makers. No wholesalers. No third markets. He hits the electronic bid on his Level II Nasdaq market screen that seems to offer the best price for the stock he wants, and it's his. No waiting for confirmation. None of the last-minute surprises that befall the inexperienced retail trader—like discovering that the 500 shares of the hot Internet stock he thought he was buying at market at $20 actually went for $88, wiping out his account.

No, what the cowboy gets for his money—an average of $300 to $700 a month for software, computer, special phone lines, and data feeds—are the tools to make an *extra* eighth (12.5 cents) or a *teenie* (half that) by "scalping" on trades of 1000 share blocks. His goal is to trade ten, twenty, fifty, hundreds of times a day. Or he may become a *momentum* player, armed with massive amounts of information and crunched data, riding the market up and down to take out quick profits within a day or a few days. He uses leverage by working on margin, borrowing two-to-one against the value of stock in his account (the holder of a $50,000 account, for example, can make a $100,000 trade).

The cowboy buys and sells in seconds. He sees his sale executed instantly on the screen right in front of him.

Given the potential rewards and the adrenaline rush, why aren't there more cowboys? And why do so many people fail at their game?

One sizable obstacle is the price of admission. Today you have to start with $75,000, $100,000, or $125,000 you can afford to lose—with enough in reserve to put any gains you do make to profitable ends. Those who don't have this kind of capital tend to trade tensely, fearfully. It's hard for them to let go of their losses and move on—a requisite attribute of the successful cowboy day trader.

Even if you've got the money to start with, you need ever increasing amounts to stay in the game. Trading costs skyrocket with this brand of staccato trading. Do the math: a hundred "round trips"—a buy and a sell order—per day, at $25 each way. That's $5000 a day—and that's exactly how a lot of the day trading firms train wanna-be cowboys. Handily for them, it's also the way the firms make the most short-term money. Five days of this training and the newcomer owes the day trading firm $25,000 (conveniently, that sum will be deducted, trade by trade, from your account). The firms charge less to those who trade at such high volume as those described here. However, the EDAT day trader also needs to check the amount of interest he's paying to trade on margin—it should be around 6.75 percent.

The mental and physical stamina demanded by this particular twitch game is mind-boggling. The top player needs the discipline of a Zen monk, the mind-body connection of an elite athlete, and the focused concentration of a chess master. One pop of the mouse, you buy; another pop, you sell. Make a mistake and you pay for it. There are no corrections, no order cancellations, as there are with online brokers.

Day trading firms, often called *SOES bandits* (for Small Order Execution System) once made their money on the fat spreads between the bid and ask prices on the Nasdaq stocks. It was like shooting fish in a barrel. But today, these firms are under assault from without and within.

To understand why the original SOES bandits' success at narrowing spreads helped dry up their SOES-order business, we first need to understand a bit of history.

THE BIRTH OF THE BANDIT

After the October 1987 stock market crash, the SEC introduced SOES to help small investors get their orders executed in times of turmoil on Nasdaq. This electronic system could execute small orders electronically and automatically.

On the New York Stock Exchange, which is known as an auction market, one *specialist* is assigned to handle all the retail trades in his one stock. But the market maker system of Nasdaq operates differently, allowing multiple market makers and ECNs to compete in offering the best prices for a certain stock, such as Microsoft. They compete for orders by *advertising*, or displaying their best prices for a number of shares on the Nasdaq Level II screen, the quote montage used by all professional traders. When a market maker is hit with an order, he either sells from his inventory or buys what he needs, making a profit on his markup. (See Figure 2.1.)

After the 1987 crash, the SEC ordered the Nasdaq market makers to use SOES. In doing so, they cleared the path for a whole new gang of cowboy traders to make their presence felt on Wall Street, thanks to an unin-

FIGURE 2.1   *This is a version of the TradeCast Level II Nasdaq screen—which I traded with in the San Francisco day trading shop. This version has all the market makers and ECNs spelled out.* (www.tradecastsoftware.com—Powered by TradeCast Limited, Houston, Texas.)

INTEL CORP				☒
INTC				
Last 135 1/2 Change 5 13/16 High 135 5/8 Q B: 1000				
Close 129 11/16 Volume 4,153,400 Low 130 1 x 10 S: 1000				

135 1/2			135 5/8		
The Island Ecn	135 1/2	15	Hambrecht & Quist Llc	135 5/8	1
Knight Securities, Inc.	135 7/16	10	Societe Generale Securities Corp	135 5/8	10
Troster Singer Corporation	135 7/16	5	Lehman Brothers Inc.	135 5/8	1
Mayer & Schweitzer, Inc.	135 7/16	1	Chicago Stock Exchange	135 5/8	10
Salomon, Smith Barney Inc.	135 7/16	10	The Island Ecn	135 5/8	10
B-Trade Services Llc	135 7/16	31	Prudential Securities Incorporat	135 11/16	10
Terra Nova Trading, L.L.C.	135 3/8	2	Goldman, Sachs & Co.	135 11/16	1
Nationsbanc Montgomery Securitie	135 3/8	10	Warburg Dillon Read Llc	135 3/4	10
Instinet Corporation	135 3/8	10	Wedbush Morgan Securities Inc.	135 3/4	1
			Needham & Company, Inc.	135 3/4	1
			Uscc Trading/A Division Of Fleet	135 3/4	2
Prudential Securities Incorporat	135 1/4	10	Dean Witter Reynolds Inc.	135 3/4	10
Morgan Stanley & Co., Incorporat	135 1/4	10	Torrey Pines Securities, Inc.	135 3/4	10
Torrey Pines Securities, Inc.	135 1/4	10	Bernard L. Madoff	135 3/4	10
Everen Securities, Inc.	135 1/4	5			
Lehman Brothers Inc.	135 1/8	1			
Merrill Lynch, Pierce, Fenner &	135 1/8	10			
Weeden & Co.L.P.	135 1/8	2			

Buy 1000 INTC Limit 135 1/2 Day Partial SOES		
◭ Action Buy ▾	Send Order	Cancel Order

tended consequence that was soon discovered by sharp traders like Harvey Houtkin at NASD-member broker/dealer firms with access to Nasdaq Level II screens. That consequence? Their computers automatically executed trades at the prices listed by the market maker. The traders needed only to keep their eyes glued to their screens; if one or two market makers were late in updating the prices they had advertised on the Nasdaq screen-based market, these cowboys could zap in between the market maker's advertised bid and offer prices—the amount they'll buy a stock for and what they'll sell it for—slicing off a small but significant profit each time.

Before SOES, small orders could be brazenly ignored. There was too much trouble and too little return involved for the wholesalers to spend their time matching up a limit order (indicating the exact price the customer is willing to pay) with other orders. But now, the computerized SOES system *forced* the market maker to automatically execute an order once he was hit electronically by a trader.

The Wall Street market makers, representing all the top firms on the Street, hated what the cowboys were doing to the spreads where they'd always made huge profits. Suddenly the stock market was transformed from the elite enclave of the pre-SOES era to the equal-opportunity, free-fire trading zone of the '90s.

"Chump change," sneered Wall Street, dismissing the money earned by the cowboys.

But relentlessly, the EDAT method of hitting Nasdaq trades ate into the profits of the Wall Street trading desks at Smith Barney, Merrill Lynch, Goldman Sachs, and Salomon Brothers—the biggest players in the old Wall Street club. Pummeled by SOES hits from the moment the market opened in the morning until the instant it closed at night, the club began to stagger under the onslaught of the cowboys.

Suddenly, elegant software allowed small traders to play the market in real time, watching the pinball of prices ricocheting between the market makers. The irascible, outspoken Harvey Houtkin, who had pioneered the cowboy style in 1988, established the All-Tech Investment Group in Montvale, New Jersey, to give small individual day traders—those who aren't licensed stockbrokers—access that was once limited to the elite. Instead of relying on a telephone call or a shaky Internet connection, customers at the All-Tech Investment Group started driving the Nasdaq market makers wild with direct buys (hits) made from the company's Level II screens.

Harvey Houtkin's new cowboy trader could turn around and sell his thousand-share SOES'd block to another market maker at a fast eighth or a quarter profit, for a round-trip take of $250 (1000 times 25 cents). Subtract the brokerage commission costs—perhaps $25 in and $25 out—paid to All-Tech (and later Momentum, Block, Heartland, Landmark, or Broadway), and the lucky new cowboy trader could pocket $200 in a minute.

Staring at the Nasdaq Level II screen, hitting on the unlucky market makers who hadn't updated their prices to reflect current market sentiment, the day trading cowboy—the SOES bandit—could hit the jackpot again and again.

"Chump change," Wall Street repeated, less loudly. And the cowboys kept shooting fish in their on-screen barrels.

Day trading shops were springing up around the country. A branch storefront in a suburban mall might have an NASD-member firm offering 10 to 40 computer seats for rent to would-be day traders. For prices of $1000 to $5000 or more, neophytes were being promised surefire trading riches while they were being trained on the complex software, Nasdaq Level II screens, and streaming data feeds in one- or two-week EDAT classes.

SOES TRADING IS A HIT

Computer nerds who couldn't get a date were now raking in thousands of dollars a day. And the software and hardware that the nerds were writing and tweaking started selling to other eager wanna-be cowboy traders about as fast as the latest Smashing Pumpkins album. Individual investors and momentum traders suddenly had an edge on the Wall Street club. Each SOES firm featured its own brand of sleek proprietary software—some created by the firm, some reverse-engineered from others' products, still others private-labeled.

By 1998, Wall Street was feeling truly beaten up. SOES and EDAT day trading were the opening wedge that made the inner workings of the stock wholesalers visible to the American investor—including the middlemen with their "payment for order flow" kickbacks paid to retail online brokers and old-line firms like Smith Barney and Merrill Lynch. SEC regulations allowed the ECNs—the new little stock markets—to post their bids up on the Level II screen with the market makers. Often, they offered a wholesale price to the retail customer, and the market makers were cut out of the loop.

The Wall Street firms' trading desks were under direct attack. Their profitable spreads, once known only to market insiders on Wall Street, were now made public on thousands of screens at the new day trading firms.

SOES TRADING TAKES A HIT

Who wouldn't want to be a day trader for $10,000 a day? The SOES bandits were so smart, so fast, and so successful at picking off their market maker targets on Wall Street that before long, the goose stopped laying those golden eggs. Margins on Nasdaq stocks—the difference between the ask and bid prices—became smaller and smaller, until the sixteenth, or teenie (.0625), was introduced. The market will soon be decimalized. There are no more easy pickings on Wall Street.

Other factors came into play, helping to narrow the spreads on Nasdaq (we'll discuss them in Chapters 3 and 4). But it's important to keep this in mind: the SOES bandits now use SOES for fewer than 5 percent of their trades. Today's EDAT day trader has to have a sophisticated and deep understanding of the markets and how they work. Add to that months or, more likely, years of very expensive training time, and you can see why day trading and SOES bandits have lost their fast-and-easy-money cachet.

New Nasdaq regulations that went into effect in the second half of 1998 have forced the size of SOES orders—once bought and sold in 1000-share blocks—down to a maximum of only 100 shares. The "actual size rule" has made it unprofitable for both the new-on-the-block day trading firms, which rely on your commissions whether you're successful or not, and the cowboy customers who haven't learned to play a quarter-million-dollar, professional-level game. (See Figure 2.2.)

As a result, the focus of the trading revolution has shifted from EDAT trading to Internet online trading. In the interim, the best day trading firms have developed a new array of techniques for snagging trading profits during a fast-moving market—both going up and going down. James Lee, head of Momentum Securities and of the Electronic Traders Association, a lobbying group that appears before Congress and the SEC (Nasdaq has not put them on any committees yet), will tell us how that works in his interview at the end of this chapter.

But here in California, the golden land of opportunity, day trading hucksters are still eager to sell you on the delights of day trading for easy cash. In May, the NASAA (North American Securities Administrators' Association) listed the top investment scams in the United States. Ranking number two on the fraud list: investment seminars on EDAT day trading.

BANDIT IN TRAINING

In early 1999 I attended one of these day trading seminars. It was held in the conference room of an airport motel. The 150 or so people in the audience—90 percent of them men, most of them blue-collar workers, the ones from India, Pakistan, Central America, Mexico, the Philippines, and China with a poor command of English—were eager to learn about this new way to get rich quick. They thought that the online brokers like E*Trade and Charles Schwab were day trading firms. Since day traders use computers, they must be online traders, too, right? Wrong. The seminar organizers were selling their own proprietary EDAT trading system: the software, the data feeds, the direct EDAT hookups to their day trading firm—and the commissions that would flow from orders.

FIGURE 2.2 *Want to read what the professional Wall Street traders read? This is the place, including listings for local broker/dealer meetings to introduce concepts like OptiMark.* (Copyright © 1999, The Nasdaq Stock Market, Inc. Reprinted with permission of the Nasdaq-Amex Market Group.)

In response to a question about return on capital, the speaker estimates that the annualized return would be 2400 percent. But if you're looking for only half that trading "accuracy," he says, on a 20-day basis a month you'd get a 280 percent return on 2-to-1 margin.

What does that mean exactly?, I ask. And what is the "system"?

"I follow about a dozen stocks, trade the same ones over and over and over," the seminar leader answers. "I could teach a monkey to trade. It's nothing but pattern recognition."

What about loans for those of us who are long on enthusiasm but short on cash? The seminar firm's loan department "will give you money to trade if you have a capital base, but only if you have a trading history. We'll lend you up to $75,000 if you've established a pattern. Trade for a month, trade for a couple months and they'll make you a loan for day trading purposes."

The margin rates offered by the firm, a member of NASD, the parent of the Nasdaq Stock Market, were less than 1 percent annualized (whatever that means). Overnight positions have a maintenance requirement of 25 percent, against the 50 percent margin requirement. "I don't have the patience to go in and out 30 or 40 times a day," he says. "I don't have the patience to take an eighth or a quarter."

"It's the perfect job," he adds. "Set your own hours. Be your own boss. You don't have to call in sick."

This is the complete package, promises the speaker: the education, the software, the brokerage house, the clearing firm, the loans, the customer support. And the EDAT ability to log on at peak times—an advantage online traders sometimes don't have.

No wonder seminars like this one find an eager audience. According to the PBS *Nightly Business News,* 96 percent of the country's mutual funds failed to keep up with the growth in the S&P 500 in 1998. Judging by the attendance at this seminar and others like it, when people realized that 96 percent of their mutual funds did worse than the market, and only four did better, they started to wonder if they'd do better at picking their own stocks for themselves. In 1999 Americans chose to invest 30 percent less in mutual funds than they'd invested in 1998. Much of that 30 percent went directly into the market through the mouse-clicking hands of individual investors and traders.

The self-empowerment messages issuing forth from the big discount brokerages serve to exacerbate this trend. It began with newspaper ads—today there are so many TV commercials for e-trading that you can barely watch a network news show without starting to think they're beamed to professional money managers. Some people, in fact, become fine stock pickers—they've read the excellent investment guide by the Motley Fool, Lynch's *One Up on Wall Street* (Penguin, 1990), or Charles Schwab's *How to Be Your Own Stockbroker* (Dell, 1991).

Others, unfortunately, end up at seminars like this one.

"Most people coming online are just waiting for people to take money from them," the teacher said without a hint of irony. "Don't let it happen to you."

BANDIT FOR TWO MONTHS

On the theory that I shouldn't write about something I wasn't willing to try myself, I put my money where my book is and opened a $5000 account at a Landmark Securities branch in San Francisco.

I take BART to the city for my first day at work. At 5:55 a.m. the sun is barely peeping over the horizon; out the train windows I'm treated to a sweeping, mystical view of Berkeley, Oakland, the San Francisco skyline. Arriving at the Montgomery Street station I find the air in the financial district quiet, contemplative. Then I enter the seventh-floor trading room and blam! The blare of CNBC from the two big-screen TVs mounted on each wall broadcasts the clatter of the trading floor at the NYSE. The trading room manager scribbles the list of hot Internet stocks that the clearing firm—JB Oxford in Beverly Hills—will not short that day, next to a list of the preopen heavy movers on Instinet.

The trading screen had a hypnotic allure. Already I could see how one could make a huge amount of money if one had a huge amount of money to start with and a lot of time to practice. But those of us who were *paper trading*—using a computer simulation to practice before jumping into the real, lightning-fast trades—quickly discovered that trading on paper wasn't the same as the real thing.

First, I learned that my favorite method of trading—and the one with which I actually did make the occasional profit—ignored the market makers altogether. Every pantingly enthusiastic article about the wild profits of day traders and SOES bandits, and the amazing "level playing field" in the Wall Street markets, involved hitting the bid of whichever market maker had the best deal for me, the wholesale buyer. (See Figure 2.3.)

But strangely enough, I found myself avoiding the market makers on my Level II screen more and more. Why? Because the new entity on the Level II screen, the ECNs—BRUT, Archipelago, Island, others—were often coming up with the best advertised price. That price was often listed with the Island ECN. And Island's electronic limit order book—the information guarded with the lives of NYSE specialists—was free online at isld.com, where anyone on the World Wide Web could take a look. This was market transparency available without paying for a Level II screen, without an EDAT connection.

Hitting Island at my day trading salon's screen worked for me, but it also made me feel a bit silly. Island was where most of my own trades,

FIGURE 2.3 *Most professional freelance traders at an EDAT shop use the Trade-Cast screen to indicate the market makers and ECNs interested in both buying . . . and selling. It helps you make a more informed decision to see where the market may be going soon.* (www.tradecastsoftware.com—Powered by TradeCast Limited, Houston, Texas.)

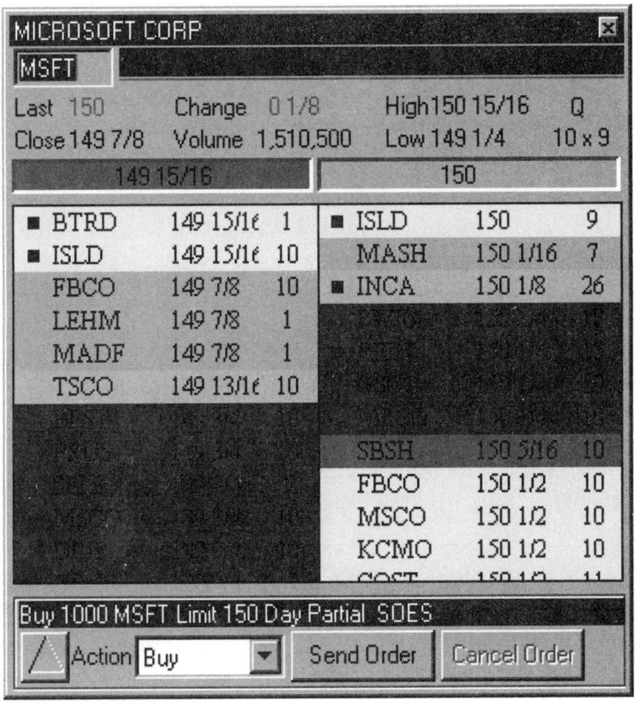

MICROSOFT CORP

MSFT

| Last 150 | Change 0 1/8 | High 150 15/16 | Q |
| Close 149 7/8 | Volume 1,510,500 | Low 149 1/4 | 10 x 9 |

149 15/16			150		
■ BTRD	149 15/16	1	■ ISLD	150	9
■ ISLD	149 15/16	10	MASH	150 1/16	7
FBCO	149 7/8	10	■ INCA	150 1/8	26
LEHM	149 7/8	1			
MADF	149 7/8	1			
TSCO	149 13/16	10			
			SBSH	150 5/16	10
			FBCO	150 1/2	10
			MSCO	150 1/2	10
			KCMO	150 1/2	10
			COST	150 1/2	11

Buy 1000 MSFT Limit 150 Day Partial SOES

Action Buy ▼   Send Order   Cancel Order

made from the comfort of my own home, were being executed by Datek, my online broker—for about $10, not the $25 or so I was paying at my Landmark terminal. Plus, at home I could put in a limit order, I could try to cancel if I had second thoughts, I could put in a stop-loss market order to cover my downside—all without buying into a dedicated communications network taking me directly to the Nasdaq cybermarket.

My orders to my online broker—at that point the only online broker offering an ECN—were shooting straight through my home laptop screen directly to the ECN without going through the hands of a wholesaler, without a slice taken out for my order flow, without another brokerage firm's trading desk getting my order in exchange for my brokerage getting its (profitable) orders. All the back-scratching and kickbacks inherent in the current system were dissolved in this electronic blast of a revolutionary innovation: opening the ECNs to the individual investor.

So why was I taking BART to San Francisco every day at dawn? Why was I paying Landmark for the privilege of trading like a bandit?

For a few days I lugged my PowerBook to the trading room, trying to invent some new style of crossover trading, a hybrid of online and EDAT. I realized I was already a wholesale trader, paying wholesale, not retail, prices for my stock—just without the expensive EDAT part. I also realized that for the level of trading I was engaged in, my homegrown method was just fine.

The people around me must have wondered why I was taking up valuable space in the trading room if I was going to do my trades on my laptop. Then I noticed another trader starting to do the same thing, drifting around the trading room, looking for an open Internet connection for his laptop's modem line. (Momentum's James Lee says point-blank that there's no way I would have been allowed to trade on a $5000 account that way at his place in Houston. I simply didn't trade enough—his minimum is $75,000. And when I did trade at the EDAT firm in San Francisco, I was getting nearly the same executions I got with my own online broker: better prices, just as fast. And I had access to Island's entire order book, sort of looking like a mini–Level II Nasdaq screen.)

I kept my day trading desk for 2½ months, from mid-November 1998 to late January 1999. In that 10 weeks, I made a profit of $132, after subtracting the margin interest costs and the trade costs of $45 or $50 round-trip.

After subtracting the $300 a month I paid for my computer station, I actually lost $618. But I learned quite a lot.

WHAT I LEARNED—WHAT YOU SHOULD KNOW

At first glance, it seems easy to make a big profit trading in and out of stocks each day. But even the most experienced, battle-scarred veteran trader can blow up: lose all his capital and suddenly find himself facing a huge debt. The SEC is prompting all investors and traders to thoroughly educate themselves about the markets and how they work. Here are some suggestions from experienced professionals for those of you who might try trading at home before going EDAT:

Fast markets mean danger. When volume and volatility are moving fast, there's little time to think. Don't be reactive and jump after the latest hot tip on CNBC or your favorite chat room. Instead, follow Troy's T3, the Three Trading Tips:

1. Always make a limit order rather than a market order.
2. Immediately go back to place a stop-loss market order, giving yourself plenty of latitude.
3. In your little black book, pencil in the price at which you'll sell. And don't get greedy.

In order to follow these guidelines, you must first learn all about *executions:* how does your buy or sell order go through your broker and how exactly is it executed? Is it sold to a middleman for a kickback for order flow? Is it moved on to an ECN owned by the firm, even if a better price is available elsewhere? Despite my limit order rule, are there ever times you might want to use a market order instead? (Check rule number 2.)

Bottom line: are you getting wholesale prices?

Compare the firms you're considering using. Call their customer service departments and ask exactly how they'll handle your order. Ask: What's the difference between a limit order and a market order? Does it go to an ECN? Do they own a middleman that they sell it to? Do they trade off with another firm and split the profits on the difference between the retail and wholesale prices of your order? What happens to a limit order and a market order during times of high volatility? During fast markets? If their customer service representatives can't answer your questions, keep calling around until you find someone who can. (Don't rely on reviews of online brokerage firms in the press. Many of them are written by reporters who simply interview firm management, not by people who actually trade and compare executions.)

Only use "play money": money you can afford to lose. There's *no* guarantee of profits. And your firm can clean out your account when you exceed your margin requirements—they don't even have to ask. (You gave them permission to do that when you signed the paperwork to open your account. Don't forget to read it.)

Go for quality. The Internet has provided access to a world of information that was previously available only to Wall Street insiders. Use this information wisely; steer clear of hot tips in chat groups. Go for quality companies and quality information services.

There are traffic jams on the information superhighway. There will be times when technological glitches delay your access to the markets. Using limit orders with online brokers can cover trading breakdowns and protect you from disaster.

These are the EDAT rules I found taped to my computer when I first tried day trading at the Landmark office. If you do decide to work with a day trading firm, consider this:

1. *Cut your losses at ¼.* No more. (The stock will *not* bounce, no matter how much you want it to.)
2. *Do not jump into trades.* This is emotional, and emotions are dangerous.
3. *Do not use intuition or gut feelings.* They do not work.
4. *Have two reasons to get into a trade.* P.S. Intuition does not count as a reason!
5. *Know when to take your profit.*
6. *Have a profit goal and stick to it!*
7. *Do not get greedy.* You will lose all profit and may turn a winner into a loser.
8. *Do not chase trades.* If you are chasing them, it is probably too late (not always).
9. *Do not hold overnight positions.* This is considered investing; you would probably not invest in the same stocks that you day trade.
10. ***Obey all rules or else!!***

Finally, lest you think these words of wisdom—or anything else—can protect you from the dangers of day trading: the trader who learned his lessons so well and wrote them out so carefully was gone soon after Christmas. I don't know what kind of profits or losses he took with him, but I do know this: few people walk away when they're winning.

We missed him.

● ● ●

INTERVIEW WITH JAMES LEE, FOUNDER, MOMENTUM SECURITIES

An MBA and former Wall Street player, Lee is an active advocate for the smaller trader going up against the market makers.

Is EDAT day trading merging into Internet-based online trading and investing?

Absolutely. We have a branded system we call the Electronic Communications Portal, the ECP. For years and years day traders on-site have been using sophisticated tools to maximize order exposure. As new ECNs, or rather points of liquidity, have become available, we've added those in. So increasingly we've moved from just having access to Nasdaq to now having access to Nasdaq and all nine ECNs. What we've been doing for years now is becoming more mainstream. There are going to be retail and institutional applications for this. What we have to do is simplify it to make it easier to take advantage of the access—make the mechanics of it easier.

Is that merging due to technological innovations like the ECNs and your software's instantaneous reach to find the best buys?

It's broader than just what we do at Momentum and Tradescape. The whole online explosion and day trading explosion was brought on by two things.

One was the SEC's order handling rules, which democratized the markets and have put customer limit orders on a fair footing and equivalent status with the professionals.

Two was enormous advances in communication capabilities and technology. You can now build networks that can get an order from our office to New York and back in ⅓₀₀ of a second! And you can do it affordably. You couldn't do that a few years ago. So out of those rule changes and technology came the ECNs. I don't think it was the other way around.

Will the EDAT traders' traditional identifying badge—a private dedicated phone line with direct access to the Nasdaq market and the ECNs—become passé with the arrival of a speedier, more robust Internet?

Yes and no. The Internet is the unknown. It is the cloud, and it is the problem with the connection that is one of two problems of online firms. Now you can improve your point-to-point through DSL hookups and even cable modems. But you're still going to have that unknown in between.

The alternative is to have a private dedicated circuit into a broker/ dealer and then from the broker/dealer onto the markets, where you have one continuous cable. If at any time you go through the Internet while they are improving the pipe, it's still the lowest common denominator link. So the slowest, weakest server anywhere in the Internet is going to be the peak performance you can obtain. You're still going to have problems.

So if you're trying to use AOL . . .

If you're going to try to use AOL on an analog system, you're going to have problems. Even if you went on a DSL point-to-point between your house and AOL, AOL on to the rest of the Internet is still a weak point. So the rule of thumb on the Internet is, your peak performance is only as good as the lowest quality server in between you and your end user on the other side of the Internet.

Isn't cable access to the Internet, like @Home, eroding the whole raison d'être of EDAT?

The Internet at times will function almost perfectly. It's just that at peak times and at times of problems, you are reduced to the lowest common denominator of the slowest functioning system between you and the other end of the browser on the Internet. I mean, Wilbur on a farm in Missouri could hit a fiber bundle with the hoe in his backyard and . . .

With a hoe? In his backyard? And it could make the system go down?

Potentially.

What's happening with order executions through online brokers? It's said that investors are getting screwed on limit orders during fast markets. Why isn't anyone saying anything?

I think they're getting screwed on market orders. It's what I call the biggest front-running operation in the history of the market. I've been calling this "front running" because that's what it is. There's a definition for it, and it's acting on material, nonpublic information about a pending block trade. Front running violates fair principles and the Fair Practice Rules of the NASD in working with customers. If you act on material nonpublic information—for your own account—of a pending or imminent block order, that's front running. Period.

What they've done here, for example, is to assemble 2000 hundred-share or thousand-share orders. Together they equal 200,000 shares. What they're saying is, that's not a block. Well I argue it is. They're all held up in a queue together.

If a wholesaler or aggregator assembles those . . .

And doesn't respond to them, yet sees them on their window and adjusts their price . . . then it's front running.

Doesn't Softbank's investment give you the global venture capital "seal of approval" by recognizing the significance of the day trading sector and its innovative infrastructure?

I think both Softbank and JW Childs validate not only our firm but the broader business.

How do you see Softbank and the world's market systems integrating Tradescape's innovative Electronic Communications Portal system? Was their shopping "bot" [robot] acquired with the other companies in the global Softbank venture capital portfolio in mind—such as E*Trade Europe, Yahoo Japan, E*Trade U.S., and so on?

My sense is that Softbank is interested in the Internet space and the major new players in it. I haven't sensed that there is an attempt to take Tradescape/Momentum software and capabilities and integrate them into one of these other players—although something like that might make sense. I think their strategy is simpler than that. It's to own the pieces and to assist major players in the Internet space. Period.

I think we all agree that what we're doing is next-generation online brokerage. The E*Trades and the Ameritrades and Schwabs, the Web players, with single access selling of order flow, was first-generation. The 10 major Web players control 92 percent of it right now. That was first-generation. What we're doing is next-generation. There was a point in time back in early '95 when owning a quarter of Yahoo! didn't make a lot of sense to a lot of observers. And now look at it! The same thing was true with E*Trade early on. This group has a track record. We believe in it. They seem to believe in it. The only people who don't get it are the state regulators.

In 1997, when I first started reporting this story, SOES trading was a niche market. Now the day trading firms are consolidating, with under 10 keeping 85 percent of the market. Do you see your firm five years from now getting into global markets?

Without question, yes. Sooner than that.

Any predictions?

We are going to leverage the good work that the exchanges are doing. Trading will follow the sun. I can see a world, just a year, year and a half from now when we're sitting here in our own trading platforms in Houston at two o'clock in the morning, trading a European stock through the Nasdaq's link to Frankfurt, to our domestic trading systems here in Nasdaq, properly settled through our settlement process. It'll be in dollars, and it'll be done in decimals.

So you've got this Euros-to-dollars problem. You've got fractions-to-decimals problems. You have certification and listing standards that have to be uniform. But those things will be ironed out a lot faster than people think. Really what we need to be looking at is not the private firms to go over and create links to Frankfurt. It's to leverage off of what Nasdaq and the New York Stock Exchange are already doing with these cross-border alliances. Nasdaq has an affiliation with Hong Kong. They're building a new market with Softbank in Japan. They've already got a joint venture agreement with Frankfurt. And that's the role of the exchanges, really, to work out. It wouldn't make any sense for an individual broker/dealer to have to go out and set up all of those linkages. We should be a member of NASD/Nasdaq and leverage Nasdaq's relationships globally.

But that's what all this after-hours trading is about. It's not about leveling the playing fields here for the retail parties trading our stocks. It's all about globalization. We're going to go 16 hours first, then on to 24. The only problem with 24-hour trading is we have to wait until the New York Exchange moves to its new floor, which it's going to do in 2005. By the way, we have a running bet here that by the time they move the New York to the new floor, the floor will be abolished and they won't have a floor. It will all be screen-based. By 2005, the floor of the New York Stock Exchange will be abolished.

So all United States markets will be "cybermarkets."
Absolutely. And continuous settlement—24-hour trading and simultaneous settlement.

What is settlement? When I was day trading in San Francisco there was a lot of paperwork involved in the backroom operations.
Well, we're still under a settlement rule where you have a trade date and three days to deliver on it. We still have some paper involved in the settlement process where people come and deliver certificates and there's a certain amount of it that's not held in the street name. We need to get to a completely paperless system. When you can do that, you can have instantaneous settlement, where the trade and the settlement takes place in the same day.

Do you feel justified and proud of yourself as the lone spokesperson for the ETA before all those Washington committees, despite your Wall Street background?

I wouldn't say "proud" just because we're too humble. We've always had a vision that this was the right way to conduct yourself, and that handling orders the way we do for customers is free of conflict. That's good. It's not bad, we have nothing to be ashamed of. I think Wall Street is warming up to the concept. You can see it in the major investments, you can see it in Merrill Lynch's opposition to the day trading suitability rules, you can see it in the Softbank investment, you can see it in a number of different places where Wall Street is ahead of the regulators.

What I'm concerned about are the state regulators who don't get it. I think it's part of being outside of the information loop, being underfunded and not knowledgeable about the systems.

And basically not being up to speed on the information superhighway?

Yeah, absolutely. They've kind of been underfunded and looking for a place. Congress moved in '87 to preempt many of the state securities boards' area of review in registration areas and investment advisory areas. So now they're fighting to justify their existence and they're taking off after day trading. They don't know what they're doing, frankly. I think Wall Street gets it. I think the Feds get it. I think that we're having a problem with the states and I think it shows a lack of knowledge in the entire area.

Who has the most to lose now on Wall Street? Does Wall Street—as opposed to venture capitalists like Softbank—get it yet? And why is this so beneficial to the individual investor?

I think those major full-service brokers, who thought they had a monopoly on information and did not provide a value-added service, have a great deal to lose. Now let me get this right. There are value-added services, such as Merrill Lynch or Smith Barney, in that they add in research (if it's good in quality), investment ideas, planning strategies, and so on. They should be paid for that. There will always be a need for that. But if they think condescendingly of their customers, and they have a monopoly on the free flow of market data and information, and they're using that to protect margins, then they're vulnerable. So they need to make sure they're value-added in an area.

I think there'll always be room for them. But if you're conducting a stranglehold on your customers because you don't think they're intelligent enough to get their information and discern it themselves, then you have a problem.

And why is this entire movement so beneficial to the individual investor?
Average spreads are off 40 percent in Nasdaq since the order handling rules. And trading costs are one-third of where they were just two years ago.

See, there are two parts to a transaction cost. There's what you have to concede in a spread. Just like when you go to Paris and you come back and there's a difference between the bid and ask when you're going from dollars to francs and vice versa. That's the bid/ask spread in that case.

If you buy a stock and sell a stock, the spread is a real cost in addition to the commissions you pay. If your spreads are 40 percent narrower than they were, then your total transaction costs have been reduced by a good percentage.

CHAPTER **3**

THE GROWTH OF MAJOR MARKETS AND THE NEW TRADING REALITIES

ECN VERSUS GOLIATH

Today the world is poised on the brink of a new financial reality: a global cyberspace stock exchange designed expressly for round-the-clock and round-the-world trading. As you read this, upstart stock markets—the ECNs, or electronic communications networks, discussed in the Preface—are already in operation. Coming soon: a battle to the death between these cyberspace upstarts and their still-dominant, almost inconceivably powerful predecessors.

We're talking, of course, about the Big Two: the New York Stock Exchange and the Nasdaq Stock Market.

WALL STREET THEN AND NOW

On a brisk Manhattan day in 1792, two dozen men were poised to make history. Over a decade earlier, strong-minded men such as these had beaten the mighty British Empire in the War of Independence. Now the little group of merchants and brokers stood in the dappled shade of a large buttonwood tree on the north side of Wall Street, talking intently about the phenomenon known as "stock trading," which allowed individual investors to buy and sell "shares" of a company, providing a ready pool of capital for the expanding nation. By the time they went off to lunch, they'd drafted the Buttonwood Agreement—the origin of the New York Stock Exchange, an association that would, by the 1990s, funnel billions of dollars into the corporations and private coffers of the world.

What emerged from that seemingly casual meeting over two centuries ago—the agreement that, among other things, decreed a standard 0.25 percent commission on all stock trades—was nothing less than the financial engine that drove the exploration and development of a new continent. In 1817, the brokers moved their enterprise indoors to 40 Wall Street. Now they had a nice place to take shelter from a rainstorm, although they continued trading outside, in an open air market sheltered by the trees, for another two decades.

At the height of the Civil War, the group changed its name to the one still used today: the New York Stock Exchange. By the end of the century, stock traders who didn't belong to the now-exclusive NYSE were looked down upon as guttersnipes and moneygrubbers. In 1908 these outsiders banded together to form the New York Curb Exchange. When the NYSE voted to deny its Big Board listings to the smaller, less-capitalized companies, those firms flocked to the Curb Exchange. The Curb Exchange, later known as the American Stock Exchange, or AMEX, ultimately merged with Nasdaq in 1998.

So quintessentially American was the idea of raising money by selling and buying shares in a company, that it raced westward across the expanding nation. At one point, almost every city worthy of the name—Philadelphia, Cincinnati, Chicago—boasted its own stock exchange. Shortly after gold was discovered in 1849, San Francisco's Pacific Stock Exchange became the centerpiece of that city's bustling economy. Several of these regional stock markets, including the Pacific Exchange, exist to this day.

In 1896 the Dow Jones Industrial Average, named for the reporting-publishing team that devised it as a market indicator, was initiated by the same publishing company that now brings you the *Wall Street Journal* and business news on CNBC. In its infancy, the Dow Jones tracked the prices of a mere dozen companies with names like Standard Rope & Twine.

BOOMS AND BUSTS

The Roaring Twenties brought a soaring stock market. The stock market ticker, a long, narrow printout emitted from a small, bell-shaped device, became emblematic of a decade of unprecedented prosperity and speculation. The origin of today's electronic ticker that runs across the bottom of the CNBC television screen, the paper teletype indicated each stock's symbol, the price and size of its most recent trade, and its most recent change of price. Ticker reading became (and remains) an art.

Throughout the 1920s, thousands of millions of dollars poured into the accounts of stock market investors. Endless coils of ticker tape accumulated on the floors of the trading rooms clustered around Wall Street, as investment fever inflated the speculative bubble and traders manipulated stock prices, while speculators swarmed into "bucket shops" where people bought stocks at unregulated prices. Investors and traders knew the latest prices at which their stocks were trading. But they didn't know about the true financial health of the companies in which they were investing: which of them practiced honest accounting and which were cooking the books.

Then, as the decade neared an end, the bubble burst.

The great stock market crash of 1929, which ushered in the Great Depression of the 1930s, led to the creation of a new federal agency: the Securities and Exchange Commission. The Securities Act of 1933 required full financial disclosure (known today as "transparency") of all publicly traded companies. The 1933 act also reined in then-unregulated brokerage houses and underwriters, legally prohibiting fraud in the sale of stocks and bonds.

America's participation in World War II created the underpinnings for the biggest economic boom in the country's history. This buoyant economy was mirrored by a climbing birthrate—the genesis of the so-called baby boom generation. By the 1960s the passions of the boomer teens began to dominate popular culture, including the booming stock market, which was characterized by a go-go mood. In 1968 the Wall Street go-go years ran out of steam when brokerage firms' back offices—those hidden, unglamorous rooms that house the paper pushing and numbers crunching that keep the stock market afloat—seized up, strangling on a hideous backlog of order slips, confirmations, carbon paper, stock certificates (lost and found), confused messengers, and pink phone message slips. The whole system nearly ground to a halt. This paperwork tsunami crisis marked the last gasp of the pre-computer-era back offices.

Besides eliminating the back offices, the fizzle of the go-go years roused some long overdue sizzle from the Securities and Exchange Commission, which finally moved to regulate the previously uncontrolled profit margins of the Wall Street brokers.

THE BIRTH OF THE NASDAQ

From the 1920s through the 1970s, every American stock customer was a retail customer. Even institutions bought their stock from brokers at large brokerage houses like Merrill Lynch or E.F. Hutton. Those brokers' commissions were sky high: Wall Street had a lock on the market and charged as much as the traffic would bear. The broker's fee for the purchase of 100 shares could be $200 or $300 over and above the stock price. In the course of a lifetime of trading, these commissions cut insidiously into profits and capital alike. Without the benefit of today's software that allows investors to run the numbers, yesterday's investors remained blissfully unaware of the compounding cost of the bite Wall Street was taking out of their retirement nest egg.

That began to change in 1970. First, the SEC zeroed in on over-the-counter stocks. These smaller OTC stocks, not listed on the New York or American exchanges, were traded in a freewheeling style reminiscent of the 1920s. To create more transparency in these transactions, the SEC nudged the NASD, the National Association of Securities Dealers, to put together a kind of electronic bulletin board. This state-of-the-art electronic network would link all broker/dealers and market makers and display the lists of quotes: the *bid* (the price the market maker will pay for the stock) and the *ask* (the price at which the market maker will sell the stock). The difference between the bid and ask, known as the *spread,* was the profit slice the middlemen took for themselves when executing orders.

During the very early days of the computer revolution, this first new cybermarket came online as the Nasdaq, the National Association of Securities Dealers Automated Quotation system. All the talk between the 500 or so dealers' computers that made up this quote-listing network flowed through private, dedicated telecommunications links. The wholesalers and the trading desks of big firms like Merrill Lynch and Smith Barney now had a central meeting ground—which completely excluded the retail customer.

Initially, the inception of the Nasdaq didn't do much for the retail stock customer who was still paying big fixed fees to his broker, still victim of a bloated, inefficient market system dating back to the 1920s. The broker collected his money from the buyer whether his tips made money or lost it, whether he gave advice or only executed the customer's trades.

MAY DAY! MAY DAY!

On May Day 1975 that system collapsed. As troops and tanks gathered in Moscow's Red Square, celebrating the anniversary of the Soviet revolution, the SEC issued new rules that ended fixed commissions on all stock trades.

Older, inefficient firms folded. New businesses were launched, as institutional investors began negotiating the prices of their stock in a new way: buying stock "wholesale." Instinet, owned by Reuters, the British financial publisher, invented the ECN. Institutions began subscribing to the service and using it to trade blocks anonymously. Used by institutional investors like mutual funds and pensions to match orders anonymously, Instinet trades in both NYSE and Nasdaq stocks without the human intervention of a specialist or market maker, without going through a stock exchange. Instinet's unspoken motto? "We can get it for you wholesale!"

An upstart eponymous brokerage in California, Charles Schwab, popularized the idea of the "self-empowered" investor who chooses not to let a broker tell him what to do . . . and to save money while doing it. Discount brokerages came into their own.

In 1980, NYSE member firms were allowed to started trading stocks newly listed on the NYSE in the so-called third market, away from the New York trading floor. This sent even more order flow to the Nasdaq-linked trading desks at discount brokerages.

Nasdaq became a Silicon Valley powerhouse, listing many of America's top technology companies. It was the hot arena for start-ups, the one reliable place where investors could buy and sell shares in new entrepreneurial companies. Nasdaq now lists firms such as Microsoft, Amgen, Intel, Yahoo!, and Dell—Goliaths in industries, or sectors, that didn't even exist in 1971. Throughout the 1980s, trading boomed on Nasdaq, but the stocks were still sold the old-fashioned way: competing wholesalers (called *market makers*) listed their best prices on the Nasdaq screen. It became so profitable to be a market maker in these hot, high-tech stocks that Bernie Madoff, a Wall Street trader, came up with the idea of *payment for order flow.* Later referred to as a "legal kickback" by some observers, payment for order flow meant brokers were paid for forwarding their customers' orders only to certain market makers. (Some believe that when an order is being handed off to a third party for payment, the implicit conflict of interest raises questions about how faithfully that third party handles that trade.)

The discount broker Quick & Reilly was the first to provide DOS-based trading software for retail customers. Investors squinting at their slow, memory-challenged desktop computers were able to make trades by going online through CompuServe, one of the first Internet service providers, or ISPs.

In 1985, the volume of trading on the smaller Nasdaq Stock Market started nipping at the heels of the NYSE. Discount broker Charles Schwab unveiled The Equalizer, a software package that linked customers' PCs directly to Schwab. Now customers could input orders electronically using their telephone keypad. The customer became the data entry clerk.

. . . AND BUST AGAIN

The first generation of online traders had just started buying stock as the bull market of the 1980s screeched to a halt on October 19, 1987. The Brady Commission report on the 1987 crash led to the institution of "circuit breakers": NYSE rules that prohibit the program (or computer-generated) trading orders from entering the electronic DOT (Designated Order Turnaround) system when the Dow jumps or drops more than 50 points. Not much attention was paid to a significant March 1988 speech by Bob Birnbaum, then president of the NYSE, in which he noted that only a few major Wall Street players—not the program trades—had been largely responsible for Black Monday. Birnbaum seemed to imply that huge institutions, in a time of panic, should not be allowed to grab all the available liquidity (the ability to continue buying and selling) for themselves, leaving the small stockholder out in the cold.

The crash inspired Nasdaq to make changes to the new Small Order Execution System. Retail investors could now automatically execute small orders on the Nasdaq screen, without a phone call from wholesaler to wholesaler. Soon the SOES bandits (described in Chapter 2) arrived on the scene, ultimately narrowing the spreads (retail markups) for all investors.

THE END OF THE FAT SPREAD; THE ADVENT OF NEAR-ZERO EXECUTION COSTS

In 1994, a paper by two unknown finance professors, Paul Schultz and William Christie, appeared in the academic magazine, *The Journal of Finance*. In it, Schultz and Christie revealed that, although prices on the Nasdaq were always listed in eighths—as in 13⅜ or 17⅞—they'd discovered that odd eighths like ⅜ and ⅝ never appeared on the Nasdaq screens, which kept the market makers' spreads fat. The trading desks of the top Wall Street firms were becoming huge profit centers, starting to usurp the status and rank afforded the investment banking side of the firms.

The professors' academic paper posited an unspoken collusion among the market makers. The Justice Department began an investigation, and the SEC instituted reforms. The SOES soon ensured that the small investor's order was executed. And the order handling rules, which went into effect at the beginning of 1997, ensured that *all* limit orders that bettered the existing *inside price* (the bid and ask price that appears on the computer screen when an individual is placing an order with an online broker) had to be displayed—put right up there on the Nasdaq Level II screen and displayed worldwide. Finally, the trading desks at famous Wall Street firms like Morgan Stanley, Merrill Lynch, and Smith Barney had to pay a total of nearly $1 billion to settle investors' class action lawsuits.

But the truly revolutionary impact on the market was made by the rules imposed on Nasdaq by the SEC.

New order handling rules went into effect in January 1997 with actively traded issues like Microsoft, Sun, Intel, Dell, and Amgen. That was "one very scary day," according to a trader I'll call "John." Any limit order that bettered the inside price had to be displayed on the screen, either by the market maker or by sending it on to one of the new ECNs blessed by the SEC. The ECNs, taking inspiration from the way the institutional investors had been able to trade at wholesale prices on Instinet, set up the same sort of anonymous, order-matching electronic systems for the customers of brokerages and online discount brokers.

"It took at least three months for people to understand the new dynamics of the marketplace," says John, who was in the middle of this SEC-encouraged revolution on the Nasdaq. "The first three months were very turbulent. People were confused. There were all sorts of wild and crazy accusations. Traders didn't understand customers' newfound abilities to change the price of stocks via the ECNs."

The broker/dealers, and the old ways of doing business, were backed into a corner. Thanks to the SEC, the brand-new ECNs—those little stock markets cooked up by the nerds called SOES bandits—were suddenly given access to Nasdaq screens and started popping up at the most inopportune times with better prices and limit orders that had previously been tucked away in a bottom drawer. Retail customers suddenly started trading wholesale on ECNs, without paying a spread to a market maker or getting clipped with a kickback. Execution costs for the small investor with access to an ECN began to drop to near zero.

The SEC is now taking applications from the ECNs to become actual stock markets. And Wall Street is still reeling.

• • •

INTERVIEW WITH ROBERT M. GREBER, CHAIRMAN, CEO OF THE PACIFIC EXCHANGE

Greber's 25-year career in securities detoured from 1979 to 1984 while he served as president and CEO of George Lucas's film and special effects studio, Lucasfilm Ltd. As chairman and chief executive officer of the Pacific Exchange, Robert Greber has presided over what some call the end of an era as the institution prepares for probable closure of its stock-trading floor. The exchange, founded in San Francisco in 1882, occupies an imposing granite building erected to house U.S. Treasury offices in 1915 at the heart of the city's Financial District. Its traditional façade belies efforts under Greber, who arrived in 1990 as executive vice president for marketing, to innovate and keep pace in a changing industry. The Pacific Exchange was the first to adopt OptiMark, an electronic trading system that debuted in January 1999. It plans to start the next century with some stock traders working off the floor as pioneering "remote specialists."

What was the exchange like when you arrived nine years ago?
There's a different kind of energy here today that's prompted by the changes in the industry. We need to be a more entrepreneurial, more flexible organization that's quicker to act than exchanges have been in the past. I think the big challenge now for an exchange is to fight to stay ahead of the volume, while at the same time understanding the mechanisms by which market forces are driving order flow. For this exchange to have built an alliance with OptiMark—that's a major departure from traditional exchange operations. Here's a complete outside party that operates as a facility of the exchange. That's to take advantage of what we believe the future is and that's more and more electronic trading.

What does it mean to be a regional exchange today?
It doesn't mean very much any more. We're all part of the national market system, so we trade with all other exchanges. The price that we guarantee here is at least as good as it's going to be anywhere. And we have competi-

tion from alternative trading systems, electronic communications systems [ECNs]—they're all over the place. We do offer price improvement, where our specialists are stretched always to improve upon a price, where that is not always the case away from exchanges. To be a self-regulatory organization still has a lot of value and as long as the SEC and the Congress care about the public, which I think will continue, exchanges will still have a major role.

When did you begin to see the writing on the wall as far as the influence of online trading?

It used to be the biggest technological leap was using your telephone keys to enter a trade. About three years ago was the first time you could do trades through a proprietary [brokerage] Web site. It became clear that the empowerment that an individual gets from that is so scintillating and so satisfying that it had to grow. Instinet was one thing, but it's a professional platform. It's really the individual that has driven this revolution and even the firms that were there have been surprised by the success.

When did you begin to consider OptiMark? What happened before the deal was agreed?

I met Bill Lupien in 1995—I knew Bill from before—and he tossed out this idea. I got a sort of a flush all over because I thought, this is a great idea and this is going to be one of the most difficult things I'm going to have to deal with in trying to get consensus from my organization to go forward with it. I took this on as a personal project because I felt it was really important for the Pacific Exchange to platform this. We were really the only ones who were willing to step up and take the heat. It took six months of talking to every single member of my board separately and going out to see all the customers that I knew would give me trouble because they would feel threatened by it. My floor members objected strongly. I basically gambled my political capital with my members and my board in order to get this through, and I think it was a good gamble.

What will OptiMark do for the exchange? Why was it important to be first?

OptiMark was a way for the Pacific to move from being a nearly totally retail-oriented exchange to one where we now have a balance with institutional and retail business. You need to differentiate yourself. By offering a product like OptiMark and showing the flexibility and aggressive nature of this organization, we do that. We make it very clear that we're a player. That's one element. The other element is that if OptiMark is as successful as we think it will be, this will be a major, major economic and financial benefit to the exchange. If OptiMark is successful based on their projections, doubling our volume is only a first step. The Pacific will be positioned better than most all exchanges, because listed business that's done on OptiMark will be done on this exchange. We also will have earned sweat equity in OptiMark, so we'll be part owners.

Has OptiMark achieved a "critical mass" of users?

No, I don't think so. Users have to build a high level of familiarity with it and it takes time. It puts a burden on users in terms of time and when you're dealing with a very volatile market, you're just trying to stay even. But the volatility seems to be evening out a little bit and this kind of environment will allow users to take the time to start using it. The critical mass is building quickly.

Did you expect other exchanges to follow your lead? How will the advent of OptiMark trading on Nasdaq affect the Pacific Exchange?

We expected other exchanges outside the United States to do that, and they are. We always knew Nasdaq was part of the OptiMark plan. At the Pacific, we only trade listed [NYSE] issues, and they only trade Nasdaq issues, so there will be very little effect for us when they start. I think it gives a lot of credibility to the product.

Can OptiMark help the exchange attract individual investors?

I think long term, yes. The individual investor, by sending their order through their broker to the Pacific, will send their order into OptiMark. The rules we have laid out state that any order coming into OptiMark through the Pacific will have priority. If you want to buy 500 shares of, say, Lucent, and a large institution puts in an order to buy 100,000 shares at the same price, normally you could be sized out. But our rules say you go first because your order came through the Pacific rather than an OptiMark terminal operated by an institution. I'm waiting for the time when people say to their brokers, here's the order but I'd like to know that it's going to the Pacific.

How would you describe the public perception of electronic trading, given past criticism of "program" trading and events like the breakdown of the Pacific's earlier SCOREX system in 1987?

The public has more confidence in electronic systems than they did. It's more understandable for people, the more they understand about computers, to know that sometimes when you hit the "enter" key, nothing happens. There is no bug-free software and no one has ever designed a system that has infinite capacity. We have redundant systems, we have backups; from the customer's point of view, they're in very good shape. OptiMark has enormous capacity and the Pacific has enormous capacity. Right now on these days when we're trading 20 million shares, we're only running at 40 percent of capacity.

How will you proceed if you get regulatory approval for your proposal to let some specialists operate off the floor?

That is what we call our "remote specialist." Once we get permission, we will move a couple of specialists and floor brokers off the floor, maybe in the same building, just to see how it works. Once we know it works, we'll certainly move farther and farther away from the complex. With full implementation we could have specialists and floor brokers anywhere. People say to me, that means the exchange is going to disappear. The exchange is not bricks and mortar. The exchange is our facilities, our technology, our regulatory oversight. We will just be able to operate more efficiently.

What has been the impact of day traders on your business?

They certainly increase the volatility and they have increased the volume. For the most part, we don't have any problem with that. I think it's more of an issue of, do these people know what they're doing. I think there are people doing this who aren't taking into account the full risks. When the market goes south, it goes south very fast. And as volatility drops, a lot of them won't be able to continue.

What do you see for the exchange in two years or five years?

Three to five years from now, the equity floors as you see them today will not be there. There will be an office building peopled with Pacific Exchange staff. There will be specialists and brokers all over the United States who are members. In metropolitan areas, there could be groups of specialists and brokers who pool their resources to trade in the same trading rooms. I think we will still have an options trading floor, augmented in a major way by electronic systems. I think you'll see the Pacific allied with more than one entity like an OptiMark, like perhaps other exchanges around the world, where we're trying to provide trading as efficiently as possible. The organization that provides the most liquidity at the lowest cost with the best technology wins, and that's our goal.

CHAPTER 4

THE NEW CYBERMARKET

THE ECNS

Neither auction market (NYSE) nor negotiated market (Nasdaq), the ECNs are a third type of market: an electronic matching system in which the individual's trades seek out a mate at the desired price. Each order goes into a networked database and hooks up with another at the same price, sort of like computer dating. The ECNs are challenging the big market makers where it hurts them most: on those popular Nasdaq Internet stocks, traded by heavy Internet users, through their Internet brokers.

As mini–stock markets, the ECNs are threatening to both the NYSE and the Nasdaq because they charge next to nothing to execute a trade. (Costs are kept low by entrepreneurial start-ups: at year-end 1998 Island, the story goes, ran on a gang of 250 store-bought networked PCs and a clutch of Compaq servers.)

But once they complete the SEC registration process and become officially recognized U.S. stock markets, as Island has started doing, the ECNs will trade both Nasdaq and NYSE stocks. And now the New York Stock Exchange is also threatening to invade Nasdaq's high-tech listings by creating its own consortium of ECNs—maybe Instinet, Bloomberg TradeBook, and BRUT—under the umbrella of the NYSE brand. They could then trade in Nasdaq stocks like Microsoft, Intel, Yahoo!, and MCIWorldCom. (Right now, the third market of NYSE stocks that routes through Nasdaq may represent 10 percent of all of trades in NYSE-listed stocks.)

The ECNs operate as matching systems for stock orders coming in electronically from online trading customers as well as institutional customers. In a way, they operate like the NYSE auction system, where over 90 percent of the orders were matched up (with no spread) in the mid-'90s, and where the electronic SuperDOT system handles the vast majority of incoming orders.

That matching system is what the ECN tries to replicate, without paying any extra fees to the NYSE or the Nasdaq. The ECN offers the best of the NYSE—order matching—and the best of the Nasdaq—open competition for the best prices—via a screen-based system viewed by hundreds of thousands of customers who can trade in many places, instead of the small group that can crowd onto the NYSE floor around the specialist's station (as seen on CNBC on mornings when Maria Bartiromo covers the opening of trading in AOL stock).

The technology behind the explosion of Internet stock chat rooms and online traders is the same technology that's fueling the new cybermarkets. These cybermarkets, like the old-line Instinet and the newer OptiMark, Island, Strike, and Archipelago ECNs, are putting both the New York Stock Exchange and the screen-based Nasdaq market to the ultimate test.

The SEC opened the cybermarket floor to the public, in essence, to help erode the price-fixing influence of the Wall Street firms. The New York Stock Exchange specialist system and the Nasdaq's market maker system both had quirks that limited the viability of the markets at times of crisis and sometimes unfairly influenced the price of stocks.

The retail customer—you and I—can now sit with an ECN alongside the market maker, and soon alongside the New York specialist, in this vast international electronic stock bazaar. Nasdaq now shows retail orders that were once brazenly ignored by Wall Street. And the Byzantine NYSE and its system of specialists will soon have to open up to ECNs that, unlike Instinet, can be used by individuals during trading hours.

Today, even the biggest and richest of the Wall Street firms aren't quite sure how stocks will be traded in the next year or so. Merrill Lynch and Goldman Sachs recently announced a new ECN, Primex. Joining forces with the big stock wholesaling firm, Bernard L. Madoff Investment Securities, the three firms will push trading volume onto Primex at about the time the stock market switches to using decimals, rather than fractions, in stock quotes. Madoff is the Nasdaq market maker who first thought up the concept of payment for order flow for discount brokers. Madoff's order-flow arrangement with E*Trade, for instance, must have been thrown into question after E*Trade's $25 million investment—with Goldman Sachs—in another ECN, Archipelago, six months earlier. E*Trade, and its individual investors and savvy traders, were getting too wise in the ways of Wall Street.

The move to create an ECN seems to make sense for Merrill Lynch, since the 15,000-broker firm pledged to make online trading available to their retail customers by year-end 1999. As discount brokers come online, more and more orders are routed to ECNs, where customer quotes can be matched or sent on to the Nasdaq screen. (See Table 4.1 for the top 10 ECNs.)

Since 1980, Nasdaq broker/dealers have been allowed to trade in NYSE stocks through third-market or "upstairs" orders (so named because brokers, in order to maintain privacy and save themselves money, used to go upstairs to their firm's trading desk rather then run an order through the NYSE's floor specialists). Thanks to the online brokers who send orders to the third markets or NASD middlemen and market makers through the Nasdaq's screen-based market, these orders now represent nearly 10 percent of the trades in NYSE stocks.

All the big upstairs Nasdaq trading desks at firms like Merrill Lynch and Goldman Sachs have become less and less profitable. These upstairs and third-market desks started making less and less money when the SEC's order handling rules went into effect in 1997. Their profits were further diminished by their continued trouncing by the SOES bandits working from EDAT day trading firms. Today, only a tiny trickle of SOES orders go through such major EDAT day trading firms as Houston's Momentum. But the upstairs desks are still shrinking.

The Chicago-based SOES firm, Terra Nova Trading, gave birth to the Archipelago ECN, which was bought into by Goldman Sachs and E*Trade. The New York–based former SOES firm Datek Online Trading spawned Island ECN, bought into by Waterhouse Securities, a division of Canada's Toronto Dominion Bank. So while SOES has lost its punch, the electronic access movement it started is unstoppable.

The roots of this thriving ECN-for-retail trend are deep in the day trading counterculture revolution that emerged with SOES in the early 1990s. Suddenly able to hack out paths through the electronic undergrowth of the Nasdaq market, these guys began to see where the weak links lay, just as the hackers who hit AT&T with their "blue boxes" had done years before.

In 1997 or 1998, had you told the great Goldman Sachs or Merrill Lynch, which labeled day trading "a threat to America," that they would be creating an ECN or going in on a deal with a day trading firm, they would have been appalled.

The young and the reckless created by the SOES era got a good look, right on their own computer screens, at how The Street's lumbering giants

TABLE 4.1   Troy's Top 10 ECNs
The new little electronic stock markets moving in on Nasdaq and the NYSE

ECN	FINANCIAL BACKERS	PLANS
1. Instinet www.instinet.com	London-based Reuters	Operates in 40 markets globally. In fall will offer after-hours trading for E*Trade customers. Competing with Datek's Island.
2. Island ECN www.isld.com	Started by Datek, now also backed by TD Waterhouse	Nasdaq trading volume surpassed Instinet Q4, 1998. Largest in U.S. Opened August 1 for after hours by Datek.
3. OptiMark www.optiMark .com	Softbank (Japan), Dow Jones, Goldman Sachs, more Wall Street firms	Sophisticated order entry takes it beyond order matching. Pacific Exchange; fall launch for Nasdaq itself.
4. BRUT (Brass Utility)	Merrill Lynch, Morgan Stanley, Knight TriMark, Goldman Sachs	Executes Nasdaq trades in closed network. Does not reveal order book over Internet like Island.
5. Archipelago	Instinet, E*Trade, Goldman Sachs, J.P. Morgan, American Century	Another ECN with day trading background. Will be used by E*Trade.
6. [Unnamed start-up]	DLJ, Fidelity, Schwab, Speer Leeds, Kellogg	An experiment for DLJdirect and others without ECNs.
7. B-Trade	Bloomberg (as in "Box")	Matching orders for Bloomberg "Box" customers.
8. Eclipse	Morgan, Salomon, Herzog Heine Geduld	Fall launch for Internet matching network linked with ECNs.
9. Primex	Merrill Lynch, Goldman Sachs, Bernard L. Madoff*	Catch-up experiment for not-yet-online giant Merrill Lynch. Launch in 2000.
10. POSIT	Bloomberg, Investment Technology Group	By 2000, sees a superECN joining with B-Trade for elec-tronic "crossing" system.

UP AND COMING SUPER ECN

CyberX	CyberTech	Developing retail SuperECN.

*Inventor of the practice of payment for order flow, also called "kickbacks" by some ana-lysts. A big factor in many online brokerage firms' bottom lines during the past few years.

divided up the spoils. After the order handling rule changes of 1997, the entire Nasdaq screen became accessible to all retail investors over the age of 21—including those 11- and 14-year-olds who convinced their computers that they were 21.

These are revolutionary times indeed. The market information and trading access that were once only in the hands of institutional traders are now used by the online trader, who can get near-instant executions at rock-bottom prices. Datek Online started ECN after-hours trading in July 1999; others followed in August.

The most established players in the country's financial markets are facing a cluster of earthquakes powerful enough to shake traditional Wall Street to its foundation. The twenty-first century will bring global, round-the-clock trading across a series of execution platforms and trading that puts the final decision making firmly in the hands of the individual (whether she or he wants it or not).

Let's look at some of the alternate markets that are populating the investment landscape today.

INSTINET

The ECNs appeared in 1997, when the SEC changed the Nasdaq rules, dictating that any price that beat the inside spread had to be posted on the Nasdaq Level II screens around the world.

In fact, the granddaddy of all ECNs had been in existence since 1969. Instinet—where all that hot after-hours institutional trading you see covered on CNBC goes on—now trades globally in over 40 stock markets, including the New York Stock Exchange. Instinet was originally designed as a private game for private players: the big institutional investors, who sought to cut their costs by cutting out the middlemen.

When Instinet was created, the ECN provided an anonymous venue that allowed the big funds to buy and sell stock at wholesale prices. Most of the smaller ECNs, like BRUT and TradeBook, that have popped up within the past three years also traffic in stocks for the funds' money managers, rather than for individual investors.

The only ECNs oriented to the individual are Datek's Island, All-Tech's Attain, and the newer Archipelago, now allied with E*Trade. For the past several years Datek has been sending all of its 200,000 customers' orders off to Island ECN. E*Trade is using Archipelago, its new ECN. This practice should muffle some of the criticism that has been leveled at E*Trade's practice of selling customer orders to middlemen.

ARCHIPELAGO

Archipelago is a Chicago-based ECN whose owners now include Goldman Sachs, one of Wall Street's most powerful players, and E*Trade, Silicon Valley's top online broker. E*Trade and Goldman Sachs each invested $25 million for a 25.5 percent stake apiece in the Archipelago ECN.

Gerald D. Putnam's day trading firm, Terra Nova, created Archipelago to allow its day trading customers to meet and trade without paying the middleman. Terra Nova Trading was one of many EDAT firms started up after the SOES traders started making money on the Nasdaq. Some of the Terra Nova traders worked out of the firm's day trading rooms on individual computer terminals; others set themselves up as long-distance EDAT customers, connected to the firm through dedicated telephone lines. Both had the opportunity to use Archipelago.

In 1998 Archipelago wasn't very liquid; in the first month of 1999, Island beat Archipelago by a factor of about 11 to 1. But once Goldman, Sachs starts using Archipelago for its institutional customers, and E*Trade starts offering Archipelago to its customers, the numbers should start to even out. Putnam's personal 25 percent stake is now valued at $25 million—yielding another important lesson: the people who invented the systems used by the day traders often come out ahead of the day traders themselves.

Archipelago charges a commission of ½ cent to 2½ cents a share, much more than the razor-thin commissions—.00075—on Datek's Island.

ISLAND

Island made headlines in the *Wall Street Journal* after Christmas 1998, when Nasdaq trades on Island exceeded the number of trades on Instinet, the oldest and the biggest of the ECNs. (See Figure 4.1.)

Island appeals to Wall Street traders who are eager to embrace the kind of razor-thin margins that the Island ECN is running on: .00075, or less than a tenth of a cent a share. (Compared to this, the 1 cent a share mar-

FIGURE 4.1 *The Island ECN came from the creative minds that brought you Datek (see www.josh.com for background). Ask your broker if they use the ECN.* (The Island ECN, Inc.)

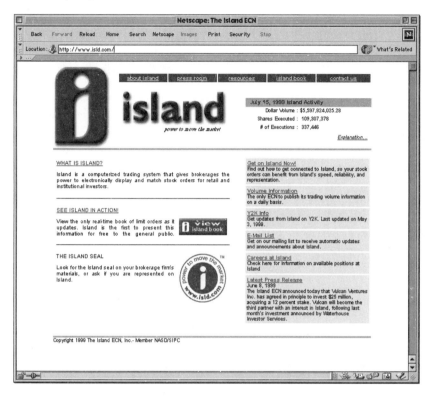

gin that caused some market makers to reject OptiMark seems absolutely bountiful.)

Driving the Island ECN volume even higher is the explosion in online brokerages, which use the ECNs to save money on their executions. As the investors and traders using these online brokers started getting more sophisticated about order execution, they began to understand that their orders could end up costing them more money per share when sold to a middleman than the money they seemed to save with their $29.95 or $7.95 discount brokers.

The Internet-generated flood of new investors has kept Island very busy. Datek Online sends all its orders to Island; if a limit order can't be matched there, it is then routed to whoever shows the best price on the Nasdaq quote montage, the Level II screen.

Island is the first ECN to apply for alternative stock market status under the new SEC regulations. Despite the recent $25 million investment by Toronto Dominion Bank's Waterhouse Securities, Island radiates an excitement reminiscent of the early days of Silicon Valley, when Apple was unveiling the Entirely New Thing: the personal computer. Like the Apple crews who worked hundred-hour weeks, eating cold pizza and sleeping on the floor, dedicating their youth to inventing the Lisa and the Macintosh, the Island boys are boys indeed. The head of Island, Matt Andresen, is a grizzled vet of 29, and Josh Levine, the computer whiz behind the Island ECN's order matching system is—yikes!—over 30! (Levine's Coney Island wedding photos are displayed on his personal Web site, www.josh.com. And should you be interested in more salient matters, you can view the entire "book" of Island, one of the cyber-floored markets, at www.isld.com. See Figure 4.2.)

FIGURE 4.2   *The Island book gives you the whole limit order book, something the NYSE specialists guard with their lives.* (The Island ECN, Inc.)

Island Book			
island home	system stats		help

GET STOCK

EBAY   [EBAY] [go]

LAST MATCH		TODAY'S ACTIVITY	
Price	119 7/16	Orders	3,392
Time	12:15:03	Volume	321,572

BUY ORDERS		SELL ORDERS	
SHARES	PRICE	SHARES	PRICE
500	119	1,000	119 7/8
15	118 1/2	200	120
125	118 1/2	100	120 1/8
50	118 1/2	100	121
17	118 1/2	500	121
50	118 1/4	100	121
15	118	100	121
10	118	500	121
50	118	100	121
100	118	1,000	122
50	118	50	122 3/16
5	118	100	122 13/16
55	118	100	123
20	118	400	123 9/16
25	118	100	123 5/8
(34 more)		(74 more)	

As of 12:15:06

OPTIMARK

Aimed at the big boys—the institutions that invest retirement funds and mutual funds, as well as banks and insurance companies—OptiMark may yet make the biggest impact on the market, with typical orders ranging in the thousands and millions of shares. Founded by Bill Lupien in 1998, Opti-Mark allows major institutions on what is called "the buy side" to place their orders anonymously, electronically, and with a detailed profile of how the buy should take place. Rather than merely matching orders, OptiMark's brain can be programmed with a money manager's complex dance, a many-stepped trading strategy. For example, the buyer may decide that 300,000 of the 500,000 shares he's buying of company X must be bought for no more than $40 per share, but the remaining 200,000 shares may be purchased at prices increasing in increments of 12.5 cents each, per 5000-share block, with various fallback positions, until the entire buy is made. The computer makes that happen cheaply and anonymously by joining all the buyers and sellers in deepest, darkest cyberspace.

The company knew they had a market, because research conducted for OptiMark showed that the extra price to a mutual fund buying a position in a midcap firm could make their order cost 9 percent more. In other words, a $500,000 purchase of stock in a midcap firm—one valued at something between $1 billion and $3 billion—would cost the fund an extra $45,000 (or 9 percent). Why? Because big buyers have a hard time moving through the markets quietly. People gossip. Traders whisper. The impossibility of keeping secrets in a human-based market allows traders to front-run a big order that they see looming on the horizon, thereby jacking up the price. (The earnings that day traders reap, staring at their Nasdaq screens, are often a direct function of how quickly they can tease out information about "the ax," the big buyer, from the market numbers flashing before them.)

The broker/dealers of Nasdaq wonder what this 9 percent savings on a midcap buy will do to *their* profits. But the holders of mutual funds see they'll be getting more for their money. One of the country's most powerful third-market traders, Bernie Madoff, has complained in print that Opti-Mark trades will only make about a penny a share, while now traders can make from between 4 and 10 cents. (See the interview with Bill Greber, chairman of San Francisco's Pacific Exchange, who first saw the promise of OptiMark's alternative trading system, in Chapter 3.)

The $150 million invested to get OptiMark up and running comes from some of Wall Street's heaviest hitters: Credit Suisse First Boston, Dow Jones (publisher of the *Wall Street Journal*), and Goldman Sachs. Trading through the Pacific Exchange, OptiMark has signed up over 150 big institutional investors and about 90 Nasdaq broker/dealers. Nasdaq itself has signed up with OptiMark to help execute trades by the end of 1999, as sort of a central limit order book, though without the transparency that the new Nasdaq team has so carefully put in place across the market since 1996— and despite the fact that this seems to compete with the NASD's own members' interests. No wonder there are tremors on Wall Street.

Interestingly, OptiMark is not itself a product of Wall Street. The jolly green giant came into being on a 1000-acre ranch outside Durango, Colorado, that once belonged to Louis L'Amour, author of all those Western novels Ronald Reagan once loved, now headquarters for Bill Lupien. From the ranch in Colorado, its big brain humming in a Toronto computer center, messages transmitted through an umbilical cord at the Pacific Exchange in San Francisco, where third-market trades for NYSE-listed stocks are often routed, running through Nasdaq's computers and servers in an office park in Trumbull, Connecticut—where a squirrel once chewed through a wire and knocked out the system—OptiMark is the perfect poster child for the new cyberspace reality of financial markets.

The NYSE is none too happy about this upstart on its flank; the big institutional trades are the bread and butter of its membership. The New York exchange has even resisted Bill Lupien's attempts to gain OptiMark access to the ITS, the main telecommunications network between the NYSE and other regional exchanges. (The ITS was cobbled together after the Big Bang 1975 deregulation in the stock markets; Lupien himself was on the committee that first created the network.) The primary goal of the SEC back in 1975 was to centralize the markets, not balkanize them; but the NYSE, powerful player that it is, is simply refusing to let OptiMark and the ECNs play.

ONLINE CONSUMER PRESSURES, OR THE DEATH OF THE STOCKBROKER AS WE KNOW HIM

The online brokers funnel significant research, breaking news, analysis, real-time quotes, and near-instantaneous trades to an increasingly sophisticated trader. The price? Next to nothing, in a world in which full-service broker Merrill Lynch can still charge several hundred dollars in commissions for executing the same trade.

What the consumer is demanding now is more knowledge and more control over how that trade is executed. The consumer wants to know what sort of a cybermarket his or her trade makes its way through. Is it an Arabian bazaar with wads of baksheesh changing hands in curtained-off rooms, or a nice, clean, bloodless white squash court in cyberspace, where costs are as tiny as the digital blips that carry the information?

Whether the brokers are scurrilous and sleazy or on the up-and-up, all this customer self-empowerment is forcing the market makers into a corner. After all, they're the ones who have to back up their buy and sell quotes on the screen of the Nasdaq cybermarket by actually putting up their own money. (Take a look at Kurt Andersen's 1999 novel about the year 2000, *Turn of the Century* [Random House, 1999]. There's a marvelous description of a market maker cornered by the fictional Ben Gould, a superrich trader modeled after TheStreet.com columnist and full-time trader James Cramer. The Cramer character graciously lets the market maker off the hook; his largesse costs him $19 million. This is the sort of old-fashioned emotional exchange that can only happen between flesh-and-blood people, not computers.)

By year-end, according to Island's Andresen, the consumer will want to tell his or her broker exactly how to execute his or her order, just as clients of EDAT day traders do now, by hitting an ECN or a firm's offer on their screen for an instantaneous execution. But industry veteran Ed Nicholl of Island's parent company, Datek Online, warns investors not to run headlong into this brave new world without an education as to how the markets work. After all, for decades brokers have been responsible for ensuring that their clients get the best execution. And now, even the big Wall Street firms aren't exactly sure how the markets work from month to month. It's fast moving. It's complex. And no one knows where the technological wave will break.

Though there have been resisters to the online brokerage revolution, they are falling one by one as they consider buying a stake in their own ECNs. Merrill Lynch, where the average compensation for a broker working on commission is still $300,000, goes online at year-end. Salomon Smith Barney is talking about it. Morgan Stanley Dean Witter hasn't yet bitten the bullet (they own Discover Brokerage Direct). And Price Waterhouse?

Whatever happens, the cheaper trading gets, the higher the volume of trading that results. Shorn of advice and hand-holding, the trade is yet another commodity today, and the value-added component comes in the execution quality.

A LOOK INTO THE FUTURE

Stock trading is now the best business on the Internet, according to *The New York Times*. The low-low commissions charged by the online brokers, combined with the elegant software that speeds customer orders to the markets, are apparently even a better business model than the online pornography that once nailed down the Internet's biggest profits.

The ECNs add even more vectors of change and efficiency to the traditional U.S. markets: the regional markets, and the American, the NYSE, and the Nasdaq. The ECNs do much of their trading in the hot high-tech issues on the Nasdaq market, where most all the new Internet issues migrate after their IPOs, from Yahoo! to eBay to E*Trade to Amazon.

Three years ago, the ECNs didn't exist. Today, 20 to 25 percent of all Nasdaq trades are being executed on ECNs—which means that 20 to 25 percent of the money, and 20 to 25 percent of the liquidity (once in the hands of the market makers), has now switched over to the less-regulated ECNs.

About one-quarter to one-third of all the retail customer trades are now being made online. And more and more of these trades are now being shuttled directly to ECNs.

So, although the ECNs and their operations may seem arcane and confusing, it's important to keep an eye on the ECNs and on the executions of your online broker as you learn about trading stock. The look and feel of today's stock market may no longer exist after 2000.

The very concept of "Wall Street" may be in for a shake-up. If Nasdaq is in an office park in Trumbull, Connecticut; OptiMark comes from Toronto in Canada; offshore trading is happening in the Grand Cayman Islands; Data Broadcasting hunkers down in Jackson Hole, Wyoming; independent investors run their lives over the Internet from Prague; and all these real-time trading quotes are zooming around overhead on shiny new satellites circling the globe—where is Wall Street in this picture? Wall Street becomes a state of mind, a sort of trademark, a brand, perhaps—a virtual, floorless, go-anywhere-do-anything cybermarket system that's circling the globe and all its people, with Internet access for all.

•   •   •

INTERVIEW WITH ALFRED R. BERKELEY III,
PRESIDENT, NASDAQ STOCK MARKET

The Nasdaq Stock Market was restructured in the mid-'90s, separating the Nasdaq from its regulatory branch, NASD Regulation, and from its parent, the National Association of Securities Dealers, Inc., headed by chairman Frank Zarb. As the country's first electronic stock market—the cybermarket without a floor—the organization selected Al Berkeley, a seasoned high-tech warrior, to lead them into the new e-commerce arena of dueling ECNs and millions of retail customers trading online. (See Figure 4.3.)

Al Berkeley had been managing director at investment bank BT Alex. Brown. Berkeley was one of the first research analysts in the country to focus on the then-new software industry (with then-unknown little companies like Microsoft). He went on to focus on information technology, much as Michael Bloomberg, creator of the Bloomberg Box and Bloomberg News, had zeroed in on IT as the direction of the future at Salomon Brothers. Before being drafted to head the Nasdaq Stock Market in mid-1996, Berkeley headed up Alex. Brown's high-tech mergers and acquisitions.

How do you see Nasdaq's new extended trading hours?

We are not rushing headlong to extend trading hours. We said in our board meeting that we thought it was more appropriate to have a full and vigorous public discussion of this issue, bringing in all market participants. We believe it's much better for the country to have all markets open at the same time. If we move to extended trading hours, everyone should do it at once.

But if someone insists on moving to extended trading early, we will bring the Nasdaq up with all its investor protection mechanisms. And we will require people to publish two-sided quotes and we'll require people to say what the last trade prices were and we will have all of our surveillance and compliance computers running.

We did that in an effort to try to slow this down until we understand the financial implications of it. It is not, as most newspapers indicated, that Nasdaq intends to open early. It is a threat that we will open early if anyone else does.

FIGURE 4.3   *Start traveling internationally: Nasdaq's site takes you on a click-through journey to over 60 stock markets around the world, from Hong Kong (set up a portfolio in local currency), Moscow, Frankfurt, to London. And, of course, links to every Nasdaq listing.* (Copyright © 1999, The Nasdaq Stock Market, Inc. Reprinted with permission of the Nasdaq-Amex Market Group.)

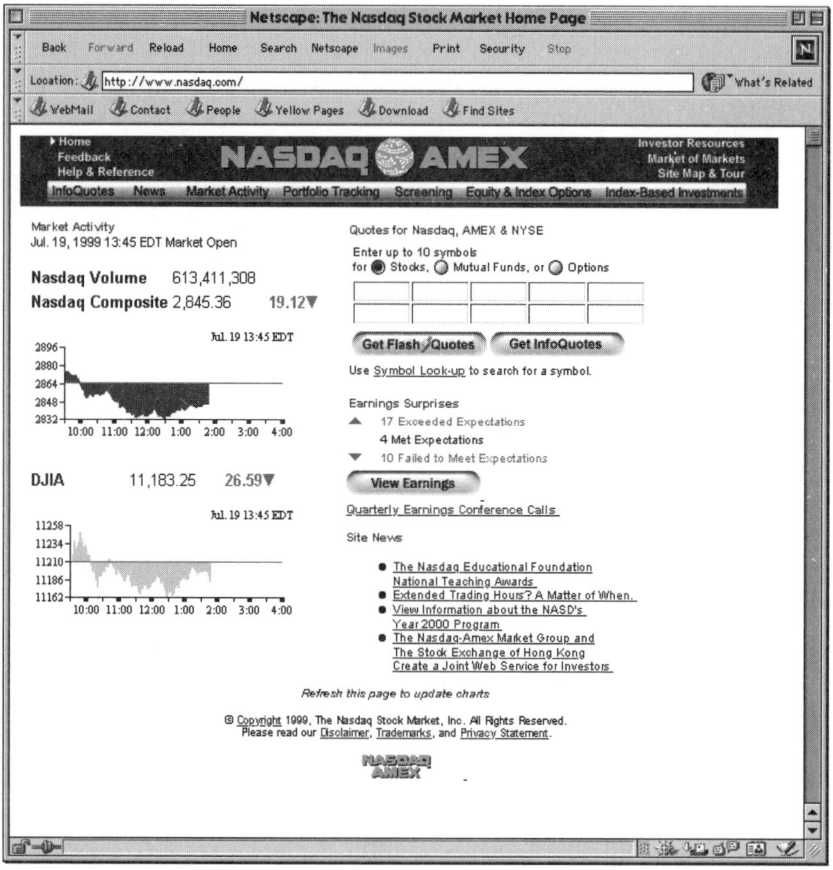

What about the New York Stock Exchange starting to trade Nasdaq stock?

We don't necessarily know all the facts about their business, but we're told that they have very few trades in most of their companies. We were told that over 2000 of their companies have less than 25 trades a day. If you look at their business model, where a designated dealer [a "specialist"] can trade the stock that he's awarded but cannot move into the ones where the action is, many of those people must be having a terrible time financially. That's why we think they want to trade our more active stocks—because the investors don't have any interest in the old smokestack stocks that populate that exchange. We also heard that half of their stocks have less than 15 trades a day and fully 1000 of them have less than 10 trades a day.

Do you think they're going to be doing this with a group of ECNs?

Well, they're certainly trying to organize a group of ECNs, but it's an interesting dilemma because the ECNs have a more efficient business model than they do. So why would an ECN want to give up its economic advantage to hook up with them? The one thing they may try to do is to share tape revenues. In other words, to rebate a portion of the fees they earn by selling quotes, which brings the "payment to order flow" issue up to the exchange level.

Now the SEC has opened an inquiry into the structure of markets and what quote "revenues" should be used for. The New York exchange and all the other exchanges have signed a document that says that they use quote revenues for the furtherance of their business, like self-regulatory functions. And if they then turn around and say, Well I don't need all this money; I can actually pay people part of it—what does that say about their attestation of needing these prices at the beginning?

So we think they're in a double bind there. But that may be what they want to do. In other words, we don't think that being affiliated with the New York on trading Nasdaq stocks is as attractive for an ECN as they think it is. And we're not sitting on our fannies either. We have rule filings in at the SEC now to take away the regulatory advantages that ECNs have, and level the playing field—to take away the unfair advantage that an agency-only ECN has over a firm who handles both agency and principal orders [principal orders are trades for the account of the firm itself, market-making trades].

And the market makers are important to keep liquidity in the stock market?

Yes. This is the great debate that's unexplored in the public conscience, that none of the press has picked up on. What you see is a classic debate: how do we as a country provide the liquidity we need in bad markets?

We're having this debate in the middle of the greatest bull market in history. So no one is paying attention to the risk side of the equation. There are three business models out there that are competing. There is a *no*-intermediary model called an ECN. There is a *single*-intermediary model called a designated dealer or a specialist. And there is a *multiple-*intermediary model called the Nasdaq.

The question is, which of those models is the right model for the country to embrace? We know from bitter history that markets do need liquidity providers in bad markets. But we haven't had a bad market for nine years.

What helped in 1987 with Nasdaq and liquidity?

Nasdaq and liquidity was just like the New York Stock Exchange and liquidity: the markets closed. But 1987 is light-years of history compared to where we are with electronic markets now.

Is Nasdaq already offering stocks from the New York exchange to the retail customer?

Anybody who's not a member of the New York Stock Exchange is welcome to trade them on Nasdaq and anybody who is a member of the New York Stock Exchange is willing to trade stocks listed on the New York after 1979 on the Nasdaq. It's called the "third market." We already have market participants who do that.

I was told by a very authoritative person that with the AOL stock that trades on the New York, only 6 percent of the trades are being touched by the New York Stock Exchange specialists. Well over 80 to 90 percent of the trades are being done away from the New York Stock Exchange, either on the Nasdaq or on the regional exchanges. The same is true of Compaq. We trade the NYSE stocks every day.

The third market is executed on the Nasdaq, on our equipment and our machines and our trade reporting. It's very complicated to most people because it's arcane and not important in most people's lives.

But it's getting to be more and more important right now, I think, as the investor gets more sophisticated.

We did an analysis for Compaq on this. Specialists [on the NYSE] look to be able to handle about 2000 trades a day. When trading surges on high-volume days, all of that surge is absorbed by the Nasdaq.

How are you going to be working with OptiMark now?

OptiMark is part of the Nasdaq. They are a central limit order book, but they're opaque. On Level II you won't see anything on OptiMark. Nobody can see what's in it.

We also hope to have a central limit order book that people can see. And we'll give investors a choice of how they want their orders displayed or not displayed. You can see everything that's in the Nasdaq. That's one of our basic tenets [market transparency], except in the OptiMark arrangement. This is why the traditional markets don't like us. We think their [NYSE] specialists should show everything that's available, too.

Yes, this is quite an interesting question. And with OptiMark, are people going to be able to put individual orders through OptiMark?
Certainly. You can do it through a broker or, if your broker gives you the electronic facility [EDAT], you'll be able to do it electronically. All firms are required to offer direct access to the market now if they offer electronic access.

In other words, because of the order handling rules, if you specify that your order goes between the bid and the ask, you create the new inside market.

There are two important things that have happened in Nasdaq. One is that anybody in the United States can set the inside price on Nasdaq from their kitchen if they want to. Anybody. Either the best bid or the best ask. If you see a stock that's selling, let's say at 20 to 20⅛, and you want to price it at 20¹⁄₁₆, you can. You can go between the bid and the ask yourself and you control that order.

The second thing we did is, if there's anything in the Nasdaq quote montage that you see that you want to hit, and you get to it first, you own it. So we have executions from the kitchen and we have inside pricing determined from the kitchen if you want to do it.

We've already talked about the fact that we display everything that's available to buy and sell in Nasdaq on Level II screens all over the world. There's no market like it.

How many Level II screens do you think there are all over the world?
Probably six or seven hundred thousand. What you've got to understand is that when you display an order in Nasdaq, hundreds of thousands of people can see it. That's very different from the New York or American where you're hoping two or three people are walking by in what they call "a crowd."

We have an electronic crowd that's hundreds of thousands of people deep and because we present it all digitally, we allow people to set their computers to beep if something hits the price they want. So we have literally millions of people who can participate in your effort to advertise your order.

This is why we're so terrifying to the older exchanges. This is why the European exchanges rose up on the political side to try to stop us from being successful with Nasdaq. Europe didn't want our Nasdaq model, did they? They wanted one they controlled. One where they could limit competition.

None of the old floors are left, but they're still run by tight groups of insiders who award monopolies to people. In our model you compete for every bloody transaction and this is what most of these other markets hate. But you'll also remember that our market is the one that's structured just like the really big markets of the world, the currency markets, which are 60 times larger than the world's equity markets.

So what are Nasdaq's thoughts about the ECNs? It seems like the ECNs are going to take over the world now.

That's a regulatory warp, not a true economic advantage. That's because of the way the rules exist.

We don't agree with that at all. What we would like to do is to mutualize the ECN functions into the Nasdaq and allow all broker/dealers to have access to those functions, all investors to have access to those functions, rather than have a handful of technology "haves" be able to carve off slices of the market for their own narrow private interests.

In other words, we think it's very logical for us to go ahead and put ECN functions across our communications network, that allows any broker/ dealer to put an order in as agent and be paid when it's lifted. That's the proposal that we have at the SEC now.

The ECNs have no economic advantage over the Nasdaq. They have only a regulatory advantage right now and that is as an agency only. ECNs are allowed to charge a commission when anybody lifts [buys and sells] their bid, whereas people who function as both agents and principal—in other words, people who make markets [Nasdaq market makers]—are not. And that's what's caused the people who make markets to not want to make markets. They'd rather be an ECN. Again, that's a regulatory warp, not a true advantage.

Why would someone not want to trade with an ECN when they can save money on their execution and get it done really fast?

You have been totally brainwashed. In fact, you're wrong. Your costs may or may not be higher on an ECN.

There are two elements of cost. One is the commission you pay. The other's the market impact that you have. And what Island, for example, is doing, is claiming to give you a very low cost. But they never tell you what your market impact is.

The other thing they do is if they can't match your order within their

ECN, they immediately hit the Nasdaq market. They're parasitic on Nasdaq's liquidity but they don't want you to know that.

Your order, then, goes straight off to Nasdaq, to one of the market makers on the Nasdaq screen?
The best bid or offer [on the Nasdaq Level II quote montage], right.

Looking five years out, what do you see? Are we going to all be trading on the Internet within five years? Are we going to be trading globally? Are we going to be trading 24 hours a day?
Well let's parse out each of those issues.

Are we all going to be on the Internet? Basically, yes. It's not clear to me, yet, how Nasdaq will be on the Internet. East Coast/West Coast has to have synchronicity. We have to deliver quotes at *exactly* the same instant. A one-second delay is too much. Because as you've seen in your visit with these [day trading] firms, we have people whose computers go off instantaneously when a stock hits a price. So, if you're on the West Coast and you're on the Internet and the prices are coming from [Nasdaq headquarters in] Trumbull, Connecticut, you'll lose every time compared to the guy across the river in Manhattan.

I can't let that happen. That's why I have a very large private intranet [dedicated private-line telecommunications system]. I have 250,000 miles of leased telephone lines running around the country so that everybody gets the information at exactly the same time. We worked with Cisco to retard the transmissions in the East Coast and get a slightly different retarding in mid-America so that everybody gets the information at the same time it hits San Francisco.

So this 250,000-mile private intranet isn't the sort of infrastructure that a brand-new ECN is going to be able to afford?
Absolutely not. That's one of the issues that we're dealing with the government.

We have over the years, for perfectly good and valid public policy reasons, built up this synchronicity. If we have synchronicity and we have surge capacity and we have hot backup, is it fair for a new exchange to come in and underprice us based on a lack of those three? Because if they want to have those three, they've got to build the same kind of network we've got. And, by the way, if the country does not care about synchronicity and backup and surge capacity, we will cut that out in order to compete with these new entrants. That sense of what the country cares about needs to come through public hearings and comments requested through the Federal Register. These democracies are truly messy, you know.

If they don't care about it, about making the markets equal for everyone?

If they don't care about it then we will have to give it up in order to compete.

So it's more expensive to run the Nasdaq than it is to run an ECN?

Because we're offering a vastly different level of service.

So, back to my question about what you see happening five years from now . . .

Well, in five years, if my team and I have been smart about it, you're going to see a lower-cost market with much more access available to everyone. With a lot more information available for investors on our Web sites. You're going to continue to see all the wonderful things that this market's brought this country in terms of capital formation and job creation. If we blow it, you're going to see a highly fragmented market with the search costs for the investor going up as he has to go to multiple systems to find the best price.

Because right now Nasdaq is paying for the individual investor's search cost, so he or she can find the best price? Is that what he or she finds on the Nasdaq Level II screen, what you call the "quote montage"?

Nasdaq now consolidates the prices that are available from many sources into one screen and reduces search cost to almost nothing. But if you have to buy an Instinet terminal and an Island terminal and an Archipelago terminal and a BRUT terminal and a Strike terminal, you're going to end up with nine terminals on your desk.

And so would Nasdaq become just one of the terminals or would Nasdaq not exist?

I think unless we're successful in producing a very low cost format for the investor to use, we would have a hard time existing with our very high reliability network with backup and synchronicity and surge capacity. In other words, if we were a high-cost provider, we would have a hard time surviving. We're in exactly an analogous position to AT&T in the early '70s when Sprint and MCI were allowed to attach themselves to those large networks. AT&T was at that time, by public policy, overcharging business users in order to support rural telephony. Right?

Right.

By public policy we overcharge our heavy users in order to support our smaller users. Small investors, small broker/dealers, and small companies are all charged less than it costs us to serve them. And the large broker/dealers, large investors, and large companies are charged more. And we cross-subsidize one from the other.

Some people have said that by the end of the year almost everybody with a discount broker will be getting Level II screens not from day trading firms, but from regular online discount brokers.

They can. If they want to pay for them, that's fine.

But don't they cost $50 per person per month?

I don't know what it is, but it's a per-person charge. Any broker/dealer can pay to provide its customers with Level II service now. That's what the day trading firms do. They pay us for every screen they produce. And they have customers with high trading intensity, who are willing to pay for that indirectly through their commission charges.

Now they're talking about people trading at home with Level II, with an Internet connection, not a dedicated line.

Well, the firm can provide that if they want. Your broker/dealer can provide you any service that we offer—by tariff, these are tariff services. They are available to anybody.

Could someone have been an electronic day trader, say, in the late '80s?

Sure. You could have gotten a Level II terminal and traded your heart out. But until SOES came in and was mandatory in the national market system in 1987—and gave you a way to execute electronically—all that information didn't do you much good. And the order handling rules that came in the fall of '96? They allowed you to set the price and they allowed you to hit anything you see.

The other thing that the order handling rules did was to preclude a market maker from trading ahead of his customer.

And if it weren't for the regulatory bodies, we wouldn't have all these individual investor protection rules?

We've got all kinds of rules in the market, none of which came to be until people began to feel that something was unfair.

You could describe all of these interactions for the last 100 years as a tug-of-war between market insiders, who want to hold their order books close to their chest, and the public, represented by the SEC, who have voted for more transparency over time. The '34 Act, the '35 Act, the Maloney Amendments, the '75 National Market System amendments, and the order handling rules are all increases in transparency in favor of the investor and to the disfavor of the market insiders.

And are the ECNs regulated now?

You've got to understand, the term "ECN" was a regulatory mechanism for describing Instinet. Instinet was an electronic agency—a limit order file—managed by one broker/dealer. And the government allegedly wanted to get its arms around that. So they defined it into a new category in the law which they called an electronic communications network. And they gave it certain responsibilities and certain privileges. The biggest thing they did is they forced them to display their best prices inside the Nasdaq quote montage.

What you have not thought about is that these are federal regulations and they apply to all markets. The order handling rules are federal law. They apply to all markets.

Then why haven't the other markets, like the New York Stock Exchange, also embraced these laws?

They've been stiff-arming them for 2½ years now. The New York Stock Exchange, the Chicago, the Boston, the American—they deny the ECNs access to their market. The Nasdaq has embraced these federal regulations because we think it's the right thing for investors and Frank Zarb and Rick Ketchum and Pat Campbell and me, this new management team at Nasdaq, have worked hard to implement these federal regulations. But you don't see the other exchanges dealing directly with the ECNs the way we are.

What's going to happen is the other sources of liquidity are going to make markets in New York Stock Exchange stocks, whether the New York Stock Exchange gives them their approval or not.

And these other sources of liquidity make markets in NYSE stocks upstairs? What does "upstairs" mean?

It's the third market. It means not down on the floor of the exchange, but on the trading desk at Goldman Sachs, for instance, instead of at the specialist on the floor of the New York Stock Exchange. The NYSE specialist is the designated dealer, the single dealer, the "monopolist," as we say internally.

Looking way out, do you think someday soon we'll be able to sit on a flight to Paris while trading through a laptop and a satellite connection, buying shares in Hong Kong or Germany?

Well, let me take you through the ways that works and doesn't work. Think of a four-layer wedding cake where the most important, biggest, juiciest layers are on the bottom. And up at the top you've got this little circle of cake that is unregulated and is something markets can do together right now and we're beginning to do a lot of, and that is to swap information. Hong Kong's a good example.

The second layer of this cake is something that we can do together with another market that is regulated and that's got dual listings. The company has to go to the effort to meet the standards of each country. And we can do that and we're doing that with Hong Kong. We're working on it. We've got more international companies on Nasdaq than all of the American markets put together and it's legal and it's fine. Everybody knows how to do it.

The third layer of this layer cake is also regulated but the cooperation that I want to talk to you about is prohibited. The cooperation to act as agents in each other's markets, to gather orders as an agent—that's against the law. I cannot have another market—or even a broker/dealer from Germany, solicit you for orders legally in this country.

Okay.

And the fourth layer of this layer cake is also regulated. What you want to do is prohibited, and that is to have markets act as principals in each other's markets, to buy and sell, to provide liquidity. We would like to be able to have the Deutsche Bank, as a broker/dealer in Germany, be able to come in and quote Intel. Provide liquidity. But it's prohibited by federal law.

Now, to the SEC's great credit, they understand that we're facing a world of globalization and they've asked the public for comments on how we, as a country, can deal with this issue. The SEC has been digesting these comments and sometime within the next year they'll probably come out with some sort of position on it.

It seems, these days, that electronic markets and ECNs can be set up so quickly, and trades can be sent to offshore entities where there

are no regulations, no investor protection . . . so "Wall Street" could
leave the United States.

This is the great risk, isn't it? That we lose our financial services market, which is one of the geese that lays the golden egg in this country,
because we're either high-cost or regulatorily inconvenient.

And then we'll have no one making sure that corporations file
according to standard accounting procedures; and we won't have
believable quarterly reports; we won't have all the other things that
go along with regulations?

Right. These are all the wonderful things that Americans take for
granted. They fail to understand that each of those were hard-fought battles
in the past that resulted in additional investor protections and have led to the
trust that we have in this market that's so important to their function. Because
you're reasonably certain that you're being treated honestly by the broker/
dealer and that the company you're buying is disclosing things accurately.

I have suggested that everyone use a limit order instead of a market
order.

You're absolutely right. And you'll get all kinds of e-mail alerts or
pagers to tell you that today.

The interesting thing is you already have the capability to put a limit
order in for Intel at 40. So you can get the transaction done if you want. But
that's not where the world and the press are focusing. They think somehow
these automatic rule-based new ways of thinking about things are somehow
new. They're not. They've been incorporated into limit order executions for
25 to 30 years.

What about payment for order flow, which some observers call a
"legal kickback" to the online brokers? Is this something that's going
to continue much longer?

You're getting into the issues that were raised by a large study in about
1989 or '90. Payment for order flow is probably the most complicated issue
you can imagine. If I give you research on a stock and charge you a commission, is that payment for order flow? Suppose Dean Witter provides
research to a local brokerage firm in return for getting the orders from
that—is that payment for order flow? You bet it is. In other words, where do
you draw the line?

These are angels on pinhead kinds of questions. A company like

E*Trade would say they provide a lot of information. And they provide custody. And they provide coupon clipping, dividend gathering, and money market funds. You get into areas where anything they do can be cross-subsidized. The economists would tell you that payment for order flow is the right economic model for the country. It just sounds bad the way we phrase it. But give me a business where there aren't inducements for order flow. The inducement for order flow is the key to order flow. What is it? Is it a fast execution? Is it a low commission? Is it research? Is it 24-hour-a-day convenience? Is it somebody to hold your hand on the phone? Inducements to order flow are what commerce is all about. IBM induces you to buy their computers by offering you a set of goods and services. If one of those is cash, is that bad? How do you draw the line between cash and noncash services? The economists would say, let the market sort it out. Now the nature of the inducement for order flow is changing. The inducement is changing to speed of execution, guaranteed size of execution, a whole slew of other noncash ways to induce order flow.

During a crash, what's going to happen to liquidity on the ECNs?

It's going to depend on how big the company is: how many investors and how much interest there is in the company. Because in the ECN model there's no one there, other than another investor on the other side of your trade. So human beings (being motivated by either fear or greed) will go away when the news turns bad. And there will be no liquidity. You'll see enormous volatility and price swings if you're dependent entirely on some other investor being there to bail you out. Stocks go to hell in a basket. They're not stupid. They're going to get out of the way.

But didn't the market makers get out of the way, too? What's to force them to do it?

They have to do it in an orderly way. If they're on the screen they've got to honor their quotes. They don't have to trade any stock they don't want to trade but if they want to trade the stock, they've got to be there with a two-sided quote. This is an enormous advantage to the investor, to have somebody there who has to buy from them.

So you don't see much liquidity, much buying and selling going on in the ECNs like Island and Archipelago, if we go into a fast downswing?

Absolutely not. Do you?

I don't know. They say the ECNs are going to be very "robust" because they have all the new infrastructure. These didn't even exist, except for Instinet, in 1987.

Infrastructure doesn't do you any good at all if there's no buyer on the other side of your seller. These are all down-market phenomena. This is when people want to sell. Who's going to be there to buy?

In 1987, didn't specialists and market makers just refuse to pick up their telephones?

That's a different issue. You're talking about the intermediaries. I'm talking about the investor on the other side, the ultimate buyer. Because if there is no buyer, a mutual fund or you on the other side, there's only so much buying the intermediaries are going to do if they can't resell it. They're not in the business of buying and holding. They will honor their commitment and move away to a new price. But you, as an investor on the other side, have no commitment at all. And you can just be gone. "I am not playing in the stock market today," you can say. "I do not like IBM at all. I'm going to the beach."

The intermediary, the market maker, doesn't have that privilege. They can increment [their prices] down but then they have to honor their quote at the next lower increment before they can move it again.

So the public policy dilemma is, what's that worth? And nobody knows right now because we've had nine good years, and nobody remembers.

You weren't actively involved in the market executing orders from your kitchen nine years ago.

No, I was in Moscow during the crash of '87 and I got on a flight back to the States and everybody was tearing apart this one issue of the *Wall Street Journal* and demanding to get off the plane in Poland to try to call their brokers.

Yes. That is panic. And none of them were going in to call their brokers to say "buy."

And none of them could get their brokers from an airport lounge in Warsaw!

Well, we've changed all that because now we let you execute electronically from your kitchen, from your laptop. We have increased the bandwidth of access to the market for individuals, probably a million times over since 1987.

CHAPTER **5**

GETTING ONLINE AND GETTING EDUCATED

GETTING ONLINE: A PRIMER

This chapter is for the beginning online trader who's looking to get up to speed on the basics. If you do all your online investing and trading on a computer at work because you've got better Web access there than at home, you might want to skip this part of the chapter. Or better yet, consider setting up your own private, convenient trading spot at home. Speedy access is getting more affordable all the time, and most bosses don't approve of online trading at the office, even though their superfast T1 connections are irresistible to the hungry employee trader. Remember: some bosses have software that tells them precisely where you're heading when you zoom off to online trading sites. (The only employees whose on-the-job trading is treated with benign amusement are those who work at E*Trade, the world's biggest online brokerage, and the world's biggest online brokerage experiment.)

ONLINE TRADING ACCESS FOR UNDER $300: COMPUTERS ON THE WEB

If you're starting from scratch as an online trader you'll want to spend your money trading stock, not racking up credit card debt buying hardware. Here's one way to do it: the iToaster, a new Internet computer, will cost you about $5 a month—when you subtract from the price the $20 a month you'll save on Internet access, which will come free with this invention. (The 15-

inch color monitor is included in the price of $200. That's about $20 a month for 10 months—about 10 Starbucks coffees a month—and you'll be the full owner of a computer.) If that deal isn't good enough for you, you're probably just not ready for the Internet!

The iToaster is made by a Seattle company called Microworkz, and you can only buy it on their Web site: www.microworkz.com, or by phone at 1-888-538-5701.

Walt Mossberg, *The Wall Street Journal*'s terrific translator of technology for the rest of us, has waxed enthusiastic about an earlier product, the WEBster. Novelist and *Wired* magazine writer Po Bronson dreamed up just such a product in his 1997 Silicon Valley novel, *The First $20 Million Is Always the Hardest* (Random House, 1997). Chasing the entrepreneurial heroism attained by computer geeks at Intel, Microsoft, Apple, and Netscape, Bronson's Andy Caspar creates a computer that sells for less than $500—but his innovation is buried alive by a syndicate controlled by Microsoft's Windows software and Intel's chips. The syndicate rightly fears that something so sensible and affordable could break their hold on the market.

Several years later, this little Seattle company is doing just that—but for $200 less. "We've priced our computers to effectively demolish the socioeconomic barriers between the 'data-haves' and the 'data have-nots,' " says Microworkz president Rick Latman. Putting its bucks where its PR is, Microworkz, which produces their computers using a just-in-time, on-demand production strategy that keeps overhead low, is also donating computers to schools around the country. Within hours of the announcement of the computer, the Web site's servers froze in the process of taking 7 million inquiries from potential customers.

PC Computing magazine gave the Microworkz WEBster Junior its top rating—five stars—among the new ultracheap PCs, citing its "sizzling dollar value and best performance," while also noting its slow CD function and extra costs for add-ons. The other cheapies *PC Computing* reviewed were:

> *IBM Aptiva D1N:* Four stars for "an IBM we can all afford, with pleasing compact size; excellent configuration for the dollar" but "dog-like performance."
>
> *PowerSpec 4321:* Four stars as well—"the only sub-$600 PC with Intel inside" has "high end configuration; low end price" but is "slower than a tax return."

BIGGER BUDGET? TRY SHOPPING ONLINE

Thanks to hearty competition among e-commerce sites, you can find some great deals on the hardware you'll need to start trading on the Web. For example, during the summer of '99 the search engine Alta Vista's online office and computer superstore was offering a $599 computer package—not quite as cheap as it seems, since (unlike the WEBster) the package doesn't include the $240 a year you'll pay for Internet dial-up access or AOL. Shipping, however, is included, so you get a complete system including 32-MB memory, a 3.2-GB hard drive, a 32x CD-ROM, and, most important, a 56K modem to get onto the Web at the fastest possible speed with a dial-up connection. Also included is a 15-inch monitor, printer cable, and a Canon color printer.

You'll find the color printer hookup important if you want to compare stock performance in a sector. For example, BigCharts (at bigcharts.com) prints out different stocks in different colors. If you'd rather keep it simple as a complete beginner, just bookmark your favorite sites on your Web browser by clicking on the bookmark button. With bookmarks, you can pursue the ideal paperless office: compare your charts, make notes in your trading notebook, and pass on the printer—a considerable saving of money as well as trees, since the color printer ink costs a bundle.

To find deals similar to this one, type in "deals.shopping" in your browser window.

YOU SCREAM, I SCREAM, WE ALL SCREAM FOR IMAC

If you root for the underdog, if you're not yet convinced that Bill Gates should own the world and all who make their living in it, you might consider getting one of these spunky, colorful, new Web-oriented computers from Apple called the iMac. (The "i," of course, stands for "Internet.") Available in five psychedelic colors—Walt Mossberg uses the strawberry one in his office at the *Wall Street Journal*—it's an all-in-one package deal. Buy it, plug it in, and you're off in great style for about $1100. (For another $100, you can get the floppy drive, or consider buying the Iomega zip drive for about the same price. Just switch the zip drive between your iMac and a Mac PowerBook, which gets wireless Internet access if you add Metricom for trading on the run.)

GETTING CONNECTED

Going online is simple. Once you've got your computer turned on and its modem plugged into a phone line, you'll need to choose an ISP—the Internet service provider that pours the digital data off the Internet and into your modem, where it's translated into your computer's language. If you've just bought a new computer, odds are it came with a CD that has the software on it that you'll need to hook up with an ISP.

If you're using an older computer, or you're not sure which ISPs you want to sign up with, try polling friends and neighbors, or your local librarian. Ask them which ISPs work well in your area and offer good customer service. Once you've narrowed in on the ISP of your choice, call the 800 number and they'll mail you a free installation CD.

Whichever ISP you choose, the account will usually cost about $20 a month with unlimited usage. Some of them throw in a bunch of goodies when you sign up—like the one that included all of this on the installation CD:

- Two free browsers (the frame on your screen through which you view the World Wide Web): Netscape Navigator and Microsoft's Internet Explorer. (You can get free downloads of the browsers any time by visiting the browsers' sites.)
- A personalized home page that loads up all the stock quotes and news you choose, with one-click access to e-mail and favorite Web sites you've bookmarked on the tool bar.
- An e-mail setup.
- A free 6-MB home page of your own on the Web—a Web site that's reached through the ISP address.
- More free software: RealPlayer for playing music, Claris Home Page Lite, Shockwave, and QuickTime for movies.
- An offer for a free $129 value digital camera to mount over your screen, to be used for videoconferences or sending snapshots and full-motion pictures with e-mail.

WHAT ABOUT AOL?

Think of AOL as a room in your house where you meet friends, read magazines, get mail from friends. But don't think of AOL as a provider of direct

Internet access. AOL is a living room you walk through before you can get onto the Internet or the World Wide Web. If you're planning to trade online and research online and chat online with other traders, you'll need to get an ISP that hard-wires you into the Internet, without requiring you to first stop off at the AOL living room to chat with your neighbors. Because of the extra AOL interface between you and the Web, many of the advanced features on trading sites don't download as quickly or don't download at all. For example, if you get your e-mail on AOL, many of the hotlinks—or Web addresses that are referred to in trading e-mails—simply will not work.

My solution? I pay my monthly $20 fee to an ISP and use Netscape as my browser. (I turn on my laptop in the morning, click on the Netscape icon, and when that comes up on the screen it makes those funny dialing squawks through my internal modem card and telephones my ISP.) The ISP is all I need for investing with an online broker, sending and receiving e-mail, and accessing all the research and chat services that are mentioned in this book. With some of the offers that come bundled with Web computers, the $240 annual ISP fee could be free—not to mention the free $129 computer conference camera and other offers. Do some research: you might even find a free year of trading online with the right ISP-computer combination.

WEB TV

If you'd rather watch television than stare at your computer screen, have we got an investing option for you: Web TV.

It's easy to set up: just plug the set-top box into a phone jack and then into your television. You can navigate the Web with the remote control device that comes with the box or, for an extra $100, you can buy a wireless keyboard that allows you to be a Web couch potato. Then you can direct your Web browser from the keyboard, which, balanced on your knees, sends an invisible beam to the box.

I experimented with a Web TV connection in 1997. I found it useful for e-mail and light Web surfing, but didn't feel comfortable trading through software attached to my television—for one thing, the more sophisticated online trading sites use Java-enabled features that don't translate well into TV. But many others disagree, including one of *New York* magazine's 1998 trading stars, who made his fortune using Web TV in his living room during his off-hours from a restaurant job in Manhattan. (He has since traded up to a real computer, modem, and ISP.)

CONNECTING TO THE INTERNET—FAST!

There are other alternatives to Web TV or the standard dial-up connection through an ISP or AOL. Here are a few.

DSL

Digital Subscriber Line gives you clean digital access to the Internet over regular phone lines—if you happen to live within three miles of your local phone company's switching office. Pacific Bell, for example, offers this connection in California at about $40 a month, guaranteeing a speed of 384 Kbps (kilobits per second).

CABLE MODEM

The usual speed of a cable modem is near the speed of the dedicated T1 lines you find in well-equipped corporate offices. (A private T1 line is the ultimate luxury—it costs around $1000 a month, not to mention whatever the phone company charges to set up the special connection.)

Now this ultimate luxury—speed—is available at about one-twentieth the price. A cable modem for your home office costs only about $50 a month. The cable company TCI (which is now owned by AT&T) is offering the service in my area—San Francisco—through @Home.

(@Home, by the way, is another of Microsoft's investments in the new world order: you pay Microsoft's @Home to get Internet access over your cable TV lines, so you can trade on a Microsoft Windows–equipped PC with Datek Online, in which Bill Gates's former partner Paul Allen just invested an unspecified amount. Datek Online may send your order to the Island ECN, the recent recipient of another $25 million of Paul Allen's money.) But Microsoft's tentacles notwithstanding, cable modems may still suffer from the rush-hour bottlenecks that AOL subscribers endure.

ISDN

Soon to be leapfrogged by new technologies, an ISDN hookup is absurdly expensive. (The joke about ISDN? Ask a telecom professional what ISDN stands for and he'll answer "I Still Don't Know.") The ISDN modem runs at least $300, the phone company gets to charge you for installing it, and then they start billing you at $60 or more a month. ISDN lines run at 128 Kbps—more than three times the speed of my current connection. But I would rather stop trading than have to call the customer service line at the local phone company—in my case, Pacific Bell—to ask for help with ISDN.

That said, ISDN remains your only choice if you decide to be an EDAT trader at home. For direct access, you'll need the dedicated line that only your phone company and ISDN can offer. Since you don't have to share your line with others, at least you won't get caught in the traffic jams of dial-up modems and DSL.

PUBLIC LIBRARY

Before going to the expense of getting online at home, you might want to experiment a bit at your local public library, local high school, or a college, many of which are equipped with that ultimate luxury, a T1 connection and Internet access, all for free. You can zoom around the Web at supersonic speeds, explore the online investing territory, and then decide whether it's worth the expense to set up your own home connection.

Try calling before you go; ask your local librarian if you can get online, and if the library has any local students—aka docents—who will teach you the ropes at no charge. If your community resources don't include Internet access, write a letter or two to your local congressperson. Everyone should have Web access today.

GETTING EDUCATED: KEEP IT SIMPLE

Now that you've got your computer, and you've gotten online with an ISP through a Netscape or Internet Explorer browser, you're ready to go exploring. I believe that information overload is the greatest obstacle to newcomers on the Internet, so here I offer a *narrow* selection of places to go and people to see, based on my own experiences and those of people I've interviewed.

If you already have an online account, or you're familiar with the market and its language, you might want to skip ahead to the next chapter. "Getting Educated" will give you a good review of classical conservative thought about investing today. In brief, that thought is this: hang onto your investments when the market goes up. And hang onto your investments when the market goes down.

Long-term investing is another luxury to me—like being able to pay $1000 a month for a T1 line. If you're considering online trading because of a divorce, because you've become suddenly unemployed, because you would like to tweak 10 percent of your 401(k), you probably don't have the luxury of the time required for the "invest and forget" approach. Like me, you may need to force the growth of your nest egg, like forcing a bulb to bloom in the winter. Maybe, if you're successful, a couple of years down the line you'll have earned the luxury of watching your "invest and forget" portfolio flower and grow.

As you educate yourself about the market, remember that the investment sites you visit may not have been created with the online trader in mind. They have been created for the cautious, middle-of-the-road investor who may prefer mutual funds to stock, even though 94 percent of those funds underperformed the S&P 500 Index, according to the Motley Fool. No matter: these sites are the investing building blocks, the grammar and syntax, of the stock market, and it's here that you'll find your start.

THE MOTLEY FOOL

Set off for your local bookstore before you hit the Internet. Buy a copy of *The Motley Fool Investment Guide* and study it carefully. This is a book by a couple of guys who grew up around the stock market—and a dad who did a lot of investing—and have completely rid themselves of fear, trembling, and awe before the great financial wizards and masters of the universe who so intimidated us during the days of the mergers and acquisitions and junk bond kings of the 1980s. These Fools prick pretension, wrenching Wall Street away from the realm of the upper classes and into a great conversation around the dinner table.

The Fool's book made me realize that I had best start investing sooner rather than later and helped me develop a useful resistance to the blandishments of easy credit and instant gratification. The book walks you through the business section of the newspaper and teaches you the basics. The most important rule, for those without the stomach for online day trading, is to *keep it simple*. Since 94 of 100 mutual funds failed to outperform the S&P 500 Index, just go ahead and buy into an S&P 500 Index fund, such as the Vanguard Fund. Since they don't have hordes of industry analysts on the payroll, the companies have been preselected for them by the people at Standard & Poor's, who put together the 500 companies on the index—and the profits can flow directly to you. Then you can pat yourself on the back for outperforming 94 percent of America's money managers.

Once you've immersed yourself in the Fool's investment book, surf over to the Motley Fool's free Web site at Fool.com (see Figure 5.1), where you'll find a king's ransom of investing information. Once I'd marked up and underlined their book to death, I went on to print out every online lesson in investing that I found on their site. The lessons, which mirror the book, are as follows:

1. Foolishness
2. Settle Your Finances

FIGURE 5.1 *The home page of the Motley Fool—which you can access through AOL—leads you straight to their priceless lessons in investing basics.* (The Motley Fool, Inc. www.fool.com.)

3. Expectations
4. Open an Account
5. Index Funds
6. Dow Approach
7. Stock Screens
8. Small Caps
9. Read
10. Growth Stocks
11. Shorting Stocks
12. Being Fully Foolish
13. Use Fool.com

After you've explored the personalities and returns of the Fool's online investment portfolios, you'll want to home in on those writers who speak to the new trading soul that's emerging from your once-uncaring consumer's heart. And you can check into several Fool portfolios that have been recorded on the site, penny by penny, for about four or five years. Read about them. They may talk you out of taking the risk involved with online trading.

MSN'S MONEYCENTRAL

You'll have to pay a monthly fee of about $10 to subscribe to the extras on this all-around online investing site, but you can experiment with a free trial by going to the "Get Started" area. Once you educate yourself, you may not need a subscription to the site, since many features can be found free elsewhere.

Microsoft Network's MoneyCentral offers an excellent introduction to researching a stock. Enter the stock symbol. (You can find these free online at *The New York Times* site—type in "nytimes.com" and click on "business"—or London's *Financial News* site—type in "fn.com." You'll need to register one time, then they're yours to explore, morning, noon, and night.)

MoneyCentral takes you by the hand to explain the five important issues you need to consider when getting into a stock.

1. *Fundamentals.* These are the basic kick-the-tire questions about the company. What business is it in? How fast is that sector growing? Look at its annual report and its quarterly reports—all to be found online at EDGAR or Nasdaq or the company's site. Is it solid or swimming in debt?

2. *Price history.* This is where the mind-bending database resources of the Web can come in handy: type in a few keystrokes, and years of the day-by-day price history of your stock tumble across the screen in a colorful chart. Another few keystrokes, and a one-day, minute-by-minute view of your stock's price volatility pops into view.

3. *Price target:* Once you've learned about the fundamentals and the price history of your stock, check the predictions about its possible price a month, six months, a year from now. Do any of the "analysts"—industry analysts at investment banks and brokerages who research and study sectors for their firms—cover the stock? (If many analysts supply "coverage" on a stock, it's an indication of possible mutual fund and institutional investor holdings.)

4. *Catalysts:* What changes in the economic and technological environment might trigger positive and negative outlooks on the stock in the months and years ahead? How will it be affected by inflation? Deflation? By weakness of the dollar against the Euro or the yen? By the loss of a key executive?

5. *Comparison:* How does this stock, and how does this company, compare to others in its sector? Here's another opportunity to let the Internet's database riches pour a digital snapshot onto your screen, putting the performance of your stock up against others in its class. With stock screens you can narrow down a list of stocks you're interested in, such as high-volatility and Internet sector.

DAILY HOMEWORK ASSIGNMENTS

Learning the market and online investing is rather like learning a foreign language: it's easiest if you're in love, and the total immersion method works wonders.

So leap in. Here's what I suggest you do every day. Read *The New York Times* online, especially the part called "DataBank" in their Sunday Business section. (You could also read the *Financial Times* of London, also free and excellent, but more Eurocentric and money-oriented, with less of the coverage of wide-ranging scientific discoveries, cultural trends, and high-tech implosions that give you great investing ideas.)

Here's an example of how you might clip out a story and follow up on some of the investment opportunities it suggests. Since we've been talking about today's markets and the sudden entry of the ECNs on the scene, let's take a look at a story that ran in *The New York Times,* "Morgan and Vulcan Invest in 2 Electronic Trading Systems," in June 1999. In the daily paper, it ran in the Business section. Online, the story ran in the Technology section. (By the way, you can set your Web browser to go to *The New York Times* Technology front page as soon as you go online. Find this story by clicking on "search," choosing "search all articles," and inputting Sholnn Freeman. By following all the links, you'll get a rich feel for the Web and its resources.)

"Morgan and Vulcan Invest in 2 Electronic Training Systems," by Sholnn Freeman, was about Paul G. Allen and J.P. Morgan & Company's investments in alternative trading systems. As you read, you might want to know who Paul Allen is and why he's investing in this obscure technology. If you type in "yahoo" and press "enter," your browser will take you over to Yahoo!'s front page. Type in Mr. Allen's name and check what comes up—don't forget to press the "Web Mentions" button across the query, since you probably don't want the Web pages. Can't find him? Proceed to his company, Vulcan Ventures. Success. The profile at *Industry Standard* looked interesting, but the links from Yahoo! didn't work. Vulcan must have a site.

What about J.P. Morgan? Who, or what, is Mr. Morgan? Typing in the name on the browser blank yields nothing, so try "yahoo." Nothing. Try again, with the name written as it is in *The Times:* "J.P. Morgan & Company." Pay dirt—sort of. The site, for one of Wall Street's most hallowed investment banks, does provide access to Morgan's research analysts—but only for paying customers. In this case, that means paying in the multimillions. But further nosing around the site, or researching stories about Morgan, will indicate why such a stuffy firm got into bed with an ECN started by computer nerds. It's like Audrey Hepburn and Humphrey Bogart in *Sabrina*—the owner of old-line corporate millions taking up with an elegant young software geek who lives over the garage.

Morgan, we read, is investing in Archipelago. What do we find when we type in "Archipelago" in the Yahoo! browser window? Only a listing of day trading firms proclaiming that they use the Archipelago ECN for trades. Pristine, for instance, will tell you they are offering a one-day day trading seminar at San Francisco's Ritz-Carlton, including a free lunch, for only $1000.

And what about Bruce W. Weber, also mentioned in the story, an associate professor of computer information systems at City University of

New York? Check out his site at the university—he may be the ECN aficionado you'll want to befriend, or he may have links from his site that will open you up to a whole new world of alternative trading systems.

Further down in the story, Island says it completes about $5 billion in transactions a day and has announced plans to file with the Securities and Exchange Commission to become an officially recognized stock exchange. This mention should bring you over to the SEC site. Use the search engine to find references to ECNs, and look for any filings by Island ECN or Archipelago. What about the Nasdaq stock market? Have they filed for regulatory relief from ECNs? What about the NYSE?

What about EDGAR, for online SEC filings? Island isn't a public company, but Archipelago's investments come from public companies. Could you find any quarterly reports or numbers on the company by looking for its parent company's quarterly reports? Nasdaqtrader.com may compare usage on this ECN to others.

When you read this story about Morgan and Vulcan in *The New York Times* newspaper, all you get is the story. When you read the same story online at nytimes.com, you get the story and you get links to three related articles—in this case, "Merrill Lynch Plans on Low-Cost Online Trading," "For Its Big Clients, Merrill Does Not Shy from Internet," and "Online Trades Rise and So Do the Complaints." You also get access to one forum, a directed flow of chat, called "Is it Safe to Trade Stocks Over the Internet?"

That's just one day. And one article. But for the curious person who loves the idea of change, who embraces the intellectual feast of the Internet, that one article can become the foundation of an entire portfolio, one year's trading ideas and an entire lifetime's investment trajectory.

●　　●　　●

INTERVIEW WITH GEOFF GOODFELLOW, PRAGUE, CZECH REPUBLIC, RESEARCHING INVESTMENTS ON THE INTERNET— FROM ANYWHERE IN THE WORLD

Geoff Goodfellow spent his teen years tinkering with computers at the Stanford Research Institute, where the Internet was born. Intrigued by the notion of wireless electronic mail, by the late 1980s he had started Radiomail Corporation in Silicon Valley. Later, his Radiomail stake freed him up to become an independent investor. He considered another start-up. He considered the 80-hour weeks. He traveled.

Visiting Prague in 1997, he fell in love with the ancient city and the Czech culture. Within a few days he had rented a loft and discovered that in the online universe, he could research stocks from Prague as if he were still in San Francisco. Here Geoff offers the secrets of a full-time online investor who eats well, listens to great music, doesn't commute, and stays fully connected—all the pleasures without any of the pressures.

Could you live in Prague and be an investor without the Internet?

I could absolutely not live in Prague without the Internet. When I'm at home I'm voraciously reading, horizontal on the couch, in front of my computer terminal, surfing, spinning vinyl, listening to music. The Internet makes it possible to be "virtual." I can go to Sydney, Istanbul. Because of the pervasiveness of the Internet I can do this anyplace where I can plug in. When I travel I use www.ibm.net. They have something like 50 to 60 dial-up nodes around the world.

How do you zero in on the fallen angel companies you choose to invest in?

I listen to the conference calls that happen after quarterly earnings along with the analysts. I find out about them by reading the press releases. The advisory says "dial this 800 number." I use my voice detection system during the conference calls. I detect the confidence level in how people speak.

How did you hear about the various software and market data feeds that are available to you?

I read newspapers online: *The New York Times, San Francisco Chronicle, San Jose Mercury News*. In hard copy I read the *Financial Times* from London and the *Herald Tribune* from Paris. I never read the Asian *Wall Street Journal,* but I do read *Barron's* through the *WSJ*. For Asia and for Japanese problems, the *Financial Times* is best. They have Japan nailed.

I'm also a die-hard fan of TheStreet.com. The James Cramer column is like having access to a trader's mind—like an IV line, or a Vulcan mind meld. I also appreciate the great writing by Greenberg and Byron.

What kind of data feed do you get?

I pay for a real-time PC Quote numbers feed. I've had that since I moved to Prague in January of '98. Before that I was being a cheap mother, using Infospace and some of the free real-time quote services. At

Yahoo! I had to type in real-time quotes—type them in again and again, hit the enter key.

I decided I wanted to try streaming real-time quotes. I think I went to DBC, or Yahoo!, for their directory of streaming real-time quotes. One of the vendors in that directory had quoted a review online from *Barron's* saying, "We're the best." I went to *Barron's* Web site, found the full review, looked at all the options, and tried PC Quote. For 75 bucks, at worst, I thought I'd gamble on it for a month.

I installed PC Quote's Real Tick. It's amazing, the difference 10 or 15 minutes makes. It's paid me back in droves. Seventy-five dollars a month is nothing for the amount of money it's made me. It allows you to totally customize your own screens, just the way I like it.

What sort of Internet connection do you have?

I have a lease line in my home, a full-time Internet connection. I have the IV needle in 24 hours a day. When I travel, I dial into IBM GlobalNet, plug in, and it's same thing wherever I go.

Why not trade directly?

I rarely trade intraday. My horizon of time is generally 18 months, playing the ratchets of a company comeback. You can't trade 30-50-70,000 shares online—that is, you can do it, but you'd be a fool.

I did do that once. My broker wasn't in, so I talked to someone in the trading room. When the ticker came in later that day, I saw just what it had done to the stock's price.

Do you get e-mail alerts through the day?

I get e-mail alerts of news all day and night through Inquisit. But I could go out to dinner and the market could plunge. I don't care about the market; I only care about my individual stocks. They're going to go up on the comeback, independent of where the market is sitting.

Why are you still using a broker when you can trade online with PC Quote information?

I trade at a big brokerage, but I pay institutional [lower] rates because of my large blocks. I could get much cheaper trades, but I read and hear such horrible things about some brokerages' "customer disservice." When something goes wrong my brokerage always makes it right. I've never had an argument, never an arbitration. I get service. I'm dealing with quality individuals. That allows me to sleep soundly at night. It's totally worth it.

What if something like the crash of '87 happens again?

If there's anything important going on and I'm away, my broker has my stocks on his screen. He likes my investing style so much, he follows me on pretty much every stock. When I was in London he called me to say one of my stocks had gone up. I initiated a couple of sells on that. But he never sells without asking.

How'd you find out about EDGAR listings of companies' online SEC legal filings?

I *love* reading 10-Ks and 10-Qs. I live on those things. They have to go through the legal scrutiny, so you can find out where things are buried in companies: how the machine works, what it's made up of.

When a company's going public they release S-1s. My favorite section is the one called "certain transactions." That's where they list who's been fired, how many people have to be paid off, mistakes they've made in hiring. Take Iridium, one of my favorite fallen angels. As part of his employment contract, their ex-CEO had use of the corporate jet. I believe that a very telling factor of the DNA of a company is represented by the "certain transactions" of the S-1. It's the portion of the filing they would *least* like to have everyone else read—like when the Starr report came out, those in the know searched for the word "cigar."

That's exactly what I do when I read an EDGAR: I search for "certain transactions." Iridium is the first one I found that had a jet as part of the employment agreement with a former CEO. That, it can be said, is an immediate short—any company losing that amount of money and giving corporate jet access to an ex-employee! When you see helicopters and jets, pull out your Richter scale and get ready for a reading. Don't get me wrong—I love a corporate jet as much as the next person. But corporations that do those things are heading for a fall.

How do you judge companies?

My mantra is, "The fish stinks from the head." You just have to look at the head: the chair of the board, members of the board. They set the DNA that replicates and mutates throughout the corporate gene pool. You want to see the new CEO; you want to see if the scum are being weeded out. You want to check the hiring process to see who they're bringing in.

I read the bulletin boards on Silicon Investor, and some on Yahoo!. I just sort of browse. There's a lot of gunk on there, but sometimes you find a nugget or a sliver.

What do you see happening in the next five years?

It's going to be a 24-hour-a-day market. People are going to have to hire people to sleep for them. That's going to be the next market: sleep futures. You're going to buy futures for someone to sleep for you so you can stay awake 24 hours a day.

Is there more to life than making money?

I should tell you, I don't do this to make money. This has nothing to do with making money. I do it because I enjoy foretelling future trends and future activities—I'm autotelic. That's a Greek word: *auto* = self; *telic* = goal. When my skill improves, I make money. I so much enjoy reading all these annual reports, 10-Ks; I love the analytical portion, the thinking portion. I'm an insatiable learner and I find the only way for me to learn is to make mistakes. I try to make as many mistakes as fast as possible. They say failing is the last thing that happens to you before you succeed.

I love knowledge. I call it mind food. My first love is eating. This investing thing is just to keep me busy between fine lunches and dinners.

CHAPTER 6

ONLINE RESOURCES
FOR ONLINE TRADING

Now that you're online, your next step is to ease yourself into a feel for the markets. Remember, this is a gradual learning process. Successful investors, frequent traders, online day traders, and EDAT traders all share one trait: they understand that the global economy is like global ecology—everything affects everything. To help you ground yourself in the global village, here you'll be introduced to the best online sites for researching your investments—preferably, *before* you make them.

CNBC CABLE BUSINESS NEWS

Now in its tenth year, CNBC will become your constant companion as you start to explore the market. If you want to know what everyone in every trading room around the United States knows—at the same time—CNBC is your best bet. (The CNBC screen is omnipresent at day trading firms, as well as at Nasdaq market makers, Wall Street trading desks, and wholesalers.) Since CNBC is allied with Dow Jones, some of the best reporters from the *Wall Street Journal* and *Barron's* appear on the show to discuss their areas of expertise. These appearances are worth paying attention to; they can and do move markets. The next day's guests who are booked for the TV show are posted daily on the online site.

The segment lineup starts at 4:30 a.m., eastern standard time. The all-important *Squawk Box* starts at 7 a.m., and *Market Watch* at 10 follows the opening of the floor of the NYSE. By noon, *Power Lunch* introduces top CEOs. Street Signs covers the close starting at 2 p.m.

THE NEW YORK TIMES ON THE WEB

Every Sunday, read the DataBank page at nytimes.com for a summary of the past five trading days and a look at the week ahead (see Figure 6.1). Here you'll find brief snapshots of the market, called *market indicators,* and vital information with a glance at the graphs on the site: major trend graphs for the Dow Jones Industrial Average, the S&P 500 Index, and the Russell 2000 Index for smaller companies, and a graph comparing the performance of foreign stocks in Europe, Asia, and the Americas in the past four weeks (with information from the *Financial Times* of London, ft.com).

This site also provides the lowdown on exchanges and currency in about 50 countries, a profile of eight big stocks in the news, the favorite stocks and funds of Merrill Lynch customers, and the hottest and coldest stocks on the NYSE, Nasdaq, and AMEX. The Rates and Yields area is a clue to bond performance, often related to stock performance (when bonds go up, stocks come down).

The most relevant area for frequent traders? "The Week Ahead" on the DataBank page pins down dates and names for the following three market-moving factors:

- Economic indicators, such as the consumer price index
- Initial public offerings, such as "TheStreet.com, financial news and commentary, $66 million, underwriter, Goldman, Sachs"
- Earnings reports, such as "Cisco Systems, reporting Tuesday, for fiscal period 3Q [third quarter], forecast per share, 30-day trend, and year ago figure," from First Call

The numbers, charts, and graphs offered by DataBank are compiled from a variety of sources. Many of them are available directly online: the *Financial Times* at ft.com, Bloomberg Financial Markets at bloomberg.com for earnings announcements, First Call at firstcall.com, MCM Corporate-watch Data Services, Bank Rate Monitor, Standard & Poor's, and Dow Jones. But what a pleasure to find it all, with no hunt-and-peck and no charge, in one central location!

In addition to perusing the DataBank page on a daily basis, it's also good to check out the front-page news, the Technology and Business sections, and the day's section focus, such as science or circuits. (See Figure 6.2.)

FIGURE 6.1 The New York Times *on the Web Business section will give you the data you need to start the day, and the week, right. And the subscription is free—just register at nytimes.com.* (© 1999 The New York Times Company. Reprinted by permission.)

YAHOO!FINANCE

Shoot to yahoo.com on your Web browser and you'll find yourself in the company of some of Wall Street's sharpest minds.

During every break at the company conferences held by San Francisco investment banks at the Ritz-Carlton or St. Francis Hotel, the conference

FIGURE 6.2 *A daily check-in with the Technology front page in* The New York Times *on the Web can get you up to speed with high tech. Promise: it worked for me.* (© 1999 The New York Times Company. Reprinted by permission.)

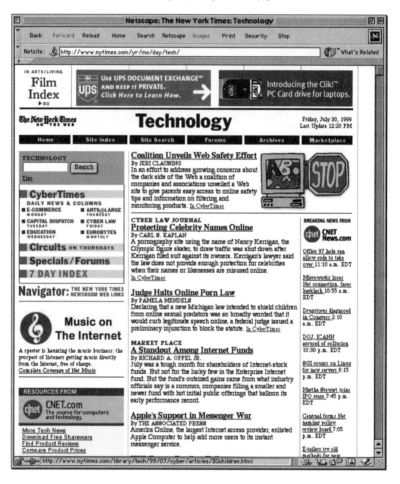

rooms are filled with industry analysts, money managers, and investment bankers who rush to hit computer screens. After all, while these investment professionals are spending the day at a Montgomery, Hambrecht & Quist, or Robertson-Stevens conference, the stock of the companies presenting at the conference will often lift several dollars in a matter of minutes, based on news revealed to the analysts in closed-door conference sessions. On bad news it may sink like a stone.

Popping up like slides on every single computer screen? The telltale blue of the Yahoo!Finance site (see Figure 6.3). These investment professionals, separated for the day from their usual word-of-mouth diet of Wall Street gossip, plug into the next best thing—while clutching their top-of-the-line cellular phones like gunslingers fingering their pistols.

You, too, can reap the benefits of the Yahoo!Finance site. To get there from the main Yahoo! page, just click on "finance," one of the three selections listed under the "business" heading, and zoom straight to one of the Web's best information and portal sites.

Yahoo!Finance's clean design and straightforward front page are part of the attraction for the analysts who want the information they need—*now*. The site is so well designed and fully integrated that you, too, are likely to

FIGURE 6.3　*The Yahoo!Finance home page.* (Copyright © 1999 Yahoo! Inc. All rights reserved.)

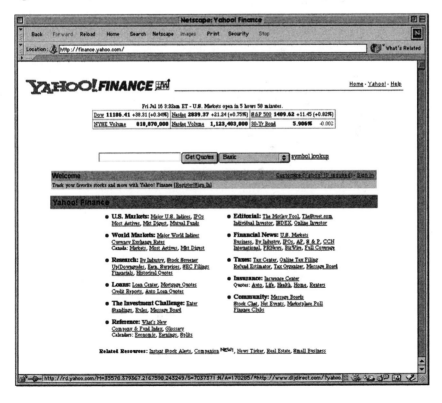

find both the financial data and breaking news you need for decision making about the day's market.

Yahoo!'s advantage as a portal site lies in its rich selection of links to other sites. Try the "shorts" link to views.com/invest/shorts/top20 to discover the 20 biggest short holdings on Nasdaq—the 20 stocks that traders are betting will move down, or short, rather than up, or long. (More about short and long holdings later.)

When you start trading stock on a short-term basis, you'll want to be aware of the following features of Yahoo!Finance. They'll keep you on top of the fundamentals, as well as breaking news on analysts' recommendations, insider buying, earnings estimates, short interest, and the industries and sectors.

CALENDAR AND ALERTS

Watch for earnings announcements, upcoming Federal Reserve moves, and splits. You can customize the process by entering dates from the *New York Times* Sunday DataBank or from the "Reference" section following, into Yahoo!'s built-in calendar. For backup on analysts' estimates—projections of quarterly and yearly earnings—you might also want to bookmark:

- Zack's
- Thomson's First Call (firstcall.com), on a pay-per-report basis
- I/B/E/S (at ibes.com), including international companies
- Argus Group (argusgroup.com) for the inside scoop on insider selling by people who work for the company. (Most paperwork is now filed with the SEC electronically, but this legally required data on insider selling is often filed by mail, on paper.)

PORTFOLIOS

These can be defined by the group or groups of stocks you're watching. Yahoo!'s alerts may lead you to buy or sell (short) a stock. Once you open an online account (coming up in Chapter 8), your broker will keep your actual cash portfolio updated to the minute, and you'll cover yourself by entering sell market orders, called *stops,* in advance. But it's a good idea to have a backup warning system for your actual trading portfolio here. (See Figure 6.4.)

FIGURE 6.4   *Portfolios run on Yahoo!Finance.* (Copyright © 1999 Yahoo! Inc. All rights reserved.)

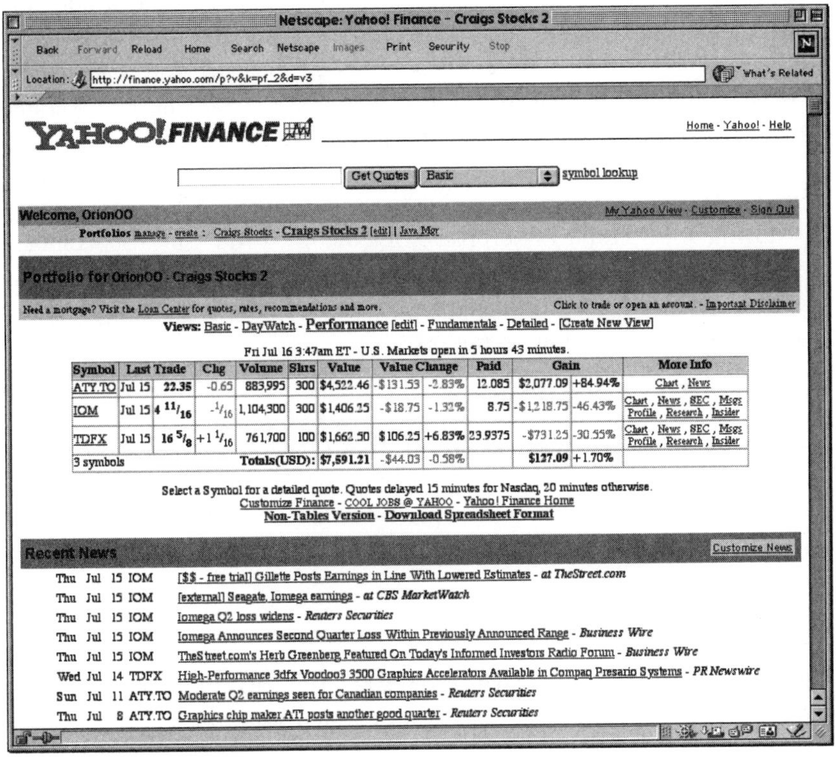

RELATED SOURCES

Click on "Related Sources" to set up your online portfolio. Start with only one or two stocks, and use Yahoo!'s Instant Stock Alerts to page you for changes (click below Yahoo!Messenger). A pager can be set off by your own specific stock price limits, or by stock split data entered in the calendar. And Yahoo! promises that Yahoo!Messenger works well behind most corporate firewalls—where all of Dilbert's friends first learn about the stock market.

Along with these data snapshots, you'll want to make use of these Yahoo!Finance areas. The ones I find most crucial for an online trader are as follows.

U.S. MARKETS

Look for IPOs and most actives. (Venture capital gives you a heads-up on upcoming companies before they get to the IPO stage—check Softbank [softbankvc.com], Red Herring, Upside, and Fisher Jurveston for who they're backing in high-tech.) Most tech stocks are on Nasdaq, and that's where most online traders have made their money. WIT Capital will send you free e-mails regarding the IPOs they're offering online.

RESEARCH

Up/downgrades, earnings surprises, SEC filings. (You can also combine these alerts with e-mails from the analyst-watch sites, as mentioned in the section on e-mail later in this chapter, although today most "whisper numbers" are already priced in on rumors.)

THE INVESTMENT CHALLENGE

Here is one place where you learn to trade online. I strongly suggest you begin by practicing on a site that is not at an actual online broker, for example, sandbox.com. Most important is learning to buy and sell using limit orders. Unfortunately, you cannot do this with any of the commercial brokers. Nor can you do it here.

REFERENCE

Glossary, and earnings and splits calendars. (You can enter these into your Yahoo! calendar—for the stocks on your watch list—along with Sunday's *New York Times* list.)

EDITORIAL AND FINANCIAL NEWS

Yahoo!Finance doesn't have its own editorial voice or pundit, like TheStreet.com's James Cramer. But for its news content it does call on some of the snappiest voices around, with news links from TheStreet.com (for subscribers), the Motley Fool, the *Wall Street Journal* (for paying *WSJ* subscribers only), MSNBC, and *The New York Times*. These stories are often grouped and headlined on the financial portal's front page, so users can link directly to the freshest news. You might, for example, find a group of 20 Internet stock stories or 20 online brokerage stories from various sources. You can also customize your own selection.

Users can link directly to the freshest news, and read back several months. The online trader should be aware of the difference between news stories reported by well-trained journalists at well-respected newspapers, and "news" written by public relations firms and published by PR NewsWire or BusinessWire. The true news stories are coming from neutral writers; the PR stories are paid for by the companies themselves. Even these press releases have their purpose, though: they often list interesting names and numbers you can use to track down further information.

Additional news sources you might consider bookmarking, especially if you trade many Nasdaq high-tech stocks, include:

- Red Herring, a Silicon Valley venture capital magazine
- ZDNet, with free stories going back through 1996 (the *Wall Street Journal,* in contrast, charges $6 a month for a subscription, then charges its subscribers $2.95 for stories more than 30 days old)
- *Inside* magazine, another Silicon Valley venture capital magazine
- The *San Jose Mercury News* at www.mercurynews.com (charge)
- *Wired* magazine (wired.com)
- *Forbes* Digital Tool (forbes.com)
- zdii, for historical news back to 1996, with some great search options for getting backdated news on your company
- Lexis-Nexis, for the ultimate search, going back up to 10 years. (Private investigators took only 10 minutes on Nexis, the newspaper database, to uncover the shady past of a Connecticut man who'd just embezzled $2 billion.)

COMMUNITY

For stock chat, Yahoo! is among the Big Four, along with Silicon Investor, TheStreet.com, and Fool.com. Never buy on a tip.

Personal Portfolio on Yahoo!Finance, your personal portfolio, uses Java to (1) display your quotes and charts, (2) show you how much money you've made—or lost, and (3) perform tricks such as displaying links to research and messages. And again, Yahoo!Finance—seemingly the first choice of financial analysts on the road—is gloriously free.

Free? How many stock market veterans hear the word "free" and snort back, "You get what you pay for!" In this case, the cyberspace glories born of the marriage of the Web and the Market are simply irresistible. You may want to supplement your Yahoo!Finance exploration with a subscription to TheStreet.com to access its lively news links at Yahoo! (at $7 a month; more later); or you might want the *Wall Street Journal,* so you can get into their news links, company briefing books, and *Barron's* ($6 a month). But while you're just getting started, you can keep it simple and keep it free.

CBS MARKETWATCH

Travel over to cbs.marketwatch.com and you'll find another successful, cleanly organized investing supersite, a 1998 alliance between Data Broadcast Corporation online—a market data behemoth—and CBS. Check in here after your morning visit to *The New York Times* and Yahoo!Finance. (See Figure 6.5.)

For the newcomer, the site has assembled a savvy introduction to investing. Unlike Yahoo!Finance, CBS MarketWatch offers a chorus of

FIGURE 6.5 *CBS MarketWatch combines the trustworthiness of Dan Rather, the editorial punch of Thom Calandra and crew, and Data Broadcasting's streaming data for total market awareness.* (CBS MarketWatch and Data Broadcasting Corp.)

experts to help the new trader recognize patterns in the market. Their writers analyze the effects of current events and global economic news on the various market sectors. This expert guidance can help the novice investor develop a sixth sense for how breaking news affects trading in the markets.

CBS MarketWatch also offers a toolbox for the individual investor's portfolio, and for technical analysis: here you should familiarize yourself with *charting,* a key element in making the comparisons that are often used in day trading. You'll find further notes on basic charting, such as support and resistance lines—terms you hear often around day traders—as well as trend lines and basing patterns.

My charting is done through my online broker via the splendidly interactive BigCharts (bigcharts.com), which supplies visitors with colorful intraday and two-day, five-day, and longer charts comparing the price and volume moves in your stock with others in its industry. I just type in the symbols for the stocks I'd like to compare, push the button, and the charts—which would have costs thousands a decade ago—appear in a flash on my screen, ready to be printed or reviewed.

If you're determined to explore becoming an active trader, you might consider signing on for CBS MarketWatch LIVE (see Figure 6.6), a nifty version of a Wall Street trade station desk—like the status symbol Bloomberg terminal on a broker's or investment banker's desk. Instead of costing $2000 a month and requiring a dedicated company intranet phone hookup, this Windows-compatible software delivers the MarketWatch LIVE trade station over the Internet with Nasdaq Level II information—streaming, real-time quotes (advancers in green, losers in red); customizable stock screens; one-click intraday charts; scrolling tickers; plus stock price alerts—delivered to you on e-mail, pager, or cellular telephone. MarketWatch LIVE also offers direct through-the-screen trading with many online brokers . . . and a free 30-day trial (you pay for the data only).

AOL features an Active Trader section in Personal Finance at keyword "Active Trader." (Bookmark it by clicking on the heart at the top right. Double-click the heart-and-folder icon of the AOL tool bar later to revisit.) But, as mentioned earlier, AOL is not the most direct Internet route to use for online trading. Instead, go directly onto the Internet with a browser like Microsoft's Internet Explorer or Netscape 4.0 or higher (which happens to be owned by AOL).

And please, don't forget the Motley Fool at Fool.com. Their introductory lessons to the market in their 1994 *Investment Guide,* and their online

FIGURE 6.6   *The CBS MarketWatch LIVE feed gives you alerts similar to a professional day trader's Level II screen, over the Internet at reasonable prices.* (CBS MarketWatch and Data Broadcasting Corp.)

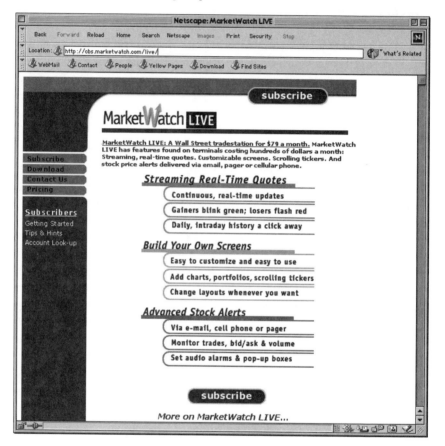

courses and market experts, can't be beat for developing the mental muscles you'll need to grow your money.

THE SECURITIES AND EXCHANGE COMMISSION EDGAR DATABASE

An acronym for "Electronic Data Gathering, Analysis and Retrieval," EDGAR was the SEC's way of creating a paperless office in Washington.

You encountered the SEC's EDGAR database in Chapter 5, as part of the fundamentals of stock picking. Links from the Research section of Yahoo!Finance will also introduce you to EDGAR, and it's worth some time to refamiliarize yourself with the filings listed there.

Publicly traded companies in the United States must file business plans, called S-1 registrations, when they go public. S-3 registrations are filed with the SEC for stock sold after the initial public offering. The company is also obligated to file annual reports, called 10-Ks, and quarterly reports, called 10-Qs. To search the EDGAR database (sec.gov), indicate that you want each of these forms. As Geoff Goodfellow points out in his interview at the end of Chapter 5, the "certain transactions" section is often the most revealing of all—that's where companies are obliged to mention the jets they lease and summer villas they rent for their top execs (and ex-execs). Also, lawsuits are intriguing. Pay attention to the experience of the management team, the contracts that management awards itself, and "creative" changes in standard accounting practices.

Also on EDGAR, you'll find the SEC filings for stocks called "penny" stocks or "bulletin board" stocks. Warning: do not trade them. Stick to stocks that are listed on Nasdaq-AMEX or the NYSE. Penny or bulletin board stocks (coded "OTC BB") are not fully under the regulatory umbrella of the NYSE or NASD.

(If you feel tempted to violate this rule, go to financial web.com/stockdetective/ and click on "Search Stock Detective" for the company index page. Familiarize yourself with "Stinky Stocks," with lots of insider selling, paid promotion, and PR masquerading as stock analysis. Look at the Stock Detective's highlights from SEC investigations, chat room scams, and "Stock Detective Light," for mining nuggets from the SEC's amended EDGAR filings.)

To learn how to analyze the financial statements in annual or quarterly reports, get out your well-thumbed copy of *The Motley Fool Investment Guide,* or check online at the Fool.com, MSN Investor, or Yahoo! links. You can also seek out the National Association of Investors (at better-investing.org) for screening and analysis information suitable to the newcomer. (The ".org" in its address tells you it's a nonprofit organization.) When you roll up your sleeves to work your way through the numbers with pencil and paper, you'll start to get a sense of the inner life of the company. As a short-term investor or trader, though, you might only want a guarantee that the company will be alive for the next four weeks or the next quarter (three months).

EDGAR-Online (edgar-online.com) gives you free access to the SEC database back to 1994, and its search engine is much easier to work with than the government's. The S-1s and 10-Ks will give you all the juicy information that Geoff Goodfellow, the investor based in Prague, and the Stock Detective, talk about: insider trading, salaries, board members, stock options, and golden parachutes. (More about the SEC in Chapter 9, on warnings.)

PREMIUM SERVICES

THESTREET.COM: MY NUMBER ONE PICK

This smart and savvy online site features James Cramer, the trader's trader, who actually used to answer all his e-mails at TheStreet.com (TSC) before they had an IPO for $66 million backed by Goldman Sachs, and before *The New York Times* bought a piece of the action. Cramer went to Harvard, then Harvard Law, then Goldman Sachs. But despite his gold-chip background, he's got a distinctly non-Establishment voice. (Read former *Spy* editor Kurt Andersen's *Turn of the Century* for a fictional portrayal of Cramer.)

TheStreet.com's editor, Dave Kansas, confesses that he still sleeps on a futon in his New York apartment. This private lifestyle tidbit, as value investor Warren Buffett would say, is a good sign of company economies.

A favorite site of active investors and intelligent traders, TSC offers a menu of information and columns that gets richer by the week (see Figure 6.7). And the tryout is free. The extremely sensible and successful Gary B. Smith writes about taking on trading at home as a full-time job and walks you step by step through the complexities of his theories of technical charting.

When the New York Times Company invested $15 million in cash and services in TSC in 1998, the company noted that in only two years, TSC had become one of the most influential investment sites on the Web, "attracting some of the country's most affluent and market-savvy Internet users." (According to the paper, the deal paired two old '70s high school pals: James Cramer went to Springfield Township High School in Pennsylvania, and so did the New York Times Electronic Media Unit's president, Martin Nisenholtz.)

Follow coverage here at TSC of online brokerage houses, and check out TSC's poll of the best online brokers—quickly becoming a favorite of online traders.

FIGURE 6.7   *Shake, rattle, and roll with the opinionated blasts coming from James Cramer's "Wrong!" columns—written during the heat of the trading day on the trading desk—plus global market news, Cory Johnson, Herb Greenberg, Gary Smith, Adam Lashinsky, and all the online stars.* (Image courtesy TheStreet.com.)

Your bulletins from TSC, including a weekend edition, hits your e-mail box daily, alerting you to stories of interest, reached instantly by clicking the link. One recent weekend report printed out at 12 pages, including a story about semiconductor packaging, a then-bullish opinion on bonds, the evening and postclose news updates, and news of Hoover's (an online database for investors, listing 14,000 companies) filing for an IPO as HOOV on Nasdaq. Plus there was information on mergers, acquisitions, and links to the TSC's economic databank.

THE RAGING BULL: ANOTHER FAVORITE

One of the fastest-growing online financial communities for bulletin board discussions, chats, news, and opinion, the Raging Bull at ragingbull.com (see Figure 6.8) was started by three college students in 1997. CMGI, the Internet investing group that bought Compaq's Alta Vista search engine, now owns a piece of the Bull.

The Raging Bull delivers Matt Ragas's weekly cyberstock report to your e-mail box, with links to weekly Internet public and private market news,

---

FIGURE 6.8 *Home page of the snorting, ground-stomping, very outrageous Raging Bull.* (www.ragingbull.com, Raging Bull Inc.)

Internet IPO filings, quarterly reports, upgrades/downgrades, and news analyst coverage, plus the most intriguing news links of the week: important stories from the *San Jose Mercury News,* MSNBC, TheStreet.com, *Upside,* the *Industry Standard* (thestandard.net), Smart Money (pathfinder.com), ABC News, *Business Week, Forbes* Digital Tool (forbes.com), and ZDNet (zdii.com). You should walk to your computer right now and bookmark all of those links.

On the Raging Bull you'll find well-organized discussions of stock trading, and you'll be able to follow leads on various new companies you encounter. But please find your stock *ideas* elsewhere, then check them out here. It's best not to rely on chat rooms in TheStreet.com or Raging Bull, the Fool or Silicon Investor (at techstocks.com) for your trading ideas.

MSN MONEYCENTRAL INVESTOR

The excellent Jim Jubak, an MSN reporter, is found here. I ran into him when he was covering the American Electronic Association meeting in San Diego in the fall of 1997, days before the Asian financial crisis really hit the markets. It was hot, it was crowded, and no tech company would admit to the slightest susceptibility to the "Asian flu." Jubak was there from New York City, taking it all in, checking out the hundreds of microcap, small-cap, and midcap companies presenting their stories to the assembled investment bankers and money managers, and filing his well-considered stories. (Available in the MSN MoneyCentral Investor archives at the site; see Figure 6.9.)

The portfolio tracker here at MSN—like the ones at Yahoo! and CBS MarketWatch—is free. Microsoft's MoneyCentral, which works best on Microsoft's Internet Explorer browser, will trigger an FYI alert.

When that happens, an FYI icon pops up next to the stock in your portfolio with (1) a technical alert, (2) a change in relative strength, (3) new fund interest, or (4) a heavy volume notice. Other triggers include new analyst upgrades, an MSN mention, SEC filings, or an appearance in one of the site's fund or stock screens (and these screens appear to be the most complex devices available online today). Price alerts will also be e-mailed.

You can move data between spreadsheets and your portfolios—a big help during tax season—with Quicken 99 and Microsoft Money 99 software. (When you choose your broker, which we'll do in Chapter 8, you might look for a broker that keeps your entire portfolio online, for immediate transfer to your tax accountant or at-home tax filing, without having to enter all the data in another place.)

FIGURE 6.9 *At MSN's MoneyCentral, you'll find the riches of "Investor," with Jim Jubak's coverage of investing moves.* (MSN MoneyCentral, www.moneycentral.com)

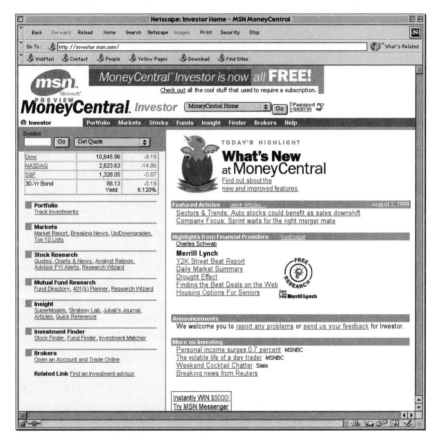

E-MAIL ALERTS: "YOU'VE GOT MAIL"— AND IT'S FREE

As you travel around these sites, sign on for their free e-mail services. Each morning you'll wake to a fresh review of all the upcoming news and opinions for the day. Start with one or two. These are the ones I swear by, and why.

Free sites

- Fool.com: Roundup of coverage, with links
- CBS MarketWatch: Roundup of coverage and opinion, with links

- ZDNet: All-inclusive preparation for the tech-trading day ahead, with links (zdnet.com/anchordesk/)
- C|NET: Their news.com has sharp, San Francisco–based tech reporting, with links
- Silicon Investor: Market alerts as news moves
- Plus . . . all alerts tied to the portfolios and watch lists you've entered at Yahoo!, CBS MarketWatch, or MSN Investor. Also zdii .com, redherring.com, and multexinvestor.com.

Free to subscribers

- ragingbull.com: A daily bulletin with links to their most interesting stock chats and analysis
- *Barron's:* Highlights of the day's coverage (free with a subscription to the *WSJ*)
- *Wall Street Journal:* Personalized news alerts

ONLINE STOCK CHAT

The Big Four online chat sites—sites for active investors and frequent traders—are, in my opinion, the following:

- Silicon Investor: You must pay $100 a year or $200 lifetime to chat online, which helps increase the quality of the postings. (And you can also activate an "ignore" button to cut bothersome people out of your chats.)
- Raging Bull: Again, you must pay to partake of the boards. Their most interesting chat threads will be highlighted with hyperlinks in your daily e-mail.
- Yahoo!: Look here to follow company threads back to the early days—i.e., 1997.
- Fool: The Internet's first and biggest online chat and self-education center. Another child of the early days. Excellent archives.

DON'T JUST DO IT!

One last note: please check the Stock Detective, the SEC's EDGAR, or NASD's regulatory site at nasd.com before jumping into any over-the-counter bulletin board (OTC BB) stock. They aren't fully regulated by the NYSE or

NASD. (Brokers and CNBC guests often don't discriminate in terminology between the "over-the-counter" market, meaning the Nasdaq Stock Market where companies are actually "listed," and the true over-the-counter bulletin board market. Ask for specifics.)

And be sure to check out any unknown broker/dealer with the NASD database. You'll find more tips on evaluating individual brokers, brokerage firms, companies, and analysts in Chapter 9.

•   •   •

INTERVIEW WITH WILLIAM A. LUPIEN, CHAIRMAN, OPTIMARK TECHNOLOGIES, INC.

Bill Lupien led Instinet, the electronic trading company, from 1983 to 1988 as president, chairman, and CEO. He started in the securities industry in 1965 and spent 17 years as a specialist on the Pacific Exchange floor.

Described as a "cybercowboy" and an "outlaw," Lupien acknowledges that his hoofbeats may have shaken a few hides. But he says he aims only to create a fair deal for as many stock traders as possible—little guys included. From a 1000-acre ranch near Durango, Colorado, Lupien and partner Terry Rickard have built a system that many believe can do just that. The supercomputer-powered OptiMark Trading System lets traders enter a profile of their desires, showing how many shares they would be willing to sell or buy at a range of prices. The system also can aggregate small orders to match big ones, making an individual investor less likely to be sized out of a deal. And with the matches made anonymously, the system avoids the price-moving market impact of big orders.

OptiMark began handling trades on the Pacific Exchange in early 1999 and launched operations for Nasdaq at year-end. Lupien now concentrates on OptiMark's future, which includes options trading and perhaps even markets for airline or event tickets.

So far OptiMark has gotten the most attention for its impact on institutional investors. How and when will it have an impact on individual investors?

I think it started doing that right away. I've heard from more than one institution that the traditional way of finding contraside investors—that is, those who buy what you want to sell or vice versa—is difficult in some sectors. Individuals have taken over, if you will, trading in some Internet securities. There's no easy way to aggregate the smaller orders to match the bigger ones, but that is one of the main functions of OptiMark. So we think we'll be a solution that brings liquidity for institutions, but maybe even more for individual investors.

How will systems like OptiMark change the actual process of investing? Can individual investors enter trades directly with OptiMark?

We're not a broker/dealer, and having a broker/dealer represent a customer is the only way to get a trade to OptiMark. Retail customers can do it through an online brokerage called Terra Nova, which is a sister to the Archipelago electronic trading system. It has a drop-down box on the screen that allows investors to designate OptiMark to handle the trade. I'm confident that there will be other online brokerages interested in offering that service. There's no reason why anybody shouldn't have access to the facility.

What do you think of predictions that OptiMark and other electronic systems will be the downfall of brokers, floor traders, and specialists, or even the exchanges themselves?

OptiMark is not designed to eliminate them, but to bring buyers and sellers together in a way that lets them do what they want to do. It should help brokers, floor traders, and specialists do their jobs by giving them added ability to rebalance their positions.

People predicted that the start of electronic ordering would be the end of the exchanges. In fact, it's made it possible for us to do a billion shares a day and not go to our knees. I remember days when 10 million shares would trade and the tape would run late. My hand would hurt, my head would hurt. That's not to say electronic systems and computers won't be the end of exchanges as we've known them. But they will go on.

If it won't eliminate them, how has electronic trading changed the role of specialists and brokers?

The function they provide—short-term liquidity—still has value. They stand willing to buy or sell at any time at prices close to the market. Markets still benefit from their ability to provide that liquidity. They just have to retool the way they interact with these automated systems.

There are always people who resist new ways of doing business and automated ways of doing business. Then there are the people who say, "Does it make me money? Show me which button to push."

OptiMark grew out of what you've described as "fundamental flaws" in the trading system. What are those flaws?

The key problem has been how to get someone to bring their desires to the market without that information causing them to experience a loss. We needed to protect that information. It was not possible to do that until the technology came along.

How did those flaws affect the individual investor? Do many individual investors recognize the problems that OptiMark wants to solve?

The flaws affect everyone by adding to the cost of investing. What's amazing is how little the average investor has understood about what happens in the trading arena. Generally they cannot differentiate between a good execution and a bad one. That's meant a lot of people don't get quite what they deserve. Day traders and online investors are rapidly becoming more sophisticated. They're demanding better services, because they make more trades and they can see how poor executions can cost them money.

Some people have said that systems like OptiMark will make the market less transparent and more volatile. What do you think?

They're definitely right when they say it will take out some transparency, but we have to look at what kind. We're talking about pretrade transparency, because all the trades are posted immediately to the tape. If you've lived off pretrade transparency, then you're going to have concerns. I'm not talking about any criminal activity; I'm talking about people in the business who have used pretrade knowledge to their advantage. The question is who's the winner and who's the loser.

As for volatility, that can be exacerbated by big traders coming into the market and creating uncertainty. It's like a barracuda swimming toward a school of fish—they turn away because they don't know what's coming. The barracuda might only eat one or two but he's caused a shift in their direction. If traders nibble here and there at a stock because a big order has been placed, it's going to move away from them. With OptiMark, those orders don't loom over the market.

Will systems like OptiMark open the door to round-the-clock global trading? How and when could that become a reality?

Our systems are ready for that now. Whenever the exchanges are, we're ready to go.

If you look at demographics, you find that 40 percent of decisions by individual investors are made at or before dinnertime. People place orders then for transactions when the market opens. If they could trade right there, they might be more likely to do so and perhaps to buy something else. That would bring more liquidity.

How will individual investors be affected by OptiMark trading on Nasdaq?

What we will do is bring more centrality to Nasdaq. I don't mean a physical place, but a centrality in the way that the Internet has centrality even though in reality it is highly fragmented. There will be more and more liquidity, some of which is available now but hard to find. It will be easier to get to.

Will exchanges that use OptiMark attract business that may have gone elsewhere?

I think so. I think that's one reason we're getting so much interest internationally. Eventually we want to allow individuals to do multiexchange trades. Maybe they think Japan is overpriced and the United States is cheaper, so they'll be selling in Japan and buying here. Ten years ago no one thought about investing in a foreign company. Today the globalization of investing is one of the fastest-growing phenomena in the business.

How likely is it that the New York Stock Exchange will eventually use OptiMark?

If the Pacific Exchange or later the Nasdaq start to take large chunks of business away from the NYSE, they will have two choices. They will either come up with their own variation on the theme—I don't mean infringing on our patents, but coming up with something to do the job—or embrace it. Historically the New York exchange has been very competitive. I think they'll continue to be.

Observers have said OptiMark needs "critical mass" to be successful. What are the main obstacles to convincing people to use it?

There are two major obstacles. One is the ease of use, which encompasses a whole range of aspects. It's a new concept and people have to ask how it integrates into their work flow. The other is the chicken-and-egg question. People say they'll use OptiMark if it has liquidity. Well, they are the liquidity. We have signed up about 155 broker/dealers and institutions; we're trying to get to critical mass every day. We started with just one stock the first four days; now we have all 2200—some listed on the Pacific and the New York boards. We're averaging 1 million shares a day and we've seen a 3-million-share day. I think maybe 15 million would get to critical mass.

Does OptiMark want to compete directly as an exchange?

Our business model is facilitating the operation of existing exchanges. We're satisfied with our position.

Where does OptiMark go from here?

Our research and development team is working on the options market. We plan to implement that facility next for the Pacific Exchange and the Chicago Board of Exchange. I can't predict now when we'll end up with a business model we're all happy with. The biggest challenge is you don't have as much fluidity in any one option. For any one security, you have many options that vary in price and time. There are a lot more variables to deal with.

We'll also look at *other* sectors outside the financial community, like airline tickets. We may not consider now that a true market exists for airline tickets, but it could.

CHAPTER 7

INDUSTRY FOCUS FOR FUN AND PROFIT

Now that you've digested the basics of researching stocks for online trading, in this chapter we'll take you through some more advanced (and profitable!) techniques—focusing your research and your trading on one industry.

DRILLING DOWN

Drilling down into an industry (e.g., fiber optics) inside a larger sector (e.g., telecommunications) allows you to pay more profitable attention to a narrower universe of stocks. If you're going to make your money work for you as hard and fast as it can, you need to find the areas of the market that are yielding the highest rewards to short-term investors—the industries and the sectors that are moving this year, this quarter.

Short-term investors, day traders, and momentum investors are all looking for the same thing: intense moves in an intense sector, a place with heat near the center of the tornado, a sector that moves up with the trends and promises a good shot at buying into upward momentum so you can sell a bit higher.

As a new trader, one of the hardest things to do is one of the most basic: moving up or down *with* the market, going along with the accepted wisdom rather than jumping out ahead. You do not want to start out being a contrarian or value investor, looking for an underpriced stock that will make money in two or three years. You want to trust the rising tide that lifts all boats, this year.

There are several ways to choose which areas to drill down after. Peter Lynch, labeled "the nation's number one money manager" by *Time* magazine, believes that nimble individual investors have a much greater chance in the market than the vast, lumbering institutional investors, and suggests you zero in on the field in which you already work. (You'll find more in his books *Beating the Street* [Fireside, 1994] and *One Up on Wall Street,* written with John Rothchild.) Others drill down into retailers, betting on the companies that get a lot of their business, such as Starbucks or The Gap or Nike.

Another option is to take a broader view of today's society and ask yourself what the big continuing trends are going to be over the next 2, 5, or 10 years. Think about the sectors that are most fascinating to you—and remember: high-technology companies (often listed on the Nasdaq rather than the New York Stock Exchange), while paying no stock dividends, are the ones that zoom around the most in value, offering the most opportunity for an exciting, albeit dangerous, ride.

In a *Newsweek* poll featured in a June 1999 cover story called "The Whine of '99: Everyone's Getting Rich But Me!," 61 percent of Americans complained that they'd missed out on the rewards of the stock market boom of the '90s. Yet over a *quarter* of those surveyed were entitled to stock options where they worked. And every American who reports a minimum of $2000 of income to the IRS (up to $100,000) has the opportunity to put $2000 annually into a Roth IRA account, which they can use to trade—a fantastic investment—with no taxes, ever.

There may be a "whine of '99" arising across the land, but even if everyone isn't getting rich, a lot of people have been getting rich enough to invest in mutual funds: the amount of money thus invested increased by about 41 percent each year between 1991 and 1998. Yet in 1999 that amount suddenly fell 30 percent below the amount invested in '98. Is this a trend? I believe it is, and I believe the popularity and profitability of online trading explains it. The money that isn't going into passive investments in mutual funds is flowing into actively researched and actively managed portfolios designed by individual investors and traders. This trend toward more and more investing self-empowerment is the outcome of the online revolution, the Nasdaq changes of 1997–1998, the SEC's recognition of the new little stock markets called ECNs, and the death of the middleman that's still unfolding today.

PORTRAIT OF A HIGH-RISK PORTFOLIO: HOT ROTATION

Since we're talking about investing money we're trying to force into growth, we'll look at this as our high-risk portfolio: money we can afford to lose at least half of. (Assuming you use Troy's Three Trading Tips [T3]—limit, stop market order, and a target price—and the markets don't collapse, you will definitely be out of your trades before losing more than you planned—or, even worse, losing more than the whole amount when you're short a stock.)

The high-risk portfolio doesn't need to balance out the safe and conservative with the fast-moving growth stocks. This portfolio goes after fast growth and rising prices, buying low and selling high, week after week. (Accomplishing that formula in three out of five or six out of ten trades keeps the odds in your favor.) So we don't need industry rotation with slow sectors and fast sectors to blunt the risk, but we do need to know which industries are hottest and which are cooling off; then we need to punch up that information with a look at volatility. Will these stocks in this industry move around enough to allow for profits?

To give you a couple of examples, I'll review the Internet stocks in the high-technology area—since you couldn't turn on the television or radio without becoming aware of the 1998–1999 phenomenon—and then focus on genetically engineered drugs in biotechnology (a high-technology sector crossed with a health care sector).

THE INTERNET FOCUS (WITH BIOTECH ON THE SIDE): USING YAHOO!

In Chapter 6 you learned to move through the Yahoo!Finance headings to get the online trading information you need. Here's a reprise of those checkpoints, with additional features that will help with your Internet focus. To begin, go to http://finance.yahoo.com, or go straight to Yahoo!, and click on "Finance" under the "Business" heading. You'll need to register at the top of the page (if you've never been to the site before) or sign in (if you have). Do not read this section until you have the Yahoo!Finance page on your screen. Now, let's walk through it together:

U.S. MARKETS

Check the major U.S. indices—but this time around, add the Internet indices:

ISDEX index (IXY2).

TSC Internet (^DOT) from TheStreet.com.

Or link to the Nasdaq home page, click on "equity and index options" on the central bar, and choose from companies in *sector indexes,* among them:

- ICX, TheStreet.com's e-commerce index. Lists all companies doing business on the Internet, such as Amazon.com, Ameritrade, E*Trade, eBay, and uBid.
- IIX, The *Inter@ctive Week* Internet Index. Lists companies cutting across infrastructure and access, e-commerce, and Internet content and software. Developed by the AMEX with *Inter@ctive Week* magazine.
- MSH, Morgan Stanley High-Technology 35 Index. Highly capitalized U.S. companies in nine high-tech subsectors.
- BTK, biotechnology index. Fourteen companies including Chiron, Genzyme, Gilead Sciences, Amgen, and Protein Design Labs.
- DRG, the Pharmaceutical Index. A cross section of "big pharma" including many big stakeholders in genetic research: Amgen (AMGN), ALZA (AZA), Merck (MRK), and Pfizer (PFE).
- CTN, the Credit Suisse First Boston Technology Index. A benchmark of high-tech performance, including Internet holdings such as AOL, E*Trade, eBay, and Yahoo!.

RESEARCH

By Industry. There are nearly 100 industries listed when you click on this hyperlink. But here on Yahoo! (remember, sectors are divided up in different ways on different sites) to find Internet stocks we click on "Internet." To find biotech research investments, rather than clicking on "High Technology," you must first go to "Medical." On Yahoo! the Internet is further divided into two industry groupings:

- Internet Services. A breakdown of listed stocks by industry, ranking them from top to bottom. For example, at this writing, Doubleclick Inc. (DCLK) is listed at number three and has hyperlinks to the charts, news, SEC filings, company profile, research, and message threads on their trader/investor bulletin boards. Others listed in the Internet Services top 15 performers are Mindspring (MSPG), Network Solutions (NSOL), Flycast (FCST), America Online (AOL), and 24/7 Media Inc. (TFSM). Since all these companies, with one exception, have four letters in their symbol, you know they're probably trading on the Nasdaq exchange. The exception? AOL. Its three-letter symbol tells you that AOL trades on the New York Exchange.

- Internet Content. Also lists Internet stocks by ranking, with the same group of links. But the Content listing includes a different universe of 21 stocks, including Go2Net Inc. (GNET), Market-Watch.com (MKTW), C|NET Inc. (CNET), Broadcast.com (BCST), TheStreet.com (TSCM), About.com Inc. (BOUT), and Ziff-Davis ZDNet (ZDZ).

Up/Downgrades. Tells you who the analysts think is hot and who's not in the Internet and biotech areas.

Earnings Surprises. Look for Internet and biotech firms that performed much better—or worse—than analysts' quarterly projections.

REFERENCE

(Across the bottom of the page.) Earnings and Splits calendars for your alerts in Internet and biotech. Please note that *Red Herring* magazine, covering venture capital in the Silicon Valley arena, has another index, not listed on Yahoo! (go to redherring.com; see Figure 7.1). And *Wired* magazine puts together a mixture of technology stocks, including the Internets, with the Wired Index Fund (wired.com).

EDITORIAL OFFERED ON YAHOO!

The Motley Fool

- Investment Opinion. You'll find editorial pieces balancing the allure of Internet stocks against the promise of biotechnology issues and explaining business models behind the two. For example, Fool writer Warren Gump notes that the biotechs—the biggest of which are Amgen (AMGN), Biogen (BGEN), Genentech (GNE), and Chiron (CHIR)—are much less expensive now than the Internets. Gump also discusses industry giants with price/earnings multiples (P/E ratios) of less than 50 times earnings. This sounds ludicrous to investors trained in the early '90s, when P/E ratios of 10 times earnings were popular. Gump goes on to remind readers that multiples of Internet stocks, on the other hand, are impossible to figure, since they seldom have earnings at all. In another article, Gump walks you through Biogen to acquaint you with product

FIGURE 7.1 *Red Herring, redesigned by Roger Black, draws you across the bleeding edge of high tech and sets venture capitalists like Draper and Jurvetson up in flames.* (redherring.com.)

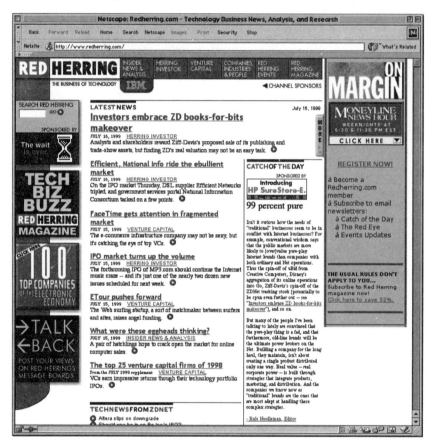

cycles, research issues, and FDA input with a successful drug, in this case Avonex, which slows down multiple sclerosis.

● The Daily Double. In this section the Fool carries a rich selection of editorial on Internet stocks. Their daily feature exploring why a stock doubled in value, and how you might have become aware of it before the run-up, recently told the story of Go2Net Inc. Last year, explains the Fool, Go2Net rated number 77 on the Media Metrix listing of most-visited Web sites. A year later it hit number 19. At the time of the Fool's writing, it was reaching 36 percent of Web users with its sites based on finance (Silicon Investor and

StockSite), search (MetaCrawler), commerce (HyperMart and Web-Market), auctions (Haggle Online), and games (PlaySite). Again, Vulcan—in the person of Paul Allen (Bill Gates's former partner)—is a big investor, with holdings at 34 percent.

- StockTalk. Here the Fool profiles some of the most interesting company presidents. In July of 1998, for instance, reporters Yi-Hsin Chang and Brian Graney interviewed Yahoo! CEO Tim Koogle. The interview focused on the business model of Web portals, the quantity of page view numbers and click-through visits, and how these numbers intrigue advertisers. Koogle stressed that Yahoo! was not in the content or editorial business, comparing Yahoo! to a television network that brands and distributes content—the word currently used in the Web business is *aggregator.* Yahoo!, Koogle explained, gathers content from independent Web sites that supply the data, news, and analysis for their financial portal (like BigQuotes, CBS MarketWatch, and TheStreet.com), puts it together dynamically, brands it "Yahoo!," and distributes it.

ISDEX. Yahoo! editorial links also jump to ISDEX, the editorial home of the Internet stock report by Steve Harmon at internet.com. Internet.com is the well-known site that was bought by Mecklermedia, when the entire world, it seemed, wanted to own the URL of "internet dot com." You might consider setting up your own ISDEX watch list after running all these companies through a screen, identifying the most important elements you seek in a stock: volatility and consistency.

PORTFOLIO

To get to this function you must start with the Yahoo! main page, then click on "Finance and Investment" under the "Business and Economy" heading. From there, click on the top listing, "Yahoo!Finance."

You might want to add two tracking portfolios here as an experiment: one for Internet stocks and one for biotech. Simply click on the "create new portfolio" button, and click on the "finished" button when you've filled in the indices and stocks you'll be following.

RELATED RESOURCES

At the bottom of the Yahoo!Finance home page, to enter in the instant stock alerts—and pager buzzes—for your experimental portfolios. Or try running one here and the other at cbs.marketwatch or investor.msn.

Or run one in the stock market trading simulation offered by CNNfn, the online presence of Time Warner's CNNfn channel (coming up at the end of this chapter). Find the simulation at sandlot.net/cnnfn_finalbell.

FINANCIAL NEWS

Here you can find your personalized news page set up to track Internet stories, indicated with icons next to the Internet tracking portfolio you set up in your portfolio section. (You can set up one tracking group for Internet stocks you're interested in, for instance, and another for online brokers to see how the market values them.)

COMMUNITY

Click here to enter the chat side of investing. This will lead you to message boards covering the Internet industry and to threads following conversations on specific companies within the industry that are on your watch list. If you feel something bubbling up at one of the companies on your watch list, you may want to lurk around the discussion area without actually signing on and joining the fray. (As a newcomer, you may be hesitant to jump in immediately—just know that you don't have to!) Later, you'll have plenty to tell the community.

BEYOND YAHOO!

THE I-WATCH PAGE

The institutional investors who manage the gazillions of dollars in mutual funds set off the sector dance: running gazillions first into the oil sector, then turning tail and heading for the financial services, then suddenly falling in love with telecommunications. A great way to check out where the institutional investors are going is found at Thomson Financial Services (thomson-invest.com), on the I-Watch page. Thomson, which has a strategic alliance with TheStreet.com and other investing sites, helps individuals understand the trading patterns of the institutional investors by creating a window into pre- and posttrade discussions between traders at large trading desks. I-Watch data comes from the AutoEx, the private network the traders use to analyze real-time trading information. The AutoEx data analysis by Thomson's in-house reporters can help small investors get a handle on the world of intra-day trading patterns.

It's intriguing to watch these huge buy orders, put in by the institutional money managers who are afraid prices will rise if it's known that they're buying large blocks. (Thanks to Bill Lupien's OptiMark system, discussed in the interview with Lupien at the end of Chapter 6, such formerly telltale moves may no longer be visible.)

CBS MARKETWATCH

CBS MarketWatch (at marketwatch.com) follows a variety of index groups, similar to those previously listed. When you click on the name of the index, it unfolds to reveal all the stocks listed in that group. And MarketWatch has started a new column called "Indications," designed to provide a premarket fix on trading trends in the hottest stocks overnight—on Instinet and other off-hours trading venues.

Like James Cramer in New York, Thom Calandra, editor of StockWatch, has become a sort of celebrity in Silicon Valley–obsessed San Francisco, where he's interviewed by local television reporters as he's emerging from high-tech conferences.

MARKET GUIDE

This site (at marketguide.com) has a fascinating method for searching through the handful of hot sectors you've discovered from your research. Click on "what's hot" at the bottom of the home page. This will take you to "hottest sectors," and within each of the hottest sectors you will discover the industries that make up the sectors, listed in order of sizzle. Click on one of those industries and discover the exact companies, their symbols, and the returns.

A recent search laid out the hottest conglomerates (which just happened to include General Electric, owner of CNBC, NBC, and MSNBC). The second hottest? Health care. The industries within health care included "biotech and drugs industry." Listed among the top 50 or so stocks here were Cytotherapeutics, Cima Labs, and Hyseq, Inc. What will today's search find?

WALL STREET CITY

Want to compare hot sectors and hot industries over days, weeks, months, years? This site (at wallstreetcity.com), owned by Telescan, is the only place on the Internet that adds the time element for analyzing heat in various sectors and industries over a period of time (see Figure 7.2). An excellent introductory discussion explains how industry group analysis can boost your returns over the market averages by using diversified portfolios, made up of *only* the hottest sectors.

At Wall Street City, first head to Industry Group Center (in the left-hand column), then click on "best and worst industries." Telescan's site bases its

FIGURE 7.2   *Wall Street City heats up your sector rotation; it's the only place like this on the Web.* (Wall Street City by Telescan, Inc.)

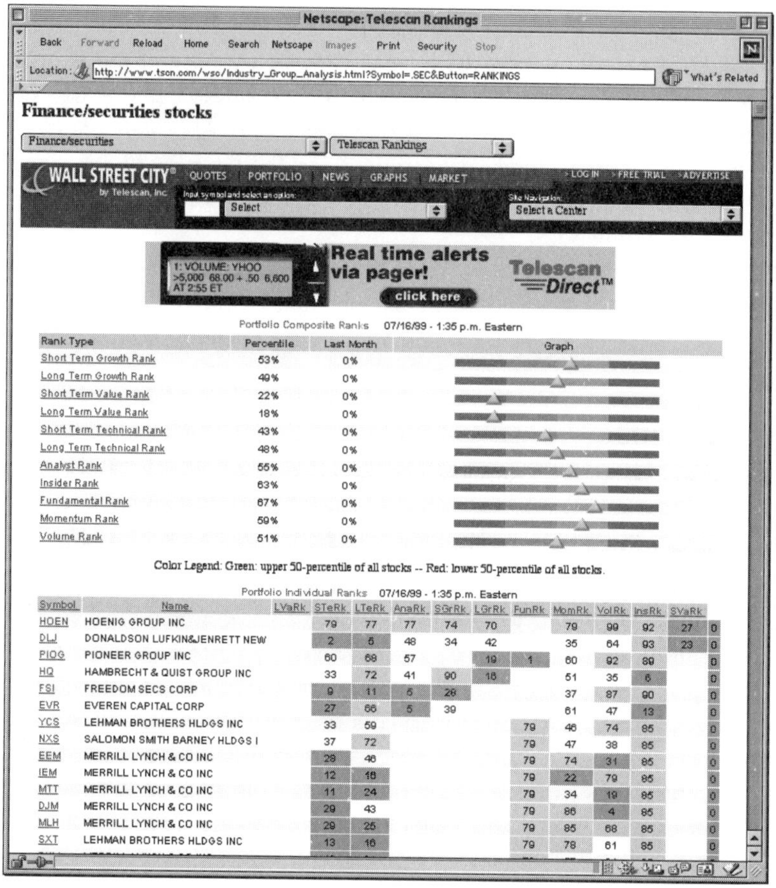

102 industries on the S&P industry groupings. But unlike the other sites, the coverage here also includes technical indicators.

Pick your favorites from among the hundreds listed. When you click the industry name, it reveals the stocks sorted within it, with best performers at the top. (For instance, if you looked at Finance/Investments, you might find the Internet-related order-entry online brokers DLJdirect (DIR), ECN-owner Lehman Brothers (LEH), wholesaler/market Knight/TriMark (NITE), and Datek Online Holdings' investor, Toronto Dominion's Waterhouse Group (TD).

CNBC ON THE WEB

Up till now, the online site of CNBC (cnbc.com; see Figure 7.3)—the network that offers the omnipresent television coverage seen in trading rooms around the world—listed only upcoming TV guests and some story links with MSNBC, a sister site and cable network owned by NBC and Bill Gates's Microsoft. Meanwhile CNNfn, whom CNBC trounces in terms of cable viewership, has had three years to build up its own personal finance site (at either cnnfn.com or fn.com), which offers the best online trading simulation, complete with limit orders and stop loss for real-world T3 practice.

FIGURE 7.3 *Maria Bartiromo is just one of the larger-than-life personalities on CNBC Cable, the ever present sight in trading rooms and Wall Street. They juiced the site in summer 1999.* (© Courtesy of National Broadcasting Company, Inc. All rights reserved.)

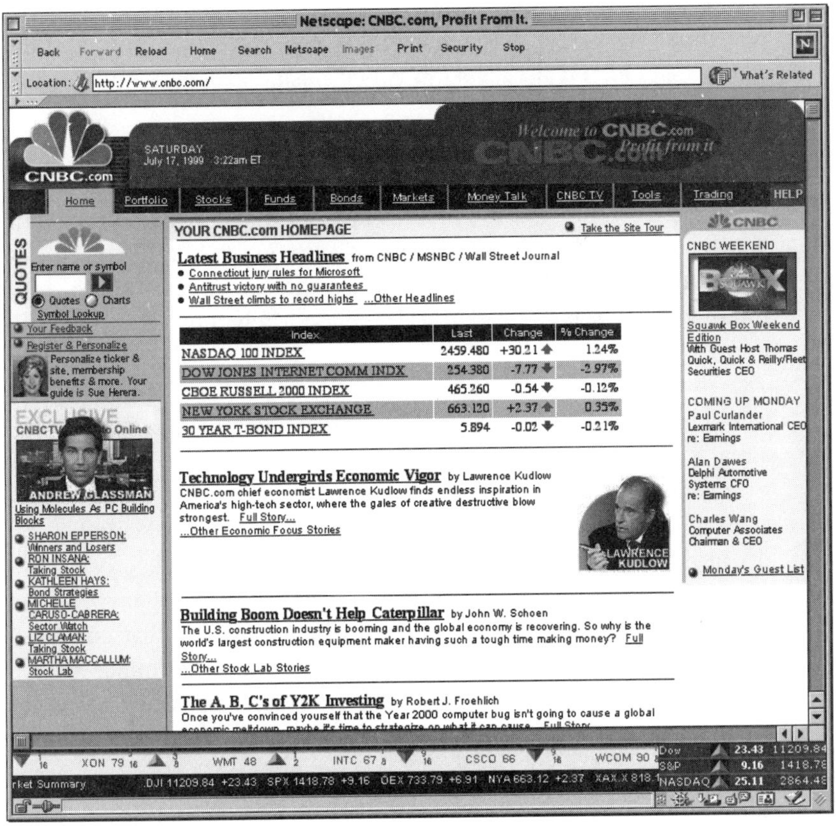

CNBC finally started a full Web service to match the excellent job they do on cable television. In the summer of 1999, CNBC began beta-testing their new personal finance hub. One executive quoted in the *Industry Standard* called this richly financed Web site "a poster child for convergence." Despite NBC's joint venture with Microsoft, CNBC is finally coming out with a site that will begin to challenge both MSN's Investor and Yahoo!Finance.

Here's what you'll find at the CNBC site:

Red and green stock ticker—just like the ticker on your TV screen, but thanks to Web interactivity, this ticker will allow you to click through on companies' symbols to hyperlink to company snapshots.

Breaking news will come from MSNBC's excellent online financial coverage. More breaking news comes from other cobranded NBC Web sites—Snap, C|NET's News.com. Plus you'll get original material developed by a new online staff of 20 at CNBC. Dow Jones and the *Wall Street Journal* already supply their business analysis and news to CNBC and MSNBC's site.

Wall Street City/Telescan (as already mentioned) is also integrated seamlessly into the CNBC site. Use their stock screener, which allows you to enter your most important signals, such as heavy insider buying or selling or a high price/earnings ratio. You can also cull stocks, matching your profile in the section of the sector you like, such as Internet content; then drop your list immediately into a tracking portfolio on the site.

Trading directly from the site. It hasn't happened yet, but this idea—for individual traders and investors—is something that Yahoo! has already been exploring with Reuters's Instinet. Currently, the site would need a broker/dealer to act as intermediary in the trade. (DBC's Alan Hirschfield, cobranded with CBS in CBS MarketWatch, discusses this possibility in his interview, later in this chapter.)

As mentioned earlier, CBS MarketWatch is offering a premium Web trading product, called MarketWatch from DBC, that combines the information flow of a less intensive trading terminal with a through-the-screen trading link with the broker of your choice. It's reasonable to expect more one-stop-shopping destinations in the near future.

INDUSTRY STANDARD MAGAZINE

If the Internet is featured on your watch list, the *Industry Standard* is a must-have weekly magazine (see Figure 7.4). Edited by Jonathan Weber, former technology editor at the *Los Angeles Times,* the *Industry Standard* (at thestandard.com, or thestandard.com/newsletters to subscribe to e-mail news) is home to a crew of terrific San Francisco–based reporters and to Media Grok, winner of the June 1999 ASBPE National Award for best original online news section. A visitor may sign up for e-mail delivery of the *Standard*'s newsletters. I strongly recommend these:

FIGURE 7.4   *The* Industry Standard, *a high-gloss weekly news magazine edited by the former tech editor of the* Los Angeles Times, *runs a not-to-be-missed, e-mailed "Media Grok" column by Mark Glazer and his team.* (The Industry Standard.)

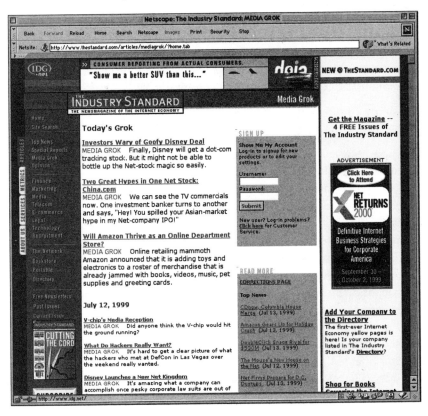

- Media Grok—a critical daily roundup with attitude, and links to globally published stories on the Internet economy.
- Stock Grok—Like the Media Grok, the weekly Stock Grok keeps an eye on the online trading world with stories about Internet and tech stocks. Again, fascinating links track stories globally.
- Shop Grok—Coverage of the world of e-commerce and e-tailing, with links.
- Metrics—This weekly look at the key indicators of the Internet economy comes with downloadable PowerPoint slides from their Web site (thestandard.com).
- Intelligencer—A Friday special report with a review of the past week's important trends and a look ahead to the next week's.
- News Alert—Lets you know the instant that breaking news gets to their site.

THE BIOTECH FOCUS

Now that we've covered the high-technology sector, we'll focus on genetically engineered drugs in the biotechnology sector.

BIOSPACE.COM

On the front page of this biotech site (see Figure 7.5), which calls itself the hub site for the "world's most exciting industry," you'll find upgrades, downgrades, brokerage ratings, and translations of terms like *buy, attractive, market perform, reduce,* and *underperform.* There are also breaking news and features on the genetic front from sources like the *Wall Street Journal, The New York Times,* and *The Washington Post,* and the market summary, including the Dow, Nasdaq, and S&P 500. Included are the Nasdaq Biotech Index ($IXBT) and the AMEX Biotech Index ($BTK). The "BioSpace movers" section lists the biggest gainers and losers in both price and volume, and "BioSpace 20," companies in the biotech arena they call the "bellwethers."

As the hub site for the biotech industry as well as the biotech investor, the site carries a wide range of career information, as well as the more investor-oriented features like "deals and dollars," a new stock sort for investors, clinical trials news, personal portfolio, IPO news, IPOs in registration, and those bellwethers.

FIGURE 7.5 *San Francisco's BioSpace.com portal is home to the biotechnology communities around the United States and is key to self-education about the field.* (www.biospace.com—The Global Hub Site for Life Sciences.)

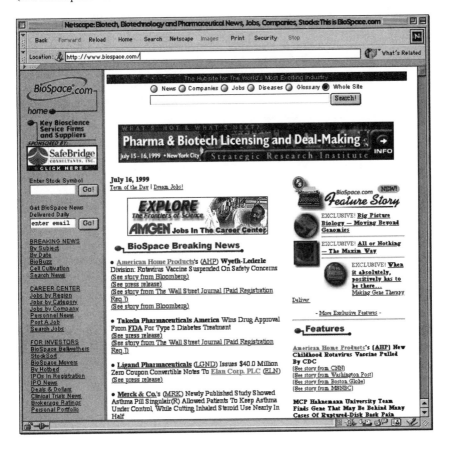

BioSpace also carries a public company directory that links you to the biotech company's sites, SEC filings, news from their team reporters, and stock quotes.

BioBuzz, with stories on subjects like cloning, biological warfare, Viagra, and arthritis, takes you to links with the latest news and press releases, plus information on conferences featuring medical stars in the field.

Should you decide to drill down to companies in your neighborhood, there is a series of regional hotbeds they call Biotech Bay (San Francisco),

Biotech Beach (southern California), BioForest, BioCanada, BioUS, BioTechxus, and about a dozen more. Genetown is, of course, Boston. Check that one out, and you'll find the market picture for the Massachusetts companies, with the local Genetown companies sorted from hot to cool. (You can even get maps for your town.)

A Boston investment banker who specializes in health care and biotech says the "GenePool" is indispensable for real-time information— "much better than waiting for tomorrow's newspaper." To join the GenePool and receive the latest biotech news by e-mail, click on GenePool at their site and register (it's free).

At this writing the list of biotech bellwethers was as follows:

Affymetrix	Gilead Sciences
Amgen	Guilford Pharmaceuticals
Biogen	Human Genome Sciences
Biomatrix	Immunex
Bio-Technology General	Incyte Pharmaceuticals
Centocor	Medimmune
Cephalon	Millennium Pharmaceuticals
Chiron	Pharmacopeia
Genentech	Pharmacyclics
Genzyme General	Sepracor

BIOCENTURY.COM

Based in the San Francisco Bay area, Washington, D.C., and England, Bio-Century—"The Bernstein Report on BioBusiness"—is an extremely well-informed and well-connected independent biotechnology analysis from Karen Bernstein, Ph.D., and her reporting team. (Bernstein knows the venture capitalists, the scientists, the investment bankers, and the money managers: she's always either on the phone with them, on a jet with them, or speaking to them at a conference, such as the Nasdaq's 1999 International Biotech and Infotech Summit on "the biotech-powered century.")

BioCentury feeds the thinking of the venture capital, investment banking, and science sectors of the industry. The biotechnology stock tables for both the United States and Europe appear here on a weekly basis. It's not cheap, but your four-week trial is free. You can choose among three newsletters, investment conferences, and their special research services. And you can find a database of $23 billion in biotech financing, IPOs, private placements, and others:

- *BioCentury* is delivered weekly by e-mail or fax and includes stories on corporate performance, scientific developments, and new technologies. Major news and trend analysis, hot new companies, and news from Washington and England round it out.
- *BioCentury Part II* is a weekly overview of all the new deals, Washington regulations, clinical trials, and investments. Also delivered by fax or e-mail on Mondays.
- *BioCentury Extra* sends out news alerts during the week for breaking stories of interest to the investor, executive, or scientist.

Fill out the online registration for a four-week trial order.

You will also need the Acrobat Reader, downloadable free from Adobe (with a link on the site). And here's a book that will help your biotech trading research: *The Billion-Dollar Molecule: One Company's Quest for the Perfect Drug,* by Barry Werth (Touchstone, 1995), which brings to life the high-wire act of starting a new biotech venture, as well as the characters who work and invest there.

Before you move on to the next chapter, where you'll choose an online broker, first try CNNfn's one-month or three-month online trading simulation to help you trade like a seasoned investor. You'll find it at CNNfn/Sandbox.net. (See Figures 7.6 and 7.7.) With this simulation you'll learn to use the T3, Troy's Three Trading Tips, to place stop-loss orders, to limit orders, and to pencil in your sales targets.

● ● ●

INTERVIEW WITH ALAN HIRSCHFIELD, CHAIRMAN OF DATA BROADCASTING CORPORATION

The former head of Columbia Pictures and Twentieth Century Fox, Hirschfield has made a surprising—and profitable—transition to the world of online trading technologies.

If you were at a cocktail party, how would you describe what your company does and why it's so hot now?

It's not easy! My wife says she was always able to understand the businesses I was in—the movie business, the TV business—until this one. This is more complex. But here goes: DBC provides real-time financial data to individual investors, which enables them to trade off that informa-

FIGURE 7.6   *Become comfortable with using the T3 safety net when you play the CNNfn market simulation at sandbox.com's game site.* (Investment Challenge and Final Bell are products of sandbox.com. © 1999 Cable News Network, LP, LLLP. All rights reserved. Used by permission of CNN.)

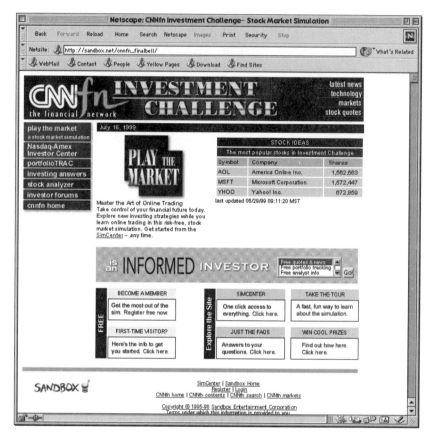

tion. Using third-party software, they're able to spot trends and momentum in a market. We give them every trade and the specific time at which it occurs on every exchange—stock commissions, monetary instruments, futures, options. The person who's monitoring his or her portfolio, who follows the market on a daily basis, can have access to news, research, and data through a variety of broadcast media, FM sideband and satellite, and so on.

Three years ago we realized that the Internet provided enough bandwidth to meet the exponential demand for data—to disseminate the infor-

FIGURE 7.7 *This order entry page trains you to think carefully about what you're buying, why, and at an exact price between the bid and ask on the Nasdaq quote. Or go for below wholesale price for your stock!* (Investment Challenge and Final Bell are products of sandbox.com. © 1999 Cable News Network, LP, LLLP. All rights reserved. Used by permission of CNN.)

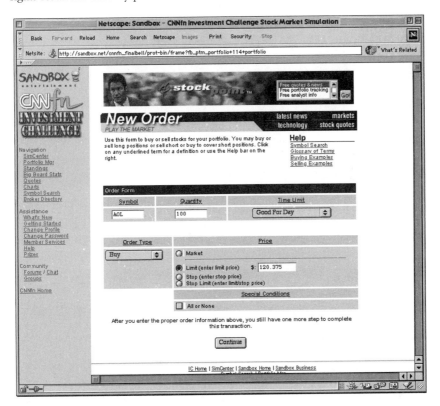

mation as the information itself expanded dramatically. This was the dawn of the electronic trading age.

Who used to buy online stock information in 1990?

It was the favored few who got the Goldman or the Morgan research—the private customer. Today you have broader access. And it's time.

Our customer used to be a person who trades at least in some part for a living—customers with $250,000 to $500,000. The Net is changing that. We're getting a more professional customer, someone who needs the information all day. We've sold the product to Schwab, Ameritrade; now we're selling it to individual brokerage houses. My broker might use eSignal rather than going through the proprietary information systems used by the old-line Wall Street firms. [See Figure 7.8.]

There's nothing really proprietary about it. Bloomberg has his own news, we have our own dedicated news organization, as does Reuters and Dow Jones. The rest is generic, public domain information if you're willing to pay for it. The question is, how do you take it and repurpose it, and at what cost?

How would you explain your eSignal product? Is it a Bloomberg Box for the rest of us?

eSignal, essentially, is another Bloomberg Box. But instead of charging $1500 to $1700 a month, we're making it available for $250. It's hard to get a banker at Solly or Goldman to give up his $1500 Bloomberg Box. But for people who can't justify the expense of having one, eSignal gives you

---

FIGURE 7.8 *Want to go upscale from the CBS MarketWatch feed (see Figure 6.6)? Trade up to top-of-the-line eSignal, real-time streaming quotes for online investors, delivered over the Internet.* (eSignal from Data Broadcasting Corporation.)

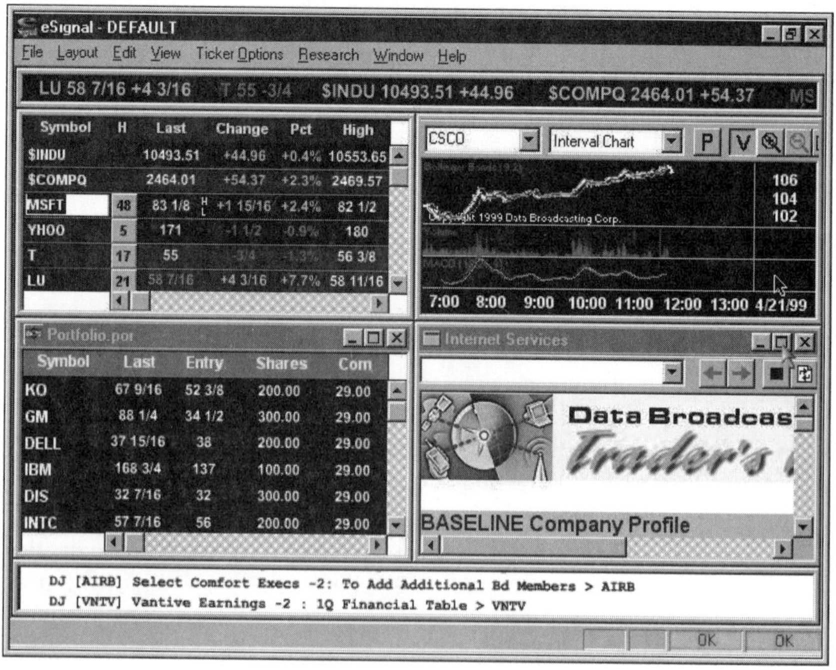

about 95 percent of what you get on the Bloomberg Box. We deliver over the Internet, not using dedicated phone lines, and we use the bandwidth available on the Internet to download all the data, which previously was only available on a dedicated, fixed, closed Bloomberg Box system.

Bloomberg's got this problem—what I call the Barnes & Noble problem. He's got this real estate with a terrific product at a terrific price, just like Barnes & Noble has all this embedded product in all this brick and mortar—versus Amazon, pumping out this ephemeral type of asset. Are you really going to trash what is at the moment a very good business?

Right now E*Trade and Schwab are running circles around Merrill Lynch. Merrill Lynch has x-thousand brokers to protect. With e-trading you don't need to call the broker. So broker-dominated firms have a problem. While they're wringing their hands, they've created this big vacuum and up through this vacuum got sucked the Ameritrades and E*Trades and Schwabs of this world. The brokers woke up one morning and . . .

How do you fit in with Schwab?

Schwab offers eSignal to its customers on a discounted basis. Or, customers can go through our service—they'll have a trading button on their screen that will automatically execute with Schwab or with 30 or 40 online brokerages: E*Trade, DLJ, Dreyfus . . . Schwab's online trading went from 14 percent to over 70 percent this year.

Can you go straight to an ECN?

To get to an ECN, you're going to need an intermediary to provide the access—in the same way that you and I can't call the NYSE and execute a trade. Those intermediaries are the Islands and the Archipelagos. They're providing the trading systems so you can see the momentum in the stocks; you can pick your best markets to buy and sell. That's what the Nasdaq Level II has done for the traders who are acquiring this information off the ECNs.

SOES bandits are really professionals. The typical day trader that [Arthur] Levitt [of the SEC] is concerning himself with is the man or woman on the street who's become enamored with day trading, who's in for $1500 to three or four thousand, has limited capital. These traders are quite distinct from the people who do this for a living, anywhere from 9 to 24 hours a day, trading in American markets and foreign markets.

You do have 24-hour trading today but it's all electronic. The NYSE is going to have to make its transition. It doesn't want to, because it doesn't want to impede on the specialist system, which is about as necessary at this point as a crank is to wind up a Ford car. Basically, they're trying to protect margins. Once you do order matching on a computer, once you have six competing ECNs, you really don't need specialists. Frankly it's not up to them to call the shots anymore. The world is going to move on without them. The handwriting's on the wall. We see it in the deals we're making.

What sort of data product do you offer the trader with CBS Market-Watch?

The CBS MarketWatch product will be eSignal very lite. It's not the kind of information for a real technical trader. It's just $19 or $25 a month, then point and click over to your broker. The investor is going to get more and more information and charts to trade with. That's the good news. The bad news is that right now people only see the market going one way. What happens with a real market implosion? You have these big infrastructures in place that could dry up, frankly.

But the e-brokers are going to be more efficient over time than the old Merrill Lynch–type operations; even though they have building overhead, they don't have high-priced personnel. There's going to be a day of reckoning in the next year or two. Who will survive? Clearly the proliferation of e-brokers is going to require a winnowing-out process. All the Web sites giving financial data will come crashing down, and a lot of entrepreneurial e-trade sites are going to disappear.

Some people see CBS MarketWatch as an entertainment portal as well as an investment site. Is your entertainment business background with Columbia Pictures and Twentieth Century Fox helping you make MarketWatch into an entertainment portal?

CNBC, AOL, Yahoo!—they're all providing trading sites. Once you have the capital to deliver full-time streaming video, 24-7, with live commentators, interviews, analysts, all day and all night, it becomes part of the media spectrum. It'll compete with other entertainment entities. I don't think we're going up against *ER* or *The Sopranos,* but if we choose to do an investment round table with five of the leading Internet analysts, we're going to take a piece of the audience from these programs. Network numbers are down because of cable and dedicated programming. The population only has so many hours in the day to watch TV or a computer screen, and the average family is now on their PC two to three hours a day. The real Death Star for network television is going to be Web TV.

What's it like, being a cybercowboy from Jackson Hole?

I'm wired in. I'm looking at my PC while I'm talking to you. I got my e-mail out to all my office locations this morning. When I moved to Jackson Hole 11 years ago I couldn't do what I'm doing now. We used to get FedEx deliveries on the back of a pickup truck. Now there's no time disadvantage in participating in the markets. I'm online all day. If we want to do a meeting, we videoconference.

One of the huge benefits of the technological revolution is that people are no longer geographically disadvantaged. I have the same access to the same information as someone with an office in the Chicago commodity pits. I can't "feel them" like someone on the floor can, but information isn't time or geographically sensitive anymore. I can sit in Jackson Hole and have quality of life at the same time.

In the future I don't think you'll need EDAT trading because you're going to get it through the Net. When you can deliver unlimited bandwidth over a cable modem through TV or live, your ISP is all you're going to need. I have a dedicated line just for the Internet. With cable modem fiber optic running over phone lines you're going to have everything you need.

CHAPTER **8**

HOME BASE: CHOOSING AN ONLINE BROKER

This chapter should be the most fun because it's here that you get to sit down in front of your computer screen and actually start sifting through potential brokers that match you and your investment style. I know what I want—simplicity, security, and excellent executions—and what I think an active trader and investor needs to focus on.

But I also realize there are other intangibles that guide an individual's choices in the financial realm. So I will lay out my ground rules: what I think you need; what my personal favorites are; but I will also lay out the entire top 10 in the online broker horse race. If nothing else, I'll know that this book helped steer you to a firm that's huge enough to survive any storms.

WHAT I THINK YOU SHOULD WANT

- A clean and simple order entry on one page, if possible (without a confirmation page for really fast traders).
- Real-time quotes. Streaming real-time quotes. Free.
- Real-time charts. Again, constantly updated. And free is nice.
- The ability to look at your portfolio and click down through each stock on a "sell" button, when necessary, without going to another screen to start again.
- A well-designed Web site that has a sturdy, muscular infrastructure to withstand those high-volume, high-volatility days without

crashing. (When your online broker crashes, it's *your* problem, too. Plan ahead. Have a backup: a Silicon Valley firm, Keynote, is running weekly metrics of the time it takes a broker's screen to load, an indicator of their tech savvy. Check them out at keynote.com.)

- A customer phone number that answers, and that can answer these questions: "I'm a new investor. Could you please explain to me the difference between a market order and a limit order? Can I place a stop-loss market order on a Nasdaq stock, and is there any charge?" The online firm with the active investors at heart will be glad to explain all potential minefields, or get their supervisor on the phone to help out. "What's the difference between a market order and a limit order?" That's your mantra.

The active investor and trader also needs a portfolio that's running real-time numbers. You always know how much money you have, exactly where your margin is getting stretched, and which stocks are nudging the exit figure you set for them when you first added them to your portfolio.

Once you're comfortable with a solid financial site such as Yahoo!Finance or Microsoft's Investor, you can do your research and run your potential portfolios there, get your alerts set there, and stay on top of all the breaking news and market developments while having access to top-of-the-line screens, analytics, and investment talk. Yahoo! even gives you free pager alerts—something many brokers are advertising as a top-flight attraction to the trader.

Bottom line? Learn about the market away from the brokers, take your time playing Sandbox/CNNfn's online trading simulation game "Final Bell," and don't budge from that Sandbox/CNNfn simulation until you have the T3 down cold: buy with a limit order, immediately go back to place a stop-loss market order, and pencil in your exit point—when you'll sell, no matter what.

IT'S YOUR MONEY, NOW GROW IT!

Since this book opened by telling you that there are times in life when an investor needs to force his or her garden to grow—a crash campaign, so to speak, before the crash, to fatten up that nut—you already know that my bias is toward the firm that will:

- Make it easy
- Be reasonably inexpensive and reliable for buying Nasdaq stocks
- Get good, lightning-fast executions

Later, you'll find that the efficiency and elegance of the top online brokers will also serve your long-term philosophy well: to develop the patience and wisdom to hang on to brand-name growth companies until you have that well-publicized courage to be rich.

Once you start to make important choices in buying stock and following your potential returns, you'll probably want to choose the online broker that gives you the best execution. If your current full-service broker is an old friend, stick with him or her until you're comfortable opening an online account, or open one of the new online accounts that most all the full-service brokers—Merrill Lynch and others—are offering now to customers they've served for 30, 40, and 50-plus years.

But you should also explore the stunning investing resources available on the Web today. Once you're online, take a look at the brokers in cyberspace. Check out the online brokers mentioned in this chapter—the best of the best in terms of size, stability, security, and infrastructure—and take your time to choose which you feel most comfortable with by exploring their sites and online order demonstrations.

Still a true-blue full-service or discount phone-order customer? Why not get online, do some research, perhaps join an investing group, then open an online account just for one experiment—saving for a trip to Paris, for example. The account experiment will expose you to the reasoning process behind setting a price for your limit orders and will also get you used to buying on margin, if you so desire. Every deposit you make in this online university of hard knocks—every experience you get—can only cost about $10 for the commission (depending on your choice of broker) plus the amount you've allowed with your T3 order.

THE CRITICAL CRITERIA

Which criteria did I use to choose these brokers? Since I'm recommending them, I went with the established top 10 online companies with the best security, the largest number of customers, the greatest assets, and expanding infrastructures: the very top firms in the online investing field. Some of them have brick-and-mortar offices you can drop in to with questions and concerns. The others, built on the online-only business model, have call centers with trained customer-service representatives. (If it makes you nervous to talk with a customer-service representative instead of a licensed stockbroker, consider reading the insightful book Charles Schwab first wrote in the 1980s, *How to Be Your Own Stockbroker*.)

The Internet unleashed a revolution in the once-stodgy world of stock brokerages and Wall Street investment houses. Around 1995, hordes of the new self-empowered investors—initially envisioned by Charles Schwab when he began promoting discounted commissions—started hitting the Web. First they came for financial information at new spots like the Fool on AOL, Finance on Yahoo!, and MSN.

The spillover to more online broker business was a natural migration: it was just a simple click from the stock quote page to a banner ad leading to an online application form with the new brand-building online brokers like E*Trade and Datek. The more established discount brokers like Schwab, determined to convert loyal discount customers who were accustomed to ordering stock over the phone—either verbally or by punching in the order on the phone keypad—were equally eager to transform traditional customers into the new, more profitable online customers.

And transform them Schwab did, managing to keep a $29.95 commission price tag on a business whose economies of scale merited more like the current average commission of $15 or $16. And as we approach the Millennium . . . that triple-zero year . . . television ads are expanding the e-commerce realm of Amazon and E*Trade into the heart of Americana.

The e-trading earthquake is setting off tremblors on Wall Street. Even John Gotfreund, former head of Salomon Brothers, tells a reporter (Cavuto on Fox) that "the market structure is changing and the markets are changing . . . we don't know how it's going to work out. On the institutional side, the people who used to make markets [at the trading desks of full-service brokers like Smith Barney and Merrill Lynch; at investment houses like Salomon and Lehman] aren't going to be, because that's not the highest profitability in the market anymore."

PROFIT TO THE PEOPLE!

What is profitable? Wall Street is extremely agitated that much of the highest profitability is flowing into the accounts of the lowest people on the totem pole: the retail investors—the newly self-empowered online investors who want to know (1) what exactly their commissions are for; (2) where and how their orders are actually executed (are their brokers getting payment for order flow, called "legal kickbacks," or using the new ECNs as order-matching systems to save the customer the price of the markup for the middleman?); (3) what sort of liquidity is available on the ECN used by their online brokers? Figures on this are hard to determine, but trading reports online at the trader.nasdaq.com site give you a general direction. There is an abstruse double-counting issue in comparing volume on the NYSE and the Nasdaq, because a matching system like the NYSE counts a transaction as one—from seller to buyer—while the Nasdaq may count it as two or three—from seller to middleman (market maker), where it is marked up, and then from middleman to buyer. You can imagine how this could skew volume and transaction figures through double-counting—though, of course, it is reflective of what goes on in the two different marketplaces.

Wall Street analysts of the online brokerage industry, such as San Francisco–based Bill Burnham, formerly with Credit Suisse First Boston, have developed complex mathematical models to help us compare apples to apples rather than apples to oranges in the amount of trades and trading volume at the various brokerages, markets, and ECNs. Since both the online and traditional financial press seem to rely on industry numbers developed by Burnham's methods—buttressed by his snappy quarterly reports on the evolving industry—I will rely on his first quarter 1999 listing of the top online brokers in this industry (to follow).

The world is topsy-turvy. What child of the '60s ever imagined stuffy old Morgan Stanley Dean Witter—whose provenance dates back to old J.P. Morgan, the man who once controlled the world's capital markets—would be so backed into a corner that they'd do *this:* splash the phrase "Power to the People" across the screens of network news shows in 1999, ads for their Discover Brokerage adopting as their own the rallying cry of the antiwar movement three decades earlier. This mood, this movement, and its soundtrack of rock-and-roll, lives deep in the tribal memory of any late-thirty- or forty-something investor. These "power to the people" ads—intended to entice new customers to their Discover online brokerage—would have been called a capitalist sell-out in the '60s. And there's one simple reason for Discover's approach: the "power to the people" retail customer—making self-empowered investing and trading decisions online—is today more profitable to the brokerage house than the very rich.

The geometric growth of online investors and traders flocking to the Web has been like a monstrous tsunami roaring in from the Pacific, sweeping everything before it. In the 1980s, Landon Jones, an editor at *Time* magazine, wrote a fascinating book about the baby boomers, *Great Expectations: America and the Baby Boom Generation,* envisioning boomers as a population "lump" moving through American society, like the body of a mouse being digested as it moves through the body of a snake. In this case, the population lump is not being digested by the snake. Rather, the snake— or, more specifically, the richly appointed, well-anointed Wall Street denizens and their institutions—is being eaten for lunch by this newly empowered lump, using the tools of the global Internet.

MY TOP BROKER FOR SAFE, SENSIBLE STOCK BUYS WITH THE T3

Stick with the highly ranked brokerages—those in the top 10—because when you start to ask pointed questions about a broker's commissions for trades, and even the extra service charges some sneak in (such as for mailing or postage and handling), you'll discover that you *do* get what you pay for.

That's why I go with Datek. I first read about Datek in the summer of 1997 in *WSJ* Interactive. The reporter had interviewed a twenty-something, new to the workforce, who had discovered that Datek's low rates and efficient order-entry interface allowed him to keep and grow the profits that standard and discount brokers ate away with commissions.

I headed over to the Datek site (see Figure 8.1) in 1997 and opened an account with the $2000 minimum. (I'll tell you how later.) By mid-1998, I'd been contacted by Stephen Isaacs at McGraw-Hill and had seriously begun educating myself about online resources. When I began writing this book I started investing/trading $25,000, and within a four-month period I was able to remove profits of about $11,500, then $5000, $5000, and $10,000 from the account. Granted, it was an extraordinary time in the market: the Internet sector went through the roof after a two-month period in the doldrums; online brokers were identifying stocks they would not allow customers to short, because of the volatility, and margin accounts were being closely monitored to prevent sudden reversals of fortune.

After heavy press coverage of SEC chair Arthur Levitt's statements about the dangers of online trading in January 1999, Americans became more aware of the importance of placing an order properly (in my opinion,

FIGURE 8.1 *Datek Online's home page with the new Market Center for visitors.* (Datek Online.)

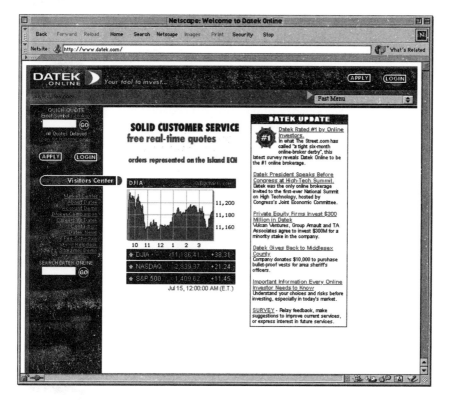

with a limit order) and monitoring executions and confirmations. Datek's guide-to-investing booklet explains it all—along with monthly statements with newsletter inserts from the Fool and *The Motley Fool Investment Guide,* the book that catalyzed the style of the new self-empowered investor first targeted by Charles Schwab.

AN ORDER WALK-THROUGH WITH AN ONLINE BROKER ACCOUNT

I have accounts at both E*Trade and Datek Online, and two years ago I opened an account at DLJdirect, without funding it. But since I learned to buy and sell stocks online using Datek, I'll use it as my example here.

Datek Online emerged as the number one winner this year after TheStreet.com's online survey of their active investor clients. Launched in 1996, it is the world's fourth-largest online brokerage, with over a quarter-million customers.

I admire the company for its clean site design, smart navigation, great prices and service, Java-enabled personalized streaming real-time quotes (free!), and, of course, the default setting (it's the first thing you see) for a limit order on the order-entry page. Long before Levitt and the SEC drew attention to the importance of placing limit orders, Datek was helping customers discover the limit order's power to protect.

Of course, all those limit orders helped funnel customer orders and create liquidity on their subsidiary, Island ECN—the only ECN to put all its orders up on the Web for every investor to see. To my mind, this is the beginner's alternative to paying for all that mind-boggling Level II information. (Instead, just look at the limit order book, the bid and ask information, in depth, on the stock you're following on the Island page at isld.com.) Island hit page one of the *Wall Street Journal* in December 1998 when this alternative trading platform first eclipsed Reuters's Instinet in volume of shares traded in Nasdaq stocks. Datek promises to offer self-directed investors a real-time market advantage in their trade executions: no commission, they say, if your market order isn't executed within 60 seconds; but I've never really tested that promise.

Their education section, along with a hyperlinked resources center and helpdesk, helped me learn the fundamentals of investing and trading, and especially how to use the limit order. You can phone the customer service number at 888-GO-DATEK until 7 p.m. EST. (Don't make the mistake of dialing 1-800-GO-DATEK; you'll hear a sex-talk come-on that is reminiscent of Spike Lee's mid-'90s movie, *Girl 6.*)

This is the routine I follow at my online broker's site:

1. Datek Online's *home page,* at datek.com, has two clear-cut *demonstrations* to lead the newcomer through his or her orders and portfolio. A series of snapshots directs you through an overview of the Datek trading experience.

   The demo shows you free, unlimited access to their premium services—cobranded real-time and historical charting services from BigCharts (see Figure 8.2); the latest headlines (which you can now personalize) from NewsAlert and news, including the *E-Commerce Times* (ecommercetimes.com), plus the pricey Thomson Investors

FIGURE 8.2 *The one-day chart from BigCharts, through the Datek trading screen.* (Datek Online.)

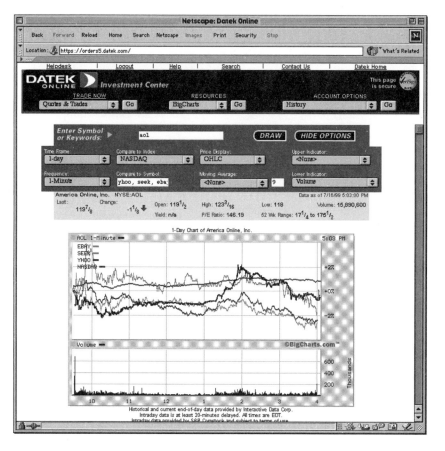

Network's comprehensive research. (See discussion of Thomson's I-Watch page in Chapter 7.)

The NewsAlert service (see Figure 8.3) also includes a clip alert e-mail feature for the stocks you're watching—convenient if you work in an office with a T1 line, because the streaming quotes feature of the order-entry page manages to shoot through most corporate firewalls, unlike the products of other online brokers.

Try acclimating yourself to the *free real-time quote feature* as well. It's on the home page. Sign up for an account, online, and they'll mail you an account password. You can then log on and

FIGURE 8.3 *The new NewsAlert can be customized.* (Datek Online.)

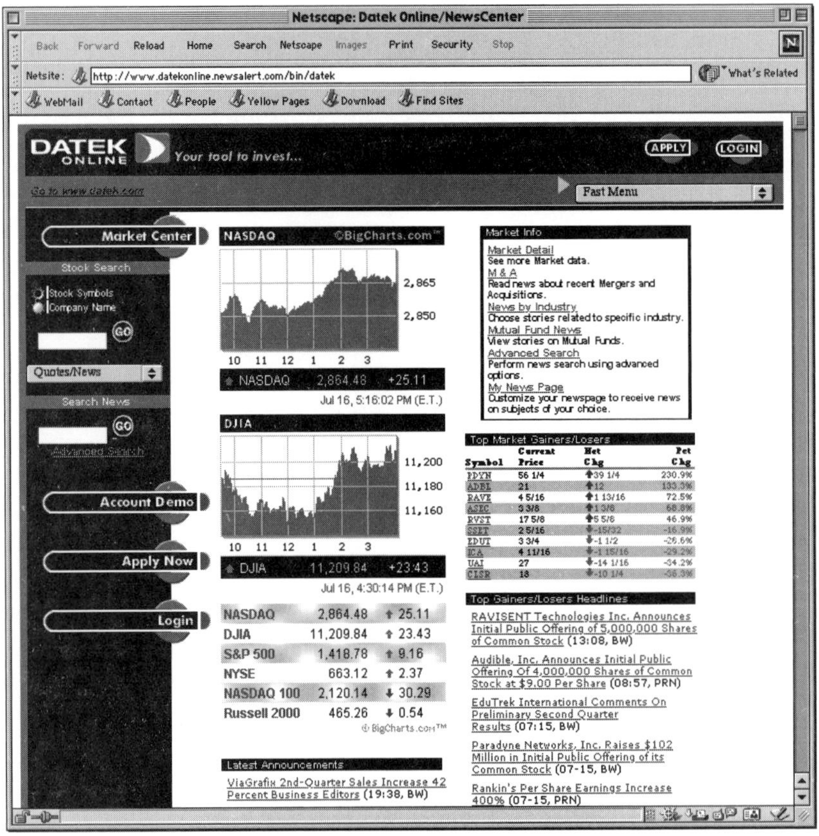

experiment to your heart's content. (You can't trade, of course, until you mail or FedEx them a check.)

2. Key: the *research resources*—especially those real-time, color-coded charts—are one click away from your portfolio, your quote screen, and your confirmation screen. If you come from, say, doing your research at Yahoo!, you can check last-minute changes that may have affected price. You can cancel your order between the time you make it and the time you've mulled it over on the confirmation screen. Or you can go back and lower or increase the price you're offering.

While you visit, take notes about volume and price moves, and you'll start to get a feel for daily, weekly, and monthly patterns. Someone who has invested in the market and has been aware of the changes for the past five years or the past five decades manages to carry a lot more market expertise and wisdom—along the lines of "what goes up must come down."

Today's explorer will find extraordinary changes afoot—changes that, in some places, stand some of that conventional wisdom on its head. I remember opening my account about two or three months before I sent in the money to actually start trading.

When I started investing online, I tried to create a portfolio of about five stocks, equally divided into \$400-size chunks (\$400 × 5 = \$2000.) This made for some pretty odd-looking orders. I probably would have been embarrassed to do it with a "real" stockbroker (and I still had trouble confessing my ignorance to the customer service staff on the telephone). But this slow, gradual process allowed me to get the hang of the order-entry page and the integration of online research into my decision-making process.

When I come to the Datek home page, I simply click right into the log-in button, either on the screen or from the drop-down menu. (Actually, I've bookmarked the log-in page, but by doing that I've missed new research features such as Thomson.)

I then choose to use either the classic Datek order entry and portfolio, without Java (some old-version AOL users can only get the classic), or the new streamlined design with icons, drop-down menus, and streamers. A third choice leads to the express servers, for the very, very experienced online traders who want their orders executed in milliseconds. "Express" features a one-click buy order—there is *no* confirmation page. (In that sense, it's like day trading—you click it, you bought it.)

You know the security encryption is in operation when you see the key—in one piece—at the bottom of your browser screen. AOL, Internet Explorer, and Netscape versions 3.0 and above are all encrypted to lock in the tightest security available for financial transactions.

3. The order-entry page (see Figure 8.4) allows you to type in up to about 10 symbols for companies you're interested in. Click "get quote" and the 5 or 10—or, in this case, 2—quotes pop up, complete with three icons to the left of each, linking directly to news, charts, and Thomson snapshots and research on that firm. Across the screen you'll read the symbol, bid, ask, and last price of the stock; the change; and the high and low for the day. Volume indi-

FIGURE 8.4 *Datek's combined quote/order-entry/research page to trade directly.* (Datek Online.)

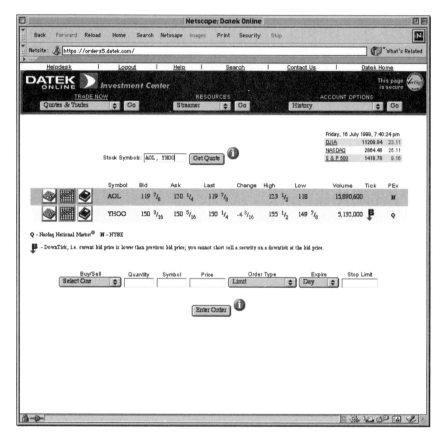

cates the thousands or millions of shares traded in that one stock so far today. The tick arrow indicates whether that last price was an uptick or a downtick—you need to know because you can't short a stock on a downtick; you can do so only when the price is going up. The final column tells you the exchange it is listed on—in this case, AOL on "N," the NYSE, and YHOO, or Yahoo!, on "Q," the Nasdaq.

You may make a last-minute visit to the charts to compare the performance of these two Internet stocks with each other and with an Internet index, for instance, by clicking on the chart icon and typing in the comparison information you want (i.e., price changes

over every five minutes for intraday, then five-day and a year).
Compare the performances. Both are established players in the
Internet space. Has one had more lift during recent momentum
than the other? You may want to invest in the other and wait for a
corresponding upward move.

The BigCharts charts are also central when investing in volatile
Nasdaq issues: a close look at the one-day chart (Figure 8.2) with
the five-day chart (Figure 8.5) helps you see where the two haven't
been tracking exactly. And those points are possible entry points.
(There's much more about charting in the archived columns of the
"Chartman," Gary B. Smith, at TheStreet.com. He's a writer and a

---

FIGURE 8.5 *The five-day chart from BigCharts allows you to compare, from
ground zero, the performance of stocks in a similar industry.* (Datek Online.)

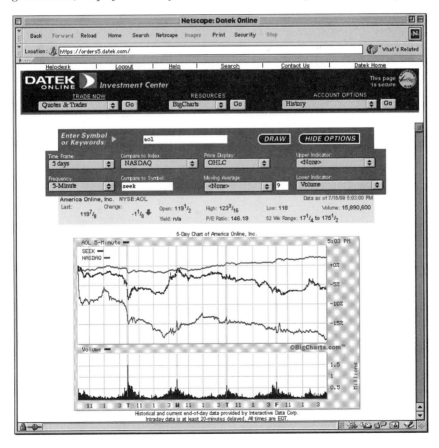

trader who quit his day job to trade at home—and who now res-
olutely stays away from day trading after being eaten alive by the
stresses of the game. Develop an approach, he advises, and stick to
it. If it isn't working, blame it on your approach, not on yourself.
Then change it.)

The price you enter for the limit order will be between the bid
and the ask—that's why you want to have the real-time data on
hand. See what happens. How soon do you get a confirmation?
Not knowing if your order will be filled until the price drops again
that day—as it surely will—is excellent training in patience and discipline. And you may make more money.

4. The Datek "Streamer," created by Big Think's chief, Peter Stern,
who studied computers at Carnegie-Mellon in Pittsburgh, Pennsyl-
vania, is a huge hit with traders and active investors (see Figure
8.6). Reading the numbers while your order-entry screen is also
up—and even hitting your order without the confirmation
screen—can get you an instant, visible change on the price carried
by the Nasdaq screens globally. Here, you can see in black and
white—or custom colors—how the person in the kitchen with a
computer can change the entire Nasdaq market price, either up or
down. Because when you offer the best price, no matter what the
market makers are saying, you get the stock. It's the automatic feature of the new order-entry rules of the post-1997 Nasdaq stock
market.

5. The Datek confirmation screen (see Figure 8.7) makes you review
your order. Type in your password again, click on "Yes, place this
order," and it's yours. Or go back and change your bid. Or cancel.
No charge for changing your mind. (Just be aware of time limitations on limit orders versus market orders. Market orders happen
within seconds; not much chance of cancellations there.)

6. Unlike many other online brokers, this site keeps your portfolio up
to the minute, including tick-by-tick changes in the value of your
holdings. You just click "portfolio" on the drop-down menu to see
how your holdings have changed with your last buy. (See Figure
8.8.) And if you mistakenly buy several more shares than you have
the cash for, the screen will immediately tell you. No mistakes here.
(Though you do want to be extremely careful with margin accounts.
Try to keep them as an experiment for your second year of trading.)

FIGURE 8.6 *Peter Stern's Streamer for real-time customized streaming quotes. You can run it through corporate firewalls and trade directly on the page.* (Datek Online.)

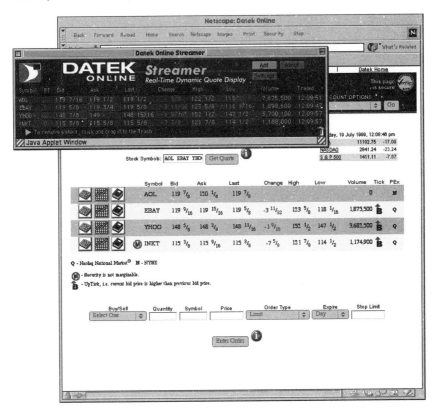

7. The firm also keeps your trading history, back to the day you opened your account (see Figure P.1). These beautifully organized records are well liked by my tax accountant and by investors who use their own tax software. Worried about capital gains tax? Personally, I rejoice in the opportunity to pay taxes on these capital gains! But for those with more complex tax situations, the Motley Fool has published an excellent tax guide, and tax law experts are coming up with ways of declaring yourself a full-time or part-time trader. There may be several tax advantages involved. (For further info, send an e-mail query to info@caroltroy.com.)

FIGURE 8.7 *The confirmation page: your password and one click. Or you can opt to skip the page if you're a fast trader.* (Datek Online.)

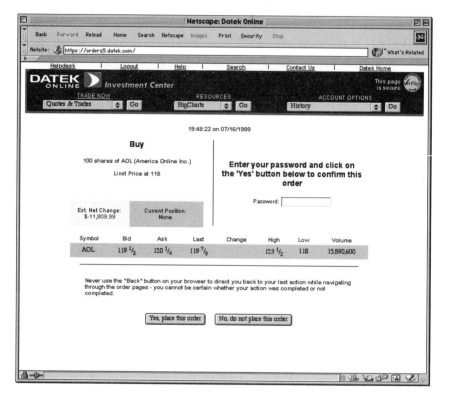

TOP 10 ONLINE BROKERS

When online brokers first came on the scene, the big Wall Street full-service brokerage houses—called *wire houses* in the trade—simply held a lot of executive meetings and let these little pipsqueaks fly in under their radar. The numbers flocking to the online brokers were dismissed as cheap deep-discount and discount-brokerage customers moving online; yet the onslaught of engaging and amusing television advertising during every network's news broadcasts, and the obvious sea change in new online customers from those "cheap" discount customers to the young, smart, big-money, self-educated and -directed customers with fat trading accounts broke the back of full-service resistance to the trend.

FIGURE 8.8   *The numbers are all real-time with the Datek portfolio.* (Datek Online.)

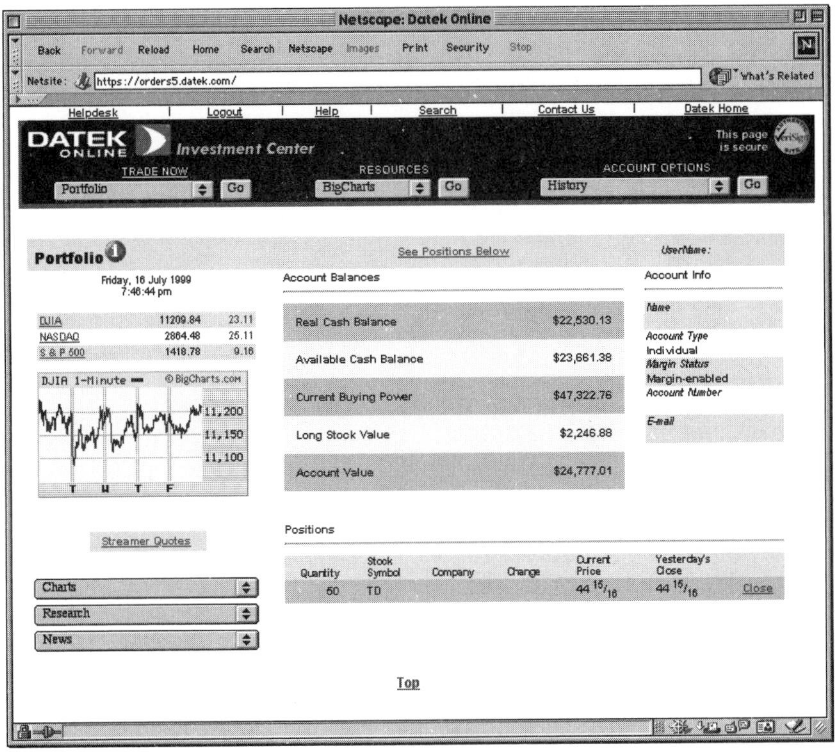

New investors flocked online despite the dangers of online-trading interruptus and the lack of a Viagra equivalent targeted to solve that occasional dilemma. Once these online customers discovered how safe and easy it was to open an account—fill out the form online, send in your check, and get your password within five days—they were hooked. Online investors often opened one account, supplemented by another with a competing online broker for insurance in case of service outages.

And by year-end 1998, the market valuation of Charles Schwab, the biggest online presence, momentarily exceeded that of Merrill Lynch, the Goliath of the Street. Schwab numbered 2,200,000 online accounts (sometimes two or three per household). Even Merrill Lynch and Smith Barney were forced to reconsider their options going into the twenty-first century.

Today, for the active investor and online trader, the primary focus is on speed and execution of orders. (Note: Check out the download speeds for individual brokerage sites at www.keynote.com.)

Following are my top 10 picks for online brokers according to the T3. Table 8.1 is a quick reference to the pertinent information on each broker.

1. DATEK ONLINE BROKERS

Phone: 888-GO-DATEK. Limit order: $9.99.

We've walked through their order-entry screens and discussed their services. You might consider calling for their informative booklet—press "2" for questions about trading and ask for their account package, which includes a great 20-page booklet called *Datek Online Investor's Reference Guide,* about trading online, limit orders, stop-loss orders, fast markets. The guide reviews everything you need to know to trade safely, in line with the SEC guidance Levitt introduced in 1999. Also, you get a Foolish wisdom newsletter from the Motley Fool with the monthly statements—always a great shot of sanity.

Datek wins in the price, execution, and design areas: for customizable streaming quotes right on the trading screen, ECN executions, price for limit orders, and all-around technological smarts, thanks to CIO Peter Stern and Island brainiac Josh Levine (www.josh.com). They can't be beat for the trader who follows the T3 and the active investor looking for both speed and quality. When you consider your overall cost per trade—not only your commission, but your execution price—Datek comes out on top.

2. E*TRADE

Phone: 800-ETRADE-1. Limit order: $19.95. Stop market order: $19.95.

E*Trade just unveiled an appealing new service for active investors called Power E*Trade. But the commission price of $19.95 and the execution are still behind the competition.

In the first quarter of 1999, fueled by a massive marketing budget, E*Trade grabbed the number two market-share ranking behind Charles Schwab. A no-holds-barred promotion campaign added almost a quarter-million new accounts, and, strangely enough, global press coverage of several February service outages seemed to polish the E*Trade name-recognition factor rather than tarnish their image. That's marketing magic. . . .

Power E*Trade's brand-new enhanced trading interface—where you can line up 10 trades at once on the Trading Desk—includes another area

TABLE 8.1   Troy's Top 10 Online Brokers
For T3 Trading

NAME (WEB ADDRESS)	PHONE	COMMISSION (LIMIT ORDER)	MIN. DEPOSIT	% ONLINE TRADING MARKET
1. Datek (www.datek.com)	888-GO-DATEK	$9.99	$2000	10.0%
2. E*Trade (www.etrade.com)	800-ETRADE-1	$19.95	$1000	12.9%
3. Discover (www.discoverbrokerage.com)	800-58-INVEST	$19.95	$2000	2.8%
4. DLJdirect (www.dljdirect.com)	800-825-5723	$20.00	$0	3.6%
5. TD Waterhouse (www.waterhouse.com)	800-934-4410	$12.00	$1000	11.6%
6. Ameritrade (www.ameritrade.com)	800-454-9272	$13.00	$2000	8.4%
7. Charles Schwab (www.schwab.com)	800-435-4000	$29.95	$5000	27.5%
8. Suretrade/Quick & Reilly (www.suretrade.com)	800-926-0600	$19.95	$0	3.0%
9. Fidelity (www.fidelity.com)	800-544-7272	$14.95*	$5000	9.3%
10. WIT Capital (www.witcapital.com)	888-494-8227	$19.95	$2000	N/A

(Source for market percentages: CS First Boston)
*Active traders only

Boutiques to consider: Muriel Siebert, the NYSE's first woman member, for a smaller, customized approach for the fully wired investor on the move; also check AB Watley, NDB, MDB, Scottrade.

High-risk only: Day Trading with direct access into the Nasdaq market. Day trading is *not* "online trading." *Day trading never uses the Internet;* day traders only rely on direct telecommunications links to the Nasdaq market.

To set off into the high-risk, brave new world of active traders, traders must be willing to lose double the capital they start with (and that's a minimum of $50,000).

Day traders' instant executions are via an expensive dedicated telecommunications line through a Nasdaq broker/dealer (a specialist day trading firm) directly wired into the Nasdaq screen-based cybermarket.

Traders work on-site, in the trading room, or solo at the trader's office or home, through wires to the broker/dealer. Traders hold no stock overnight. Try CyberCorp.com (see Figures 8.1 and 8.2), Momentum/Tradescape, and Broadway for EDAT connection platforms; DataBroadcastingCorp. (eSignal) and TradeCast for software and streaming data.

called the Pulse, a dynamic screen with streaming Level II quotes, streaming real-time quotes, and charts, through a partnership with Bridge. The power traders, at over 25 trades a month, are allowed more perks than the 10-times-monthly traders.

The current drawback? The decision-making area of the Pulse isn't really integrated with their trading screen. The Bridge streaming quotes are a separate computer applet; you must change screens and go to a separate page to trade. And the price for a limit order Nasdaq trade is still the same as it is for regular E*Trade customers. But the team, headed by Doug Doyle and Brent Blackaby, is currently working on evolutions. CEO Christos Cotsakos invested in Archipelago, an ECN, and started after-hours trading with Instinet. Trades once routed through Knight/TriMark wholesalers—in which E*Trade had an interest—should soon be routed with a lower price and improved execution for active traders. Ask their customer service reps.

Current E*Trade offerings are more full-bodied for the long-term, long-haul investor, and Japan's Softbank investment makes them a global player. Their trading simulation—while not allowing for the limit orders which are a key element of T3 trading—gives you an overview of how various trading strategies work. Destination E*Trade offers a range of investing tools—free to visitors—much like Yahoo!Finance and mySchwab.com. And E*Trade invested in former Robertson Stevens cofounder Sanford Robertson's E-Offering as a delivery vehicle for online IPOs.

In a March 1999 *New York Times* story, Cotsakos envisioned E*Trade as "a digital financial media company"—a sort of money hub or financial supermarket. Rolling out globally, E*Trade will remain the hot company to watch. Cotsakos, who joined E*Trade just before its 1996 IPO, injected a gung-ho leadership style honed in Vietnam. In 1988, he had helped unroll FedEx in Europe, aiding the computer-heavy company's expansion from U.S. to global reach. Today, he is introducing E*Trade to the global village, working in over 30 countries with dynamic President and Chief Operating Officer Judy Balint.

Back when Cotsakos opted for the new green-and-purple logo in 1998, E*Trade left the stodgy brokerage image in the dust. Visiting their Palo Alto offices in mid-1999, I saw him vectoring around the cubicles, encouraging the troops at their computer screens. The active traders may yet join him.

3. DISCOVER, MORGAN STANLEY DEAN WITTER

Phone: 800-58-INVEST. Limit order: 19.95. (See Figure 8.9.)

FIGURE 8.9 *Discover takes off this year with active traders.* (Discover Brokerage Direct Inc.)

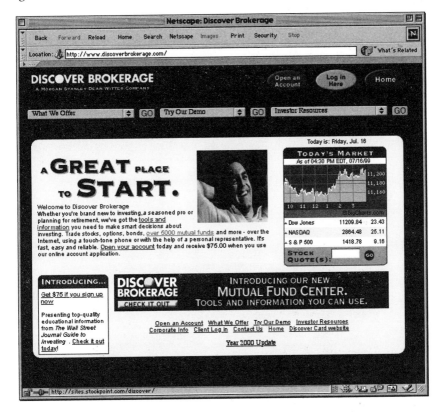

Remember those mind-bending television commercials of 1999 featuring the high school student with the helicopter on the front lawn, the trucker with a private island, the woman bailing out the small principality? These commercials were the sparks put off by Discover, in its surge to come from the back of the pack into one of the top five spots. Helping them advance through the competition: a mid-1999 initiative that makes Discover more appealing to the active investor, plus power from the backing of Wall Street investment bank Morgan Stanley, now combined with Dean Witter brokerage house. With $2000, you can open an account. They offer information from Zack's, S&P MarketScope, Reuters, and Lipper, as well as long-range planning tools with rippling muscles, but with limited access to IPOs. They also offer Morgan Stanley research for a fee.

4. DLJdirect

Phone: 800-TALK-723. Limit orders: $20.00. (See Figure 8.10.)

Open an account before you deposit a dollar here at DLJdirect. The first Wall Street investment bank to go public in the 1980s, Donaldson, Lufkin & Jenrette now has both a DLJ stock listing and a tracking stock for their DLJdirect Internet brokerage. Their online chief, Blake Darcy, was one of the first visionaries to recognize the growing power of the online

FIGURE 8.10   *DLJdirect is the online trading home of one of Wall Street's most respected research and investment banking operations, Donaldson, Lufkin & Jenrette.* (DLJdirect home page, the online brokerage firm of Donaldson, Lufkin & Jenrette.)

investor. Their services are also first rank, including all the research and amenities a first-class investment bank affords its private clients.

DLJdirect was also one of the first to open outside the United States. Their Japanese online brokerage can be found at www.dljdirect-sfg.co.jp.

DLJdirect has heavy-duty long-range planning tools as well. "Research" and "Ideas" guide newcomers to self-directed market research. They offer limited access to IPOs.

5. TD WATERHOUSE

Limit order: $12.00. $1000 to open an account. (See Figure 8.11.)

FIGURE 8.11 *Waterhouse offers both a full-service approach and limit order trades at $12.* (Waterhouse Securities, Inc.)

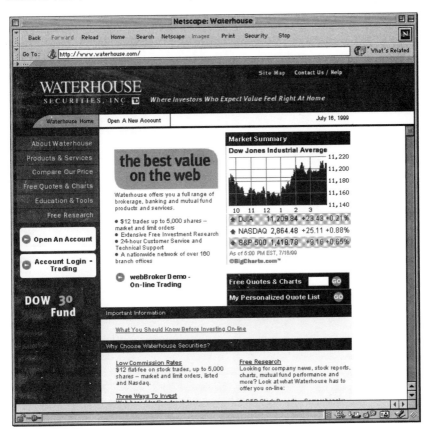

Move your funds easily between checking and brokerage accounts. Waterhouse has the look and feel of a more full-service brokerage house, with an extremely good $12 price for limit orders. They will be using Island ECN for trading.

6. AMERITRADE

Phone: 800-454-9272. Limit order: $13.00. $2000 to open an account. (See Figure 8.12.)

Ameritrade offers commentary by one of America's favorite market observers, the former *New York* magazine columnist Andrew Tobias, author of *The Only Investment Guide You'll Ever Need* (Harvest, 1999). Yet they were

---

FIGURE 8.12   *Ameritrade features low flat-rate commissions.* (This Web page is published with the permission of Ameritrade Holding Corporation. The rights in all copyrightable content are owned by Ameritrade Holding Corporation. Ameritrade is a registered trademark of Ameritrade Holding Corporation.)

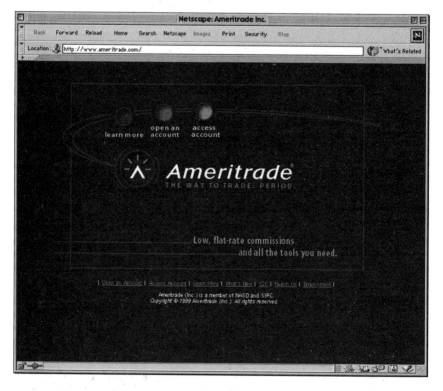

signing on new customers at such a rapid rate that their technological infrastructure was bursting at the seams. So, very deliberately, Ameritrade set out to cut back the ranks of its new customers . . . while at the same time running some of the most amusing TV ads, hitting Middle America in the funny bone.

7. CHARLES SCHWAB

Phone: 800-435-4000. Limit order: $29.95 a trade. $5000 to open an account. (See Figure P.2.)

Schwab's focus remains on the long-term, slower-moving investor; their personal assistance and hand-holding—and $29.95 trade price—reflect that focus. This is an extremely comfy place to start your online adventure. And they may be going after the more energetic investors as well: they have registered the Web domain "activetrader.com." Look for announcements. . . .

MySchwab.com, powered by customization technology from Excite.com, offers a selection of tools, quotes, chat, news, watch lists, and research akin to financial portals such as Destination E*Trade and Yahoo!Finance, and, like them, free to all.

For $30 a month, you get research from high-tech investment banking specialists Hambrecht & Quist and Credit Suisse First Boston. They offer limited customer access to IPOs.

8. QUICK & REILLY'S SURETRADE

Phone: 800-672-7220; Q&R 800-926-0600 (24-hour broker available for Q&R). Limit order: $19.95.

Quick & Reilly is the parent of Suretrade; Q&R also has its own online operation. The less expensive Suretrade division gives you low margin rates and it ranked, along with Datek and DLJ, as one of the top three online brokers in *Barron's*.

9. FIDELITY

Phone: 800-544-7272. Limit order: $14.95 (active). $5000 to open an account. (See Figure 8.13.)

Fidelity rules the mutual fund roost from Boston; their Peter Lynch was one of the first writers to convince individual investors they could choose their own stocks rather than relying on the expensive mutual fund

FIGURE 8.13   *Fidelity has that Boston aura.* (Copyright © 1999 FMR Corp.)

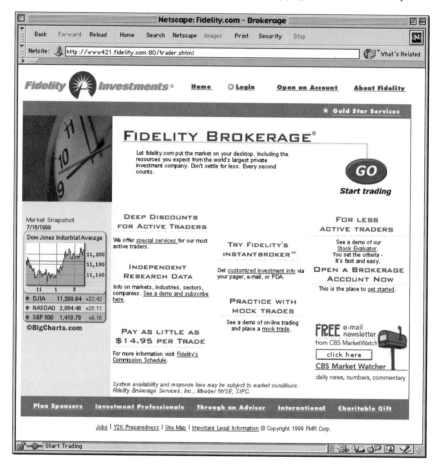

solution. They now allow trading at their Web site, probably to keep their profitable mutual fund customers from straying far from home. A comfy place for you mutual fund believers to break into online stock investing. They offer good telephone support staff, research from Smith Barney, and limited access to IPOs.

10. WIT CAPITAL

For those interested in IPOs, $2000 to open an online account. Phone: 888-494-8227. Limit order: $19.95.

Open an account and you have as good a chance as any WIT Capital client to snag 100 shares of an IPO. Look at online discussion groups on IPOs at Silicon Investor and Yahoo! for discussions of IPOs and your chance of getting your piece of the action.

COMPLAINTS

Problems? Be careful to type in the correct stock symbol and order amount. Use a limit order. If you still have problems, make computer copies of your trading data. Send a letter to the brokerage plus instant e-mail. Notify the SEC at www.sec.gov and NASD at www.nasd.org, and add a note to the online chats that discuss trading, such as Gomez Associates (at www.gomez.com), Silicon Investor, Yahoo!Finance, Raging Bull, Motley Fool, and TheStreet.com.

FINAL WORD ON THE TOP 10 BROKERS AND THE TOP 10 ECNS

The two lists may soon join as one (see Table 4.1 for top 10 ECNs). How?

Portals—like Yahoo!—aggregate content and make life easier by putting all the choices in one area. In the real world, *The New York Times* is a place that clumps together all the news you may think is most important. In the markets, the New York Stock Exchange clumps together all of their listed stocks, and the Nasdaq Stock Market offers a screen-based cyberfloor, linking all the broker/dealers and ECNs in their system. Clumping is good.

As a Datek customer, I was one of the first to be able to take advantage of the ECNs, the little stock markets that allow you to meet orders at prices better than those offered on Nasdaq. On the horizon is yet another possibility opening up: As the Yahoo! portal made centralizing your financial information a relatively simple operation, the ECN aggregator portal will make stock trading across *all* the ECNs a possibility for the online trader, by hitting whichever ECN offers the best price for your stock.

Day traders, of course, with their direct electronic access to the market, dedicated phone lines, and monthly cost of $500, were able to choose among any of the ECNs that offered the best price on the Nasdaq Level II screen. But the $500 price was high for someone who wasn't trading in 1000-share blocks. Yet online traders, increasingly sophisticated about the extra costs of trading through an online broker's own middleman (the market-making, or wholesaler, firm) were looking around for a way to escape the middleman, the "kickbacks," and shave off some savings to increase their trading profits.

Meanwhile, the online brokers had been drawing customers away from sites like Yahoo!Finance and MSN Investor by offering nearly the same panoply of free services as the portals themselves. Datek started up the Market Center, Charles Schwab took out two-page advertisments in *The New York Times* to promote their free info center, and E*Trade spent millions promoting Destination E*Trade to drive their numbers up.

In the fall of 1999 a whole new style of online trading appeared: the Web-based broker that may allow the online trader to choose among ECNs and the Nasdaq market maker quotes and hit the best price. CyBerCorp's CyBerXchange has been linking to the BRUT ECN. (They cut commissions to a flat $15, from $20, and integrate with Data Broadcasting's streaming eSignal.) BRUT is expanding into the active investor and day trader area. Datek is offering free after-hours trading to all customers.

The ECN advantage? No middleman in the middle of the transaction, making a market and creating a spread. The next generation of execution technology over the Internet should result in faster executions and lower transaction costs by offering retail customers access to not just one ECN, but a variety of ECNs and the Nasdaq quote montage. Let the best quote win!

Since the ECN after-hours trading revolution got under way just as this book was going to press, I thought it was important to give you a sense not only of what after-hours trading *feels* like, but of the actual dangers of trading during times of very low liquidity (not many people out there ready to trade) and high volatility. The following are the words of Wall Street trader Jim Cramer, who tells you about the dangers of after-hours ECN trading, even for the professional.

The After-Hours Gunslinger: Trading on Instinet
"Wrong!" Column by James Cramer, TheStreet.com.

Join me in a trip to the Badlands, the strange after-hours market in stocks, the last great trading frontier. I was there tonight, alone, armed only with an Instinet machine, intent on trading Yahoo! (YHOO:Nasdaq) after the conference call was over.

I liked what I heard. Oh, it wasn't only the guidance and the firm tone of management, or the buzzwords and the letter-perfect execution. What I liked about it—and what I would despise about it if I were short—were the effusive congratulations offered by each analyst before questioning the company. That's a security blanket that makes you want to take stock with gusto.

Except that's not the Instinet game. After-hours trading is an art form, one that exists at a level that rivals the most rigorous poker games for their bluffing and outrageous bidding. Your confidence in your hand must be supreme, and your judgment of your nameless and faceless opponents, both on the buy side and the sell side, must be perfect.

For those of you who have never traded after-hours, Instinet is a customer-to-customer market in which you can advertise where you want to buy and where you want to sell, just like in Web trading. Tonight, as the Yahoo! conference call drew near its conclusion, I wanted to buy 2,500 shares.

On the screen was someone who wanted to sell 1,000 shares at 214 and someone who wanted to buy 1,000 shares at 210. That's a pretty typical market for after hours, wide enough to drive a Peterbilt through, yet so thin as to be impossible to get anything "real" done. As much as I trade after-hours, I find myself constantly on the defensive, and rarely as confident as I would like to be, and I regard myself as being fairly good at the game.

My goal: to get 2,500 shares in as cheaply as possible. First, we type in a 211 bid for 1,000 shares. We wait a minute and nothing happens. But someone offers 1,000 shares at 212. Here's the first decision. Do I take it, knowing that the call is going well, or do I wait to see if the seller hits me?

Before telling you what I did, picture this. There are maybe 25 people looking at this trading. If I take it, that will be a sign, an aggressive sign, that someone is betting this stock is going to go higher. If I wait, and I get hit, that might be a signal that someone believes the stock is going lower.

Now, add another dimension, the short sale. You can short after-hours without waiting for a higher stock price (a plus tick, as it is known). So, it is possible to be hit by a short-seller and have that short-seller create an impression that this stock is going lower in after-hours trading.

I chose to pounce and take the thousand at 212. Immediately, right at that very moment, the seller offers 2,500 shares at 212. (Or at least I think it is the same seller, as you can't tell.)

Ooooh, I think to myself. A gamesman. The guy wants to make the stock look heavy. That's a master ploy, meant to both frustrate the buyer and establish the market as one that doesn't lift. Very demoralizing for the buyers. Great for the shorts.

I bid 211.5 for a thousand.

Whack. I'm hit. Brutal. Now the pattern has been established. There are sellers, they want out. I am cannon fodder, I think to myself. Maybe I am wrong. Maybe the call's not that good. Second-guessing. Maybe a downgrade coming? GeoCities (GCTY:Nasdaq) deal not closing in time? Dot-com run over? (Told you you had to have confidence to play this game.)

I bid 210 for a thousand. For three minutes, nothing happens. So I get more bold. I move up to 211 for 1,000. Nothing. Nobody whacks me. I am like the mouse jumping out for the cheese, and the cat/seller seems to be asleep. Next I take the 212 offering for 1,000 shares. Now I have bought more than I want, but that's okay, because I like the stock. I feel like the cheese is mine. Gorgonzola.

Next thing I know, someone comes in and takes the stock that is still being offered at 214. Then another buyer sweeps the stock, taking everything at 215, 216 and 217, all the way to 218.

I'm in like Flynn, I figure. Ready to rock. Holy cow, I am up six points in three minutes. Even for the Net, that's something.

And then what happens? Guy comes back, offers 2,500 at 212. Told you this was the Badlands. I am cursing the guy because he's the master. He knows how to make a buyer feel like a moron. He's good. He's very good. He has wrecked whatever good feelings may have been caused by that stunning sweep.

I bid 210 for a thousand. If he hits me, then I know the Badlands are going to bleed red.

And then I wait. Nobody hits me. And he waits. Nobody takes him. Two minutes. Three minutes. Five minutes—this is a lifetime in the after-hours business. An eternity.

Ten minutes later, that's still the market, 212 last.

The number of people viewing the screen has gone down. The number of people who want to play rapidly diminishes. It's 6:15 p.m.

Time to go home. My time in the Badlands is over. Looks like the stock's going out about where I bought it. Until tomorrow,

when the authorities re-emerge and the rules change and all of
this trading won't mean a thing.
    Good night.

Reprinted by permission, TheStreet.com, April 7, 1999.

James J. Cramer is manager of a hedge fund and cofounder of TheStreet.com. At the
time of publication, his fund was long Yahoo!, although positions can change at any
time. Under no circumstances does the information in this column represent a rec-
ommendation to buy or sell stocks. Cramer's writings provide insight into the
dynamics of money management and are not a solicitation for transactions.

HIGH-RISK ONLY: DAY TRADING

This is the Real Thing, only for traders with the Right Stuff.

In my book, there is no such thing as "day trading online." True day
trading requires a dedicated telecommunications line to the markets. And
that, dear reader, is *not online trading*.

I've met a group of women in San Francisco who call themselves "day
traders," yet they trade online with Charles Schwab—33 trades a month
there runs you about $1000. That's relying on your ISP—Internet service
provider—to speed your order on its way to market, with no weak links in
the Internet chain. Trusting in the middleman. And it's relying on Schwab's
infrastructure to hold steady, something it was incapable of doing several
times in 1999. No, buying and selling stock at Charles Schwab—or at Datek,
as I did—is *not day trading*.

Real day trading is for the high-wire, high-risk players able and willing to "blow up," to lose double the capital they start out with (and that's a
minimum of $50,000, right?). Hit the wrong button, it's yours. To become an
EDAT day trader, your Level II screen must be so wired into your nervous
system that there is no momentary hesitation, no blip between pattern
recognition in the brain and the order to sell—or buy. No $5000 seminar
can teach you that. It's hard-wired into your nervous system, a peculiar sort
of genius that would be recognized by Harvard professor Howard Gardner's
theory of the "seven intelligences." Sure, it's easy to buy into a stock that's
floating up; it's devilishly hard to unload a stock that's crashing—especially
to unload 1000 or 5000 shares . . . that you bought on borrowed money. All
the buyers disappear. The world seems to stop momentarily on its axis. And

if you can't take your losses instantly and move on, you're not cut out for the unemotional, accountant-like approach you need for stability in the business.

To repeat, know your software instinctively, and know how to get out of a trade without a second thought. My estimate is that 93 to 94 percent of the experimental day traders across the country trying out the EDAT Level II screens and trading at day trading firms will slink away from the trading room . . . just like me! (Would I be *writing* this book if I'd been making the sort of money I've read about in the *Forbes* cover story?)

Sign on for a Nasdaq Level II screen (see Figures 8.14 and 8.15) and data feed to go one step beyond the real-time limit order book you can see on Island ECN and real-time streaming quotes—best bid and ask—at your broker's site. This screen (see Figure 8.16) shows you the actual lineup of buy and sell orders being placed by market makers and ECNs for Nasdaq stocks. This moving data stream helps you decide whether your stock is going up or trending down. And your limit order price calls can be even more precise and profitable. (But remember, I made only $132 with a $5000 account in two months—it's not easy.)

To set off into the high-risk brave new world of active online traders, search out even faster executions via a dedicated telecommunications line through a Nasdaq broker/dealer, then directly into the Nasdaq screen-based cybermarket. You can work on-site, in the trading room, where it's often good to consult before you leap, or you can work solo at home. Try CyBer-Corp, Momentum/Tradescape, Landmark, and Broadway for EDAT connections; DataBroadcastingCorp (eSignal) and TradeCast for software and streaming data; PCQuote for quotes.

●   ●   ●

INTERVIEW WITH MATT ANDRESEN, HEAD OF ISLAND

A former Olympic fencing champion, Andresen has become the champion of the ECNs, operating from his headquarters in a funky office in the shadow of Wall Street, where he and his colleagues are burrowing away at the system from the inside.

Explain to new investors why Island helps them save money on executions—to buy stock wholesale instead of paying retail.

FIGURE 8.14   *CyBerCorp's consumer version of the professional trader's Nasdaq Level II screen: for boom-box appeal, CyBerX Trading System. They're also working on a superECN.* (CyBerCorp, Inc., http://www.cybercorp.com.)

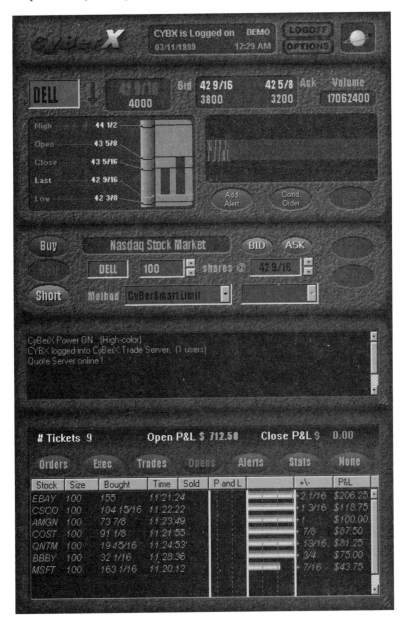

FIGURE 8.15   *Explore the edges of the EDAT trading game with CyBerCorp's trading simulator. Just don't get hooked!* (CyBerCorp, Inc., http://www.cybercorp.com.)

Everyone's getting the same price. Three years ago, when it was a retail environment, there was no way to have customers' orders represented in the marketplace. With Island, their orders can be instantaneously represented in the market [instantly advertised on the worldwide screens]—at 60⅛, not 60. Bam, bam, the entire market changes in that stock. That's an incredibly powerful idea, and really underscores the extent to which we have a more level playing field.

The advantages of using Island are speed, reliability, low cost, and liquidity. Why should that make any difference? Let me give you an example. My mom says, "I'm so proud of myself—I only paid $15 in commis-

FIGURE 8.16 *The Island "book" on NITE, the symbol for Knight/TriMark, owned in part by E*Trade and Ameritrade.* (The Island ECN, Inc.)

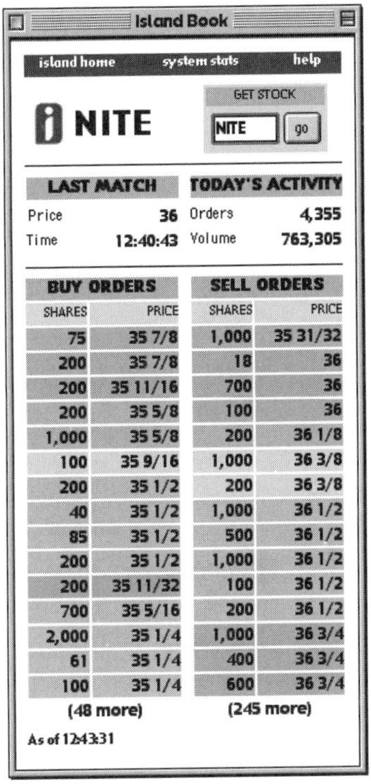

Island Book

island home   system stats   help

NITE   GET STOCK NITE go

LAST MATCH		TODAY'S ACTIVITY	
Price	36	Orders	4,355
Time	12:40:43	Volume	763,305

BUY ORDERS		SELL ORDERS	
SHARES	PRICE	SHARES	PRICE
75	35 7/8	1,000	35 31/32
200	35 7/8	18	36
200	35 11/16	700	36
200	35 5/8	100	36
1,000	35 5/8	200	36 1/8
100	35 9/16	1,000	36 3/8
200	35 1/2	200	36 3/8
40	35 1/2	1,000	36 1/2
85	35 1/2	500	36 1/2
200	35 1/2	1,000	36 1/2
200	35 11/32	100	36 1/2
700	35 5/16	200	36 1/2
2,000	35 1/4	1,000	36 3/4
61	35 1/4	400	36 3/4
100	35 1/4	600	36 3/4
(48 more)		(245 more)	

As of 12:43:31

sions. I save $15 every time I trade." So I ask her, "Would it make a difference whether you get filled for 24 or 24¼?" And she says, "Nah, it doesn't make a difference—I'm not going to sell it for 10 years." Then I say, "Mom, let me put some math to you. That quarter point cost you $124 and you saved $15. What if you'd put it in Yahoo! and it had gone up 5000 percent?"

The investor has become much more sophisticated, and the level of the sophisticated investor today is going to the level of the average investor in six months to a year. Even the most passive investor knows the values of his stocks, either through CNBC or by tracking them online. There's so much more awareness than there was three years ago. Investors have really taken control of their finances. The investor decides what and when to buy, and now we allow them to decide how: "I want my order to be displayed directly in the marketplace; I don't want to turn it over to my broker."

Why does everyone keep talking about used cars? That doesn't sound much like the stock market we all learned about.

If you want to sell your car, which way would you go? Option One is, you take a for-sale sign, paste it in the back window, and hope that someone drives by with a pencil, a paper, and a cell phone. Option Two is that you place your ad, with a picture, so that it's transmitted over the Internet, in newspapers, on TV, to the broadest possible audience. Which gives you a chance to get a quick and optimal sale?

Your bid or offer of a stock [your limit order] is an advertisement of your intention. Is it better if it's only shown to a small segment of the market, or better if it's shown to everyone in the world?

How would you describe the difference between a market order and a limit order?

If a market order is marketable, that means there's a price on Island or somewhere else for a person who wants to sell that stock. Every broker/dealer must comply with "best execution," which means they have to make their best effort to give their clients the best execution.

Orders often arrive at Island because Island is that best price. To the extent that Island drives the inside market [Level I quotes], we're often the best. Or sometimes it's Goldman, Merrill, Knight, Instinet.

If it's a market order, brokers will have to route it—but some don't route it at all. They sell to third-party aggregators [wholesalers]: like E*Trade sells to Knight/TriMark. They sell their order flow. The SEC has been having lots of questions about the practice recently.

[Arthur] Levitt, quoted in *The New York Times,* said it's very important that people start using limit orders. I think that's sage advice. Specifying a price has its advantages. There were people who wanted an Internet stock under 20, put in an order, and it got filled at 90. You don't go to a car dealer with a market order! You'd never go in there and say, "Buy me a car." You'd have a price in mind. Why should it be any different with your investments?

Why are investors and traders just now learning about how to get their best execution prices and how to use limit orders?

If you don't know anything about the market, you have no idea. What's changed in the last two years is that people have information, which gives them the ability to make rational decisions. With the Internet they have information at their fingertips.

Part of that is us putting our Island book on the Web, available to all in real-time. (See Figure 8.16.) Three years ago the dealers and market markers made their money by keeping that information secret. Imagine going to a specialist in New York and asking to see their entire book.

The needs of the dealer are contrary to the needs of the investor—that's why going to an impartial agency like Island is so powerful.

Who actually uses Island ECN?

About 150 day traders, market makers, full-service brokers, discount brokers, and quant firms.

Why have institutions traditionally paid so much for anonymous executions in terms of commissions and markups?

They pay in the hope that their market impact will be mitigated. But individuals are much more aware now. They ask, "What price are you getting?" What's evident is that sometimes you can get both: a low execution price and a lower fee. Everyone has to go for the best execution. Some do it themselves, others sell their orders to a third party. Everyone understands the word "disintermediation" [cutting out the middleman]: do you want a human with a profit incentive between you and the market?

How would the trader or investor, who's now more sophisticated about choosing the broker who can give him the most economical, efficient execution, go about choosing an online broker?

No matter which broker they choose, they should make their choice based on: (1) where they can get the best commission price and service and (2) how their order is executed.

Who chooses EDAT and who goes with online trading?

It depends on how much trading you do, and how sensitive you are to price. The more active you are and the more sophisticated, the better you'll do. Investors have to learn about the market. It's not like they're learning about sixteenth-century Florence or anything. They're learning about their personal finances. I expect them to demand more and more access.

What's holding back all this demand for change are the exchanges, because they make a tremendous amount of money from market data revenue [selling information about real-time quotes and volume]. Island is trying to get registered as an exchange. Every time you click on Schwab, they get charged by Nasdaq for the quotes. It's the second or third business line item despite the fact that the information was generated by them. For Level II it was $50 per user per month. The question is, when does it become cost-effective for the broker?

You've just turned 29. What do you think about warnings that executives your age have no experience with a crash?

I was in high school in 1987. I didn't trade in high school. But I'm sensitive to the issue. I saw the Nasdaq fall to 1300 last fall. It's at, what, 2600 now? That's pretty bad. I saw the market have to shut down because of trading halts in the fall of '97. Volatility means up and down. There have been plenty of up months, and plenty of down.

What do you think causes a market panic leading to a crash?

Inability to access the market is the cause of volatility. We have a more robust trading environment today than we had in '87. There were no information systems and no access for the investor. Today online brokers put the market at your fingertips and electronic networks allow them to exchange stocks without humans with a profit motive in between. Computers don't have mortgages.

One last tip: buy low, sell high. For as much effort as you put into selling your stocks, be sensitive to how your orders are executed. Why would you spend three days tracking and deciding when to sell your stock, then an hour picking the right time—then hand it over to someone?

There will always be a place for dealers. Take Biogen Q convertible bonds. They haven't been traded in 15 months. You need a dealer for a thing like that. There'll always be a place for that.

But—quote me on this: there's no longer a place for a dealer monopoly. Not with books or cars and not with stocks either.

CHAPTER 9

WARNING: IF YOU TRY THIS AT HOME . . .

WHEN BAD TRADES HAPPEN TO GOOD PEOPLE

1999 was a year of unprecedented growth in online trading. Not surprisingly, it was also a year of unprecedented growth—330 percent, to be exact—in complaints from traders who got badly burned, trading in a fast market without learning about the role of the market order, the limit order, and the stop loss. The following are a few recent true horror stories.

True horror story number one: On November 13, 1997, when The-Globe.com, a hot new Internet stock, launched its IPO, the stock opened at $9 a share. That morning, an investor we'll call "Fred Doe" turned on his computer, signed onto his online brokerage, and placed an order for 2300 shares "at market." Fred figured he'd get the stock for $15 to $25 per share (at a total cost of about $45,000), sell it off quickly, and make a nice profit. When Fred got his bill for the transaction, he was in for a not-so-nice surprise. His order had been executed "at market" all right—but "market" turned out to be $90 per share. Between its opening at $9 and closing at $63.50, TheGlobe.com had hit $90. The cost of Fred's $45,000 transaction? $207,000.

True horror story number two: A second investor we'll call "Jill Smith" placed an online order to sell all 30 shares of a stock she owned. She never received the confirmation notice she'd come to expect after placing a sell order, so she placed it again. The result? According to her online brokerage, Ms. Smith had sold 60 shares—twice the number she'd owned.

True horror story number three: After placing an order of 45 shares, "Bob Jones" changed his mind and cancelled it. Although he received acknowledgment of the cancellation, in fact the sale went through—so the stock was Bob's, whether he wanted it or not.

Trading online from home or office, it's easy to feel that you're part of some bustling trading room in cyberspace, with your buy orders shooting instantly to the markets. But the reality is somewhat different—and somewhat more dangerous. Today's online trading, in essence, is no different from trading as it's always been; you simply have a high-tech front end where you enter your trades yourself. From the order-entry screen, that order of yours can wend its way through your brokerage house's "back room," just like any phoned-in order. And just like the old-fashioned stockbrokers, your online broker is legally responsible to get you the best execution on your stock order. You rely on the broker's trading desk or his wholesaler to get you the best possible deal.

What happened to Fred could happen to you. You could easily come up with a bill for $207,000 instead of $46,000 if you don't understand how orders work, and how markets work. To avoid disasters like Fred's, Jill's, and Bob's, you have to know—and use—Troy's Three Trading Tips (T3): the limit order, the stop market order, the target price.

IF YOU DON'T BELIEVE ME, BELIEVE THE SEC

In a statement released on January 27, 1999, SEC chairman Arthur Levitt announced that by the end of 1999, the number of online brokerage accounts was expected to exceed 10 million, accounting for 25 percent of all retail stock trades, and cautioned small investors to beware of the seeming ease of online trading. "Online investors should remember," he warned, "that it is just as easy, if not more so, to lose money through the click of a button as it is to make it. The SEC will do everything it can to protect and inform investors during this time of great innovation and change. But investor protection—at its most basic and effective level—starts with the investor."

Levitt laid out "three golden rules" of online investing:

1. *Know what you are buying.* Learn as much as you can about the company in which you're investing, as discussed in Chapter 6.
2. *Know the ground rules under which you buy and sell a stock or bond.* Understand your broker's responsibility to you and the mar-

ket in which you're buying the stock. As discussed in Chapter 3, the NYSE with its specialists works differently from the screen-based Nasdaq market. Many orders from order-entry firms (the online brokers such as Ameritrade) are sent straight to wholesalers instead of shooting into the Nasdaq market to set a new price, as your limit order can.

3. *Know the level of risk you are undertaking.* Fred thought he was in for a maximum of $45,000. That assumption turned out to be a $150,000 boo-boo. As Matt Andresen of Island ECN said in his interview (see Chapter 8), ordering a stock at market is like walking into a car showroom and ordering a car with all the options without asking about the price. Why would you trust your online broker any more than you'd trust a car salesperson?

Levitt's statement also warned investors to be aware of other "issues and limitations" of online trading: delays in getting online and/or receiving timely execution confirmations, and quickly changing prices that might result in traders "paying much more for a stock than you intended or can afford."

And what does Levitt recommend to circumvent these problems? The same thing I recommend with the T3, Troy's Three Trading Tips: *Use limit orders* to establish the maximum price at which you'll make a purchase. If poor Fred had taken that advice, he would've saved himself a big chunk of change. Let's say he'd entered a limit order for TheGlobe.com at $20. He would have bought the stock only if it stopped at that precise price as it rocketed its way up the charts. But whether he got the stock or not, he would have avoided that $150,000 surprise.

Levitt warned, too, against buying securities with borrowed money. "In volatile markets," he said, "investors who have put up an initial margin payment for a stock may find themselves being required to provide additional cash (maintenance margin) if the price of the stock subsequently falls. If the funds are not paid in a timely manner, the brokerage firm has the right to sell the securities and charge any loss to the investor.

"When you buy stock on margin," he added, "you are borrowing money . . . you should make sure that you do not overextend."

Finally, Levitt expressed his dismay about people trading online with money they can't afford to lose, advising people to use the stock market for investment, not trading, and warning against using student loan money, second mortgages, or retirement funds. "Investment should be for the long run," he said, "not for minutes or hours."

To which I say: do two days, two weeks, two months count as the long run?

FAST MARKETS AND NEW TRADERS

In response to the extreme price and volume volatility of the online markets, wholesalers started trying to keep themselves from losing money by placing orders manually, rather than using the computerized automatic execution systems.

The manual handling led to delays, which meant that the prices shown on home traders' screens were often far from the market price—which in turn led to big losses like the one Fred experienced.

In the winter and spring of 1999 the NASD issued a series of warning notices in which they laid out several ground rules:

1. Member firms were reminded to ensure that their systems were sufficient to handle high-volume and high-volatility trading days, and "to treat customers fairly."

2. Order handling firms and integrated firms (those that not only do retail business but also do market making) were reminded to make the following types of disclosures:

   Delays: Customers have the right to know how order executions are handled by market makers, including the fact that they may execute orders manually or reduce their size guarantees during volatile times.

   Types of orders: Firms should explain to their customers the differences, risks, and benefits of market versus limit orders, including the information that limit orders will be executed only at a specified price or better. (If that price isn't met, the order won't be executed at all.) For hot IPO stocks traded under fast market conditions, Levitt asked that undefined "additional disclosures" also be made to customers.

   Access: Customers should know that during periods of volatility, when they have problems accessing their accounts due to high Internet traffic, they might suffer losses or be unable to trade at all.

   Communications with the public: Claims made in advertising or any other contact with the public must be supportable and honestly represented. "Misrepresentation or omissions of material facts in public communications violate NASD [rules] which [require] members to observe high standards of commercial honor and just and equitable principles of trade."

3. Traders should be warned that "modifications to order execution algorithms or procedures designed to respond to turbulent market conditions may be implemented only when warranted by market conditions." And trading firms were warned not to use such modifications "excessively" or without documenting the basis for using them.

4. Broker/dealers were advised to ensure their systems won't be overwhelmed by high volume and that "frequent activation of modified order execution algorithms or procedures because a firm has failed to maintain adequate system capacity to handle exceptional loads may raise best execution concerns."

5. Companies that do manual order handling were advised to operate "an over-the-counter order room or other department assigned to execute customers' orders" to ensure order execution in "the best available market . . ."

If you trade at Datek or any other brokerage that uses an ECN, your online broker should supply you with "warning notes"—some of which appear on the front page, some of which appear on a pop-up screen you must see before you trade.

STATES' RIGHTS

Although the SEC, not the states, has jurisdiction over regulating day trading, so many new traders got burned during 1998 and 1999 that several states started looking into the problem. At a hearing on Internet stock trading in California's state Senate, a representative of Charles Schwab told the Senate Finance, Investment and International Trade Committee that its primary focus should be on educating the investor, not imposing new regulations on online trading. The committee chose to focus on day trading, without differentiating between EDAT day trading and trading online with a broker like Schwab. Everyone's trying to get educated, including the lawmakers, as the field continues to shift at breakneck speed.

In the spring of 1999, the New York State Attorney General's Office began investigating what happens to the online investor and trader's order when overload sets in, the servers go down, and traders can't get online to sell, to buy, to confirm that their orders have gone through, or to cancel their orders. "The public knows that there are always risks involved in investing in the stock market," said Attorney General Elliot Spitzer in a statement. "But part of that risk should not include questions about whether trades will be executed promptly or whether online brokerage firms can deliver on the services they've promised." Spitzer's office investigated E*Trade for its peppering of service failures in March of 1999, when traders stood helplessly by as their portfolios gyrated wildly. But E*Trade's contract, like the contracts of all online brokers, says the company is not liable for problems with its electronic systems.

Despite government investigations, the law seems to provide little protection for traders who place *market orders,* executed at the best available price at the moment when the wholesaler or broker puts it through. The solution? Once again: limit orders specifying the exact price you will pay.

The state regulators were mostly concerned with "day traders"—the EDAT sort, who take expensive training courses to learn how to trade stocks during the day, making an eighth or a teenie ($\frac{1}{16}$) on the trade, and selling out or "going flat" by the end of the day. The Clinton administration, too, weighed in on the Internet fraud and day trading front, promising in the spring of 1999 to move against the bad guys who fall through the cracks between regulatory agencies.

DAY TRADING FIRM BOOM AND BUSTS

Texas-based Block Trading, one of the splashiest of the "franchise" breed of shopping-mall day trading shops, had a spectacular flameout in the fall of 1998 because the company didn't have enough infrastructure to keep it going. According to *60 Minutes II,* the CBS news magazine, 67 of Block's 68 clients lost money. The Texas state securities regulator began an investigation.

Massachusetts regulators felt that the branches of the New Jersey–based All-Tech in their state seemed to promise traders would make money, while downplaying the risks. Some All-Tech clients, according to newspaper reports, claimed to have lost tens of thousands of dollars; clients' funds were commingled instead of being kept in separate trading accounts—an illegal way of allowing margin calls to be met, according to investigators.

All-Tech's Harvey Houtkin—a 1989 EDAT pioneer—claimed he had received only one letter of complaint about All-Tech's Watertown, Massachusetts, office. He called the investigation a "witch-hunt," and told a *Boston Globe* reporter, "We provide market information and direct access to the market (EDAT). What people do with that information and access is an individual thing."

Day traders do need education so they can protect themselves. After all, trading in an EDAT shop can be like standing downhill from a boulder in an avalanche and trying to stop it from falling. If you haven't gotten out in time, you can find yourself unable to sell while it's dropping because it's moving so fast.

The fact is that most of the 100 million Americans invested in the stock market aren't day traders. Momentum Trading estimates that there were only about 4000 real day traders working EDAT systems in 1999. That's one EDAT trader for every 24,999 investors (only 80 per state). According to that figure, the industry is as clean as Ivory Soap, with its promised purity of $99^{44}/_{100}$ percent.

CHAT ROOMS, E-MAILS, AND ONLINE TIP SHEETS

Recently, the SEC went after a clever if devious gentleman who used a Bloomberg News template and set up a hyperlink (that resembled Bloomberg News) to his fake story about a merger with an Israeli technology company. The technology company stock soared. The next day, it sank. Two weeks later, our clever antihero was arrested by federal agents.

The Big Four of online trading chat—Yahoo!, the Fool, Silicon Investor, and Raging Bull—all warn traders, in effect, to "watch your back, because we can't watch it for you." To be more specific:

- *Beware of e-mail stock hypes.* When you sign up for free services or trial subscriptions, offer no more than the information absolutely required—usually the fields that must be filled in are marked in some way. Wherever you encounter a box indicating that you'd like to be informed about new services (the default setting is usually something like, "Yes! Send me everything! I'd love to hear it all!"), uncheck it! The good news is, as my experience tells me, that these sites do stand behind their privacy policies: in all the time I've been online, registered with a broker and with various investment sites, I have not received one piece of spam (indicating that a site had sold my name to marketers).

- *Stick with the winners.* If you stay with the stocks on the NYSE, Nasdaq, and AMEX, and if you stay with one of the well-established online brokers (as described in Chapter 8) and the Big Four chat rooms, you should be just fine. Remember, the get-rich-quick schemes are just that—schemes.

OPTIONS, PENNY STOCKS, BULLETIN BOARDS, AND SHORT SHORTS

If you've chosen an online broker from a list of the top 10 brokers with the largest market share (who therefore have the greatest chance of staying in business), and if you stay away from the fly-by-night online chat rooms, avoid stock-promoting e-mails by registering only on secure, private sites, and do your homework—congratulations! You're inoculated against online stock promotions.

OPTIONS

Checking your online brokerage listings, you might notice that I haven't included options. There's a reason for that: this book is not called *Learn to Manage a Hedge Fund in Seven Easy Lessons.* Options are big gambles—they're hard to master, they're highly leveraged, and they're an easy way to wipe out all your cash in one shot. If you've built a big nest egg by next year, you might consider taking 5 percent of it and investigating options. But that's another year.

PENNY STOCKS

In late January 1999 the SEC stopped trading in six companies, five of which—Citron Inc., Electronic Transfer Associates Inc., Invest Holdings Group Inc., Polus Inc., and Smartek Inc.—were tied to a stock promoter who'd been banned from the brokerage industry in 1998 because of previous securities laws violations. The six stocks were listed, not on the NYSE, not on the Nasdaq, but on the OTC Bulletin Board (sometimes called "the pink sheet")—the small-capitalization (meaning the company is capitalized at under $50 million) "penny stock" market that doesn't fall under Nasdaq's regulatory arm. Trading in stock of the sixth company—whose shares increased nearly 300 percent in the first month of 1999, but which was not involved with the stock promoter—was also halted for two weeks.

SHORTS

In 1997 I bought 20 shares of Yahoo! at $40. Actually, I didn't buy them, I shorted them, believing the market was sure to go down because of the trouble with the Asian economy. But the problems in Asia didn't hit for a while, and when they did, they didn't seem to make a dent in Yahoo!. As a beginning student of the markets I had read about price/earnings ratios, realized Yahoo!'s was out of the ballpark, and waited for everyone else to discover the same information. (Actually, it injured my ego to realize I'd done such a stupid thing, and I didn't want to let go of it and take the loss.) By the time I sold out (by buying back the shares I'd initially sold—or getting out of my short position), I had to pay about $189 a share. (You can see this buyback on my account figures for the month of November in the Preface.)

This experience—holding onto a Yahoo! short position for a year and a half—taught me a valuable lesson: *never short without using the T3, Troy's Three Trading Tips.* If for some reason you haven't applied the T3 going in, get out as soon as you've passed a 15 percent or 20 percent increase in value, depending on the volatility.

In the case of my Yahoo! debacle, if I had not been an active trader and had simply held onto the stock, I'd be a much calmer investor. But as I've said before, those buy and hold strategies are for the time—next year, two years from now—when you're finished with the superaccelerated phase of growing your retirement nest egg and can relax into an intelligently managed portfolio, maybe something like the batch of high-tech stocks mentioned by Geoffrey Moore and his coauthors, Paul Johnson and Tom Kippola, in the paperback of their newly revised book, *The Gorilla Game* (HarperBusiness, 1999)—a must-read for the tech investor.

CREDIT CARDS WILL KILL YOU

When I've bought stock on Datek in the past, my margin has been 6.75 percent—though it's now gone up to 7.25 percent. If you really want to make money fast, before you start paying interest on margin accounts, wipe out all your credit card debt and pay the cards off month by month. Nothing is more important. Here's the step-by-step recipe for avoiding the cost of margin:

1. Start trading with, say, $25,000.
2. Use your first profits to pay off your credit cards. Leave the original $25,000 untouched.
3. Calculate the interest on any of your other loans. Perhaps you are paying off a luxury car. If so, consider selling it and buying a cheaper car outright with the cash.
4. Now that you're not paying interest on your loans, you can concentrate on putting cash (from trading profits, or any other source) into your trading account.

Why so stern? Recently I saw a television commercial from a national computer manufacturer, promoting their $2000 model. Take advantage of the low monthly payment plan the ad offered. And the interest on that plan? The commercial neglected to mention that, naming only the monthly payment. But if you'd taken the company up on its offer, you would have paid $1000 in interest. That's a 50 percent interest rate.

If you got as intense as I did in trading online, in a year or so you might have built the $1000 you saved by paying cash for the computer into $5000. Then you'd have your fully paid computer, plus the $5000 in cash. Or, after four years, you might have an old computer, no cash, and no nest egg.

Cash in hand is wonderfully valuable when you are able to invest it—in online trading or anything else. Cash in credit cards is always a shame.

ILLUSION AND ADDICTION

The cover photo of *Forbes*'s April 1997 issue on day trading pictured an exultant twenty-something—a recent Russian immigrant, no less—winning at the day trading game at New York's Broadway Trading. Surely, one might think, if this kid could make hundreds of thousands, anyone could—right?

Sure. Just like anyone can win the lottery.

In 1999, another day trading gambler showed up on a *60 Minutes II* episode, wondering how he could have lost his entire inheritance. He didn't seem to have read the release forms every investor and day trader must sign before doing business with a registered broker/dealer. And he seemed to think that the money he'd borrowed by investing on margin could be paid off over a period of years, like a school loan.

The reality, of course, is that if you've invested in a volatile stock that's just dropped 50 percent in value, and you've bought it on a two-to-one margin, you'll be getting a margin call. That money will be due in your account the very next morning, or your account will be liquidated to pay off the margin call. When a $500,000 tab is called and the trader can't pay, it can bring down the entire day trading operation. There are day trading firms no longer in existence for exactly that reason: their clearing-houses weren't keeping up-to-the-minute tabs on the margin figures in various highflyers' accounts.

Morals of the story? First, you don't want to get caught in a margin call. Always think ahead on the downside as well as the upside of any trade you're considering. Second, don't get caught trading with a small firm that can be put out of business by one big margin call. (Checking your brokers with the NASDR site, or choosing an online broker/dealer from among the top 10 I've listed, and making sure you're covered with SIPC (Securities Investor Protection Corporation) insurance will help you make the right choice.)

After spending some time at a day trading shop, I could pick out the guys who were most likely to go down in flames. They were the ones whose macho pride wouldn't let them let go of a loser; instead, they rode it and rode it down and further down, while leveraged to the hilt. The next step was to "win back the money." That goal laid even more stress on the guy (we already know how much he hates to lose), so he'd place a few ill-considered "bets" on some initials standing for a company he knew nothing about.

The traders who can't let go of their losers, who can't wear their losses like a loose garment, who don't realize that winning 6 out of 10 times means coming out ahead—these are the traders who shouldn't be involved in day trading. Often, after a few days or weeks, their money is gone.

Recently, CNBC covered a twenty-something day trader who was living at his grandmother's house, trading for eighths and quarters, who had started to wonder if he was becoming addicted to the adrenaline rush of EDAT day trading. As Dr. Kimberly Young, author of the Internet obsession book, *Caught in the Net* (Wiley, 1998), told reporters, ". . . if you're doing that every day at the expense of other things in your life, you would call that an addiction."

Dr. Young, an Internet addiction specialist at the University of Pittsburgh, describes day trading addicts this way: "You're constantly thinking about your next session—strategizing about when you're making your next investment. . . . It takes away from your life, that's the scary thing: people sitting in their room for 10 hours a day in front of their computer. They try harder to get their money back—just like a gambler would."

TAKE THE ADDICTION TEST

If you're wondering, you can take this addiction quiz, from a Web site for compulsive gambling addiction (www.800gambler.org).

1. Are you trading in the stock market with money you may need during the next year?
2. Are you risking more money than you intended to?
3. Have you ever lied to someone regarding your online trading?
4. Are you risking retirement savings to try to get back your losses?
5. Has anyone ever told you that you spend too much time online?
6. Is the way you are investing affecting other areas of your life (relationships, vocation pursuits, etc.)?
7. If you lost most of your money trading in the market would it materially change your life?
8. Are you investing frequently (day trading) for the excitement and the way it makes you feel?
9. Are you becoming secretive about your online trading?
10. Do you feel sad or depressed when you are not trading in the market?

After answering these 10 questions—honestly!—ask yourself if online day trading, especially EDAT day trading, is something you should be considering at all. Or call 1-800-GAMBLER for advice.

SURVIVE AND THRIVE

You should have read enough in the preceding pages to convince you to proceed cautiously. Keep these warnings, and the T3, Troy's Three Trading Tips, in mind and you'll survive—perhaps even thrive.

If, however, you feel you've been the victim of cyberfraud, or you want to educate yourself so you can avoid it, you might want to check out these Web sites.

- The SEC, at sec.gov. Now publishing information on the stock frauds coming across the SEC desk in Washington.
- Nasdaq's regulatory arm, at nasdr.com. Remember to check out the name of your broker and your brokerage firm with the NASDR site (nasdr.com), where you can fill in an online query. (See Figure 9.1.)
- NASAA, the North American Security Analysts' Association. Good information about how to protect yourself.
- Fraud.org. A wide variety of Internet fraud schemes.

FIGURE 9.1 *Check out your broker and your brokerage house: the online questionnaire gets you the complete story within a matter of days. And the front page keeps you up to the minute with any new SEC or NASDR rules with Nasdaq broker/dealers, wholesalers, and market makers.* (© NASD Regulation Inc. (NASDR). Reprinted with permission from NASDR.)

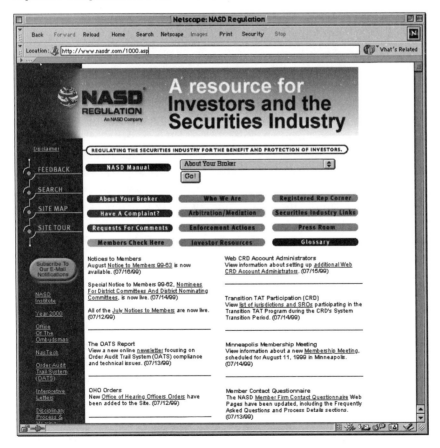

•   •   •

BILL BURNHAM
ONLINE BROKERAGE ANALYST

Bill Burnham, the 28-year-old Internet commerce analyst recently moved from CSFirst Boston. According to an estimate by the *WSJ*, Burnham was making approximately $4 million a year as the nation's favorite online brokerage expert. The chairman and founder of Japan's Softbank Masayoshi Son—a noted Internet investor in companies such as Yahoo! and E*Trade—recently hired Burnham for his newest California-based venture capital team.

Do you think the extended trading hours at the NYSE and Nasdaq will happen soon?

Well, I doubt they'll come into being before 2000. They've got too much to resolve in terms of Year 2000 issues prior to that.

What do you think the new hours will be?

I assume that what they're going to do is extend the edges of the trading session, perhaps by an hour or two on either end. They're talking about a separate evening session on the New York Stock Exchange after a one-hour break. I suspect that whatever's decided about the Nasdaq, the NYSE will decide on the same time period to make things simple for everybody. A whole series of meetings is going on as they try and coordinate the change. I suspect that what will happen, barring any kind of major disagreement, is that both the Nasdaq and the NYSE will agree on a schedule.

Do you think the Nasdaq will become for-profit?

Potentially. A lot of people inside the Nasdaq are very excited about the idea. If you see other exchanges file and go public and get big valuations, the Nasdaq may try and do it. But I don't think that doing it preemptively makes a lot of sense for them in the short term.

This spring the SEC was doing quick visits to different brokerages to check up on the way they were executing trades for retail customers. Was this just with EDAT day trading firms or was this with regular brokerage houses?

This was with all the big brokers.

As you say in one of your quarterly reports, the practice of "legal kickbacks" to the big brokers from the market makers or wholesalers—the whole area of best order execution—is very questionable and ill defined. I've personally always used limit orders, for both safety and economy. So my whole perception of how online trading works has been very much shaded by that. The idea that people have been putting in market orders—with no price specified—during fast markets, in hot stocks, just terrified me. Do you think the SEC will actually start making some changes in how orders must be executed?

They're under pressure to do something. They thought that by doing some investigation they might be able to scare up some easy scores for political gain. But I do believe they're on to something. [These problems] aren't only the brokers' fault. They're the market makers' fault.

Ultimately it will be a huge story if the SEC figures out what's going on. But it's very hard to figure out—it's basically the biggest organized front-running operation in the history of the market, but nobody understands it.

It's very hard to explain.

Yes, it is. It is very hard to explain to investors why they're getting screwed. They're not necessarily getting screwed by bad executions. Where you get screwed is *not* getting executed. So there's a huge opportunity cost that's very difficult to quantify that's happening every day in the markets.

When you say "not getting executed" do you mean at that time or with a limit order?

With a limit order. Let's say you put in an order to buy or sell stock [with a broker who sells your order] to a big market maker [also called a wholesaler or middleman]. Normally, a market order comes in, let's say that your limit is the best ask in the market—a hundred. You should get hit, right? Your trade should be completed. What's happening is that at the exact instant that that market order comes to the market, *if* the market maker, based on their knowledge of all the other order flow in the market, believes that the stock is going up, they'll do what's called "step in front" of your limit order. They'll step in front of your limit order and they might bid 99.999 [offer to buy] just to step right in front of your limit order.

They jump ahead of you in line? They speculate.

Yeah, that's correct.

It's a guaranteed investment.

There's not a 100 percent guarantee but they've got a pretty good idea what the picture looks like. That's what's going on in the market, time in, and time out.

Does this happen on the New York Stock Exchange?

There's a long history of arguments about specialists being at the trading booth and seeing some guy running toward him with what's obviously a big order and all of a sudden he cleans the book out because he knows he's just about to get a big buy or sell order.

What about the "upstairs market," the third market?

The same principle holds in the third market. Actually the New York Stock Exchange is losing some volume to the third market, so perhaps that indeed is what's happening. I'm not as in touch with the third market as I am the Nasdaq market. But there has been a shift, and the same exact principles that are at work in the Nasdaq market could indeed be at work in the third market.

The average investor has no clue what's going on and to be honest, when it comes to an eighth or a sixteenth, doesn't really care. It doesn't make a huge difference to their trading style. That's why it goes on.

The brokerage houses make it sound extremely complicated.

If it was straightforward, it wouldn't be happening.

I can't believe the SEC doesn't understand.

What we're talking about here is basically plumbing, right?

What do you mean?

Plumbing and execution type issues which, as we've said, are very hard to understand. So if you come out and you say, "We've taken this great regulatory action against the plumbers," nobody really cares, because they didn't understand what the problem was in the first place. Whereas if you take action against, you know, a brand name on my trading firm—*Wow!* That everybody knows. Right?

Right. But there are plumbers, and then there are plumbers . . .

I don't think the problem is high profile enough to attract a lot of political scrutiny. And the market makers will give you lots of arguments as to why their services are great. For every limit order they don't execute, some-body just got price-improved, right? When they step in front of an order, they actually are giving somebody a better price than what they thought they were going to get. That's how it is on one side of the trade. Of course, that means they're not executing somebody else.

When CNBC celebrated their tenth anniversary on air, Mark Haines, who hosts *Squawk Box* each morning before the markets open, told a fascinating story. When the SEC's market maker investigation was coming out in 1995 or '96, he made a point of reading it out loud on CNBC because it was ignored in the press. Why? Because, again, it's plumbing—it's back rooms?

That's absolutely right. You're an experienced markets reporter and you've taken a lot of time to understand this and will take more time researching and understanding it. For the average beat reporter, it just doesn't make sense to spend all the time to understand what's going on. Here's the thing. I'm saying I think this is going on, and I can say that because I talk to a lot of people and I'm pretty damn sure it's going on. But to *prove* it would be another thing. Actually I think it would be quite easy, to be honest with you, but it's just a difficult thing to assemble and get into and it's not that high profile.

But I think it's important to the investor today, the so-called "retail" investor, to get his or her stock at a wholesale price, without some-one stepping in front of the order. Can you do that on an ECN?

But remember: most ECN orders usually aren't matched because most people won't put a limit order in that matches. Most people who are trying to buy won't put a limit order in on the ask. There's always a spread [the difference between the best current buy and sell prices]. There's a natural tension between buyer and seller. But that said, there are a lot of crossed orders [matched up] ultimately. But a lot of the "hits" on ECNs are actually from market orders that are coming in at the market, and the ECN happens to be the best bid [best current buying price] in the market. And ECNs have played a very big role in collapsing the spread inside markets—which mar-ket makers hate, of course.

I rented an EDAT day trader's seat at Landmark Securities' San Fran-cisco office. I day traded with direct access to the markets, using a Level II screen, choosing exactly where I wanted to execute my

order, and "hitting" it. It was absolutely terrifying. I made $132 in two months.

In two months, really? How many trades?

I only traded 20 or 30 times. So $132. But then you have to subtract the $300 a month fee. Of course, the trading commissions are included already, leaving me the $132 profit. I only had a $5000 investment. Most traders need something like $50,000. But, using all the expensive equipment, I would always hit Island.

Yeah, everybody does.

I thought, why should I be paying all this money when I could be doing this on Datek at home?

Right.

What do you see as the future for day trading firms? What about the SOES orders?

In the early '90s the SOES arbitrageurs? You could really make lots of money quite easily. Those days are gone, as you saw, sitting in a [EDAT] day trading firm. It's really just speculation right now. Very informed, intelligent, disciplined speculators can actually make money but pure arbitrageurs are largely gone. What's to hit? It will continue to be a very small niche market that has very high turnover, much like the locals at an options exchange.

If you go to any open outcry pit, like commodities or options, there are lots of speculators who are called "locals." Eighty percent of them are not successful; they blow themselves up in the first six months. Twenty percent are successful over the long term. The same thing will happen in the day trading arena.

Do you really think it's 80 percent and not 97 percent?

Successful is defined as not actually losing all your capital and going bankrupt. There are some people who just sort of hang on and finally quit because they can't make a living at it. The people who are truly very successful at it? I think you're right—it's the top 5 or 3 percent who really are quite good. I have a friend who's quite good at trading IBM options and he makes a fortune but he said he sees people come in and leave every week. Some people come in and stay for six months and leave.

Yes, it seems to me it must be a 3 percent success rate. I went to one of those free day trading seminars advertised in the newspaper. They

were telling us how we could get rich quick, and they were selling their SOES trading system and talking about 10-to-1 margin.

Wow.

Doesn't that mean you have to have a proprietary account with the firm?

That's illegal. You can't do that. You can't buy stock on 10-to-1 margin. You can't margin stock below 25 percent. Period. The Federal Reserve won't let you. And you can't initially buy stock for less than 50 percent of its value. Or, you can't buy it on more than 50 percent margin. That's also illegal. Doesn't matter who you are. A broker/dealer cannot margin you stock on initial sale less than 50 percent. The Federal Reserve sets those limits and I believe the lower end of the limit is actually 25 percent. If you go below 25 percent, they *have* to call your margin so you could never do a 10-to-1 margin. Now if you're a hedge fund, you can actually borrow money from people for the fund and then reinvest the fund in the stock market.

But that's totally different, isn't it?

It depends. But a broker/dealer cannot extend margin greater than 25 percent of stock. That's illegal. Hmm. That's interesting. Maybe they have. Sounds like they have.

I'm still most interested in the executions.

It's a very important issue for traders to understand. They can lose a lot more—or make a lot more—on the execution than on their commission. You get what you pay for in some respects. Routing orders through ECNs makes the most sense because nobody's playing with your order. You want to go to a firm that doesn't have a conflict of interest, that's not selling its orders or things like that. Today there are very few [online brokers] that are doing that.

I've read complaints about Datek as well having bad executions, maybe in the beginning days when there wasn't that much liquidity on Island. What about Datek and Island ECN?

They attract some of the most active traders, period. Any . . . Wall Street traders, they never got a good trade, right? They're always getting screwed on every trade they do, right? I think in Datek's case, because it has all these aggressive traders, there were some specific periods, especially at the open, in the morning . . .

But stay away from the open . . . stocks can gap up or down . . .

. . . where they had huge amounts of activity pouring into the system and they did have some systems limitations that prevented good executions at the open. But all things being equal during a normal day, they clearly have the best execution. As I like to say, truth will out. The reason they're so big and growing so fast and all those big traders hang out there is that they are getting good execution.

When you say all the big traders hang out there, do you mean at Datek Online or do you mean Broadway Trading?

I mean the most aggressive online traders are hanging there at Datek. I'm not talking [EDAT] day traders. But to be honest with you, if you're really serious about day trading, you probably should be in a day trading room. . . . At least have a dedicated connection.

When you say "really serious about day trading" you're talking about having capital of $100,000 or $150,000?

Trading 50 times a day, and doing trades in a very small group, it's quarter points/half points.

But if you don't choose to be a professional EDAT day trader, you will use an online brokerage firm. What are Charles Schwab and the other online brokers doing for execution?

Schwab owns its own market maker, Mayer Schweitzer. They internally sell almost all their trades to Mayer Schweitzer. It's called payment for order flow. They do sell to a couple of other firms if Mayer doesn't make a market in the name [trade the stock]. Most firms send their orders to people [market makers/wholesalers/middlemen] who give them the best deals. So . . . Schwab has Mayer Schweitzer. And Waterhouse has an equity stake in Knight/TriMark, though it recently took a $25 million equity stake in Island [ECN]. E*Trade also has an equity stake in Knight/TriMark, although they sold about 40 percent of that recently and spent $25 million to buy a stake in Archipelago, an ECN. They made a $25 million investment for 25 percent of Archipelago. Datek has Island ECN. Fidelity also owns its own market maker. Very similar to Schwab. Sends almost all its trades directly to its own market maker. Ameritrade is very much a Knight/TriMark shop. It's a big owner of Knight/TriMark and traditionally directs much of its volume there. . . . Most firms send their orders to people who give them the best deals.

You say online brokers often sell their customers' orders to middle-men who give them the best deals. By "the best deals" do you mean the best order executions for the customer? Or do you mean the best payment for order flow—what's sometimes called "kickbacks"?

The best payment for order flow. They don't care about execution. They say they do, but my impression is that they're talking about who's willing to pay the most for the order flow.

10

THE FUTURE IS NOW

In the summer of 1997, a San Francisco futurist gave the word to a Texas convention of full-service stockbrokers: you will soon be obsolete, he told them. By the end of 1998, Merrill Lynch sold off its in-house group of NYSE specialists to punch up a sagging bottom line.

At the MIT Media Lab, a young Dutch professor, Patty Maes, thinking about the all-electronic London stock market, realized that her "shopping bots" might morph into "stock bots." These stock bots could zip globally through the digital stock bazaars and ECNs worldwide, tracking down and bringing back the best prices for traders.

The Nasdaq Stock Market hopes to ensure the liquidity of worldwide electronic exchanges and private markets, the ECNs, by bringing the competing systems together in the Nasdaq tent. (Check out their links to the global markets at nasdaq.com, and take a look at their experiment with the Hong Kong stock exchange: you can even input a sample Hang Sen portfolio in Hong Kong dollars.)

In late 1998, SEC chief Arthur Levitt announced new rules for the new ECNs—the upstart alternative to the traditional NYSE, Nasdaq, American, and regional stock exchanges. By 1999, online trading accounted for one-seventh of the stock trades in the United States. And the SEC decided to move forward with facilitating the change to electronic trading. By summer, New York Senator Charles Schumer asked for a five-year budget for Internet policing by the SEC. He voiced concerns about after-hours trading, "which traditionally could increase 'market manipulation,'" reminded investors that the same rules apply to day traders as to individual investors (the broker/dealer has the responsibility not to allow the client to do "rash and outrageous things"), and asked for regulatory relief for the NYSE and Nasdaq-AMEX. "There has to be some regulatory parity," he said. Schumer proposed "lifting some of the more outdated regulations that [the traditional NYSE and Nasdaq] have lived under" and talked of an "uber-ECN."

Was he worried about day trading? "Most of the people lose money, and the word will spread that this is not a way to get rich quick," he said.

Depending on the amount of trades they do, the new electronic exchanges in the United States can be regulated as either broker/dealers or as stock exchanges. This SEC ruling cracks open the time-honored lock the older exchanges had on the American market. The new ECNs, rather than setting themselves up as nonprofits like the NASD, the Nasdaq Stock Market, and the NYSE, will now be allowed to operate as businesses for profit. Both the NYSE and the Nasdaq will be doing their own IPOs—transforming themselves from membership organizations to publicly traded firms.

For online investors, jumping in and out of global electronic stock exchanges will be as easy as leaping from the Yahoo!Finance site to Silicon Investor. Trading, now restricted to market hours of 9:30 a.m. to 4:30 p.m. EST, will become round-the-clock, round-the-world entertainment. Want to make an after-hours trade? Day traders will no longer be restricted to phone calls through their broker/dealers or clearinghouses to make after- or before-hours trades on the illiquid Instinet system. In fact, day traders will no longer be restricted to "day," as the world morphs into a true global village.

These changes, further blurring the line between professional institutional traders and the individual day trader, are happening right now. Trading at any time of the day or night in markets worldwide, negotiating the price of a stock trade with the buyer or seller, even executing an individual version of the complex, computerized program trading once available only to Wall Street—these revolutionary opportunities will be in the hands of individual day traders this year and next.

Several of these new ECNs, already alive and kicking, promise to revolutionize the way individuals buy and sell stock. And just as the rules allowing SOES trading created multi-billion-dollar savings for all investors by narrowing the bid-ask spreads, this new wide-open world of electronic markets promises to save online traders even more. These ECNs may enhance an individual's annual returns by 10 percent. That 10 percent will be taken from the pockets of old-line NYSE specialists, Nasdaq market makers, and the big brokerage houses that need fat fees to enhance their bottom lines.

If 10 percent doesn't seem like much, consider the numbers worked up in an article comparing fees on a simple mutual fund. A fund with a low management fee, at 2 percent, created $170,000 less in 10 years than a fund with a management fee of 1.2 percent. That's the amazing reality of compound interest over the years.

In talking about executions, I've gotten off into some clanky, backroom, plumbing-diagram sorts of explanations of screen-based cybermarkets and ECNs and Level II quote montages. I, myself, had to put up with scores of these plumbing metaphors back in 1995 and '96, when high-tech experts and journalists were desperately trying to explain why this mysterious new being called the Internet had now become the World Wide Wait. There was a night on the MSNBC show *The Edge,* with Soledad O'Brien, when a Ziff-Davis computer expert stood there with two lead pipes—in his left hand, a fat pipe; in his right, a skinny pipe. The fat pipe was the 56K modem which would soon speed the download of our graphics-rich multimedia Web pages; the skinny pipe was the 14.4K or 28.8K modem that was the reason our pages downloaded in a slow dribble. I got it: Eureka! All these data, these mysterious electronic blips, flow through the pipes! Okay, it's down to plumbing. Plumbing is boring. But when it's my data that are flowing around in those pipes, I get very, very interested.

In late 1996, I first heard the phrase "big iron." Again, more plumbing, more infrastructure, and the word "robust" usually lurked in the wings, but "big iron" had a certain ring. Java applets wiggled down those pipes and onto our computer screens in 1996, slowly at first, then faster and faster. Anyone investing in the market was probably getting quotes from the newspaper business section—all those teensy, tiny rows of numbers the over-forties were finding difficult to read. By 1998, Peter Stern, the CEO of Big Think, cooked up the Streamer for Datek—the favorite online broker for active investors, and number one in TheStreet.com's reader survey. The Streamer could be personalized: big type for the over-40 set; hip, teensy-weensy type for Generation X. Stern's creation even came in chic, personalized colors. Who could resist?

Technology had come so far, so fast, that our "pipes" were bringing us real-time quote streams dashing across the screen—news of an electronic stock market we had scarcely been aware of in 1996—with a little window through which we could trade. By 1999, the clunky phrase "electronic communications network" began to pop up in the business section, with equally clunky attempts to explain what the ECN, the alternative trading system, actually does.

I hope this book has helped expand your understanding of these little automatic order-matching stock markets, and the crucial role they can play today on the Nasdaq Level II screen's quote montage. The "disintermediation"—that horrible seven-syllable business school word for getting rid of the middleman, brought about by removing the human element from the middle of the trade—has forced the profit spreads, the difference between wholesale and retail prices to the customer, down by over 40 percent since the SEC order handling reforms transformed every investor into a potential trader. In this revolutionary time the "investor in the kitchen," as Nasdaq stock market chief Al Berkeley calls her, can improve a price quote on screens around the globe simply by entering a better price with limit order into the screen-based cybermarkets linked by Nasdaq.

So not only do we become enamored of plumbing and the magic way it can improve communications into home and office, we also become curious about those clanky mechanisms hidden behind the curtain, the tricks and magic and colored smoke the Wizard of Oz used to deflect our attention from the simple reality of what was going on—in this case, the ECNs. These are the 800-pound gorillas transforming the stock market arena now—in the United States, and in the global market.

•   •   •

INTERVIEW WITH GEOFFREY MOORE, AUTHOR OF *THE GORILLA GAME*

Geoffrey Moore is the author—with Tom Kippola, a colleague at The Chasm Group, a Silicon Valley consulting firm, and Paul Johnson, an Internet analyst at San Francisco's Robertson Stevens investment bank—of a top-selling business book of 1998, *The Gorilla Game*. *The Gorilla Game*'s lessons on creating a savvy, long-term portfolio in the technology sector are the best philosophy to help today's active investor create a steady, stable portfolio for life after one or two years' quick growth with the T3.

Here are Moore's thoughts on the "global village" ahead of us.

Geoff, what's your quick take on the Internet and electronic commerce in general, globally, five years out? You've predicted that e-commerce—all facilitated by the Internet—will not only be making all of us more efficient, but will be creating strange sorts of new per-

mutations that we can't even imagine yet. What is our payoff from all this new efficiency?

The double headline for the Internet and e-commerce is that it (1) makes existing markets more efficient and (2) enables markets that heretofore could not have existed.

Number 1 is very much a two-edged sword. In business-to-business e-commerce, where we are taking costs out of asset-intensive supply chains, there is net new wealth created. Why? Because vendors were typically eating those costs, and now they can take some portion to the bottom line while still passing on some savings to the customers. That's the virtuous side.

Then what's the less than virtuous side?

In business-to-consumer e-commerce, where the Internet has set off a land grab, we are creating a hyperefficient market that may lead to profitless prosperity positions.

In business-to-business e-commerce, where there are no physical assets, we are somewhere in between. Take retail stockbrokers: to the degree that profits were a function of inefficient markets, there is going to be a net loss overall. But to the degree that the new markets attract more investors and enable new kinds of investments, there is a net new add.

So you see the pure information itself—the 3-D virtual reality world that William Gibson's *Neuromancer* [Ace Books, 1984] jacks into— may be more valuable itself than any bread-and-butter transactions?

The general winning idea going forward appears to be that information about an asset has greater wealth-creation capability than asset ownership. In that context, using the Internet to collect the information is hugely net positive; using it to execute transactions upon that information is modestly net positive.

So the key to sustaining competitive advantage may well lie in patenting information-based wealth-creating processes (such as PriceLine's patent on its approach to transaction creation).

As retail customers—buyers of stock through online brokerage services—what will be exciting about the Internet over the next five years? And will we find marvelous, as-yet-uninvented companies to invest in?

The Internet will put two constituencies seriously at risk: a bunch of incumbents who have made their money off of market inefficiency in the past, and new institutions who make land grab plays, and either fail, or suc-ceed—but without creating insufficient barriers to exist—in either case win-ning a profitless position.

But in conjunction with the "new" economy, in which virtual compa-nies can be assembled from multiple outsourced functions, these things will enable a myriad of new creations. (There are too many nutrients not to attract whole new phyla of organisms.)

So your global outlook for all these organisms . . . ?

In this context, the U.S. head start on the Net, I believe, foreshadows decades worth of wealth creation domination on a worldwide basis.

The U.S., and its markets, remain a great space for global investment then?

Yes.

INDEX